PC System Architecture Series

MindShare, Inc.

Please see our web site (http://www.awl.com/cseng/series/m

80486 System Architecture: Third Edition
0-201-40994-1

AGP System Architecture
0-201-37964-3

CardBus System Architecture
0-201-40997-6

EISA System Architecture: Second Edition
0-201-40995-X

FireWire® System Architecture: Second Edition
0-201-48535-4

ISA System Architecture: Third Edition
0-201-40996-8

PCI System Architecture: Third Edition
0-201-40993-3

PCMCIA System Architecture: Second Edition
0-201-40991-7

Pentium® Pro and Pentium® II System Architecture: Second Edition
0-201-30973-4

Pentium® Processor System Architecture: Second Edition
0-201-40992-5

Plug and Play System Architecture
0-201-41013-3

Power PC System Architecture
0-201-40990-9

Protected Mode Software Architecture
0-201-55447-X

Universal Serial Bus System Architecture
0-201-46137-4

Protected Mode Software Architecture

MindShare, Inc.

Tom Shanley

ADDISON-WESLEY
An imprint of Addison Wesley Longman, Inc.

Reading, Massachusetts • Harlow, England • Menlo Park, California
Berkeley, California • Don Mills, Ontario • Sydney
Bonn • Amsterdam • Tokyo • Mexico City

Library of Congress Cataloging-in-Publication Data

ISBN: 0-201-55447-X

Copyright ©1996 by MindShare, Inc.

Sponsoring Editor: Kathleen Tibbetts
Project Manager: Deborah McKenna
Cover Design: Barbara T. Atkinson
Set in 10 point Palatino by MindShare, Inc.

3 4 5 6 7 8   MA   01 00 99 98
3rd Printing December 1998

Addison-Wesley books available for bulk purchases by corporations, institutions, and other organizations. For more information please contact the Corporate, Government, and Special Sales Department at (800) 238-9682.

To my pal—Nancy.

Contents

About This Book

Part One—Background

Chapter 1: Single-Task OS and Application

Chapter 2: Definition of Multitasking

Contents

Chapter 3: Multitasking Problems

Part Two—Register Set & Real Mode

Chapter 4: The Control Registers

Contents

Chapter 5: Real Mode Operation

Part Three—Protected Mode

Chapter 6: x86 Protected Mode Intro

Chapter 7: Intro to Segmentation

Contents

Chapter 8: Code Segments

Contents

Chapter 9: Data and Stack Segments

Chapter 10: Creating a Task

Contents

Chapter 11: Mechanics of a Task Switch

Contents

Chapter 12: Interrupt Sources and Handling

Contents

Contents

Contents

Contents

Figures

Figures

Tables

Acknowledgments

Kathleen Tibbetts, our editor at Addison-Wesley, remains calm and reasonable when faced with all manner of calamity: repeatedly slipped schedules, unreadable files, an author threatening suicide, etc. For her calming influence, I remain thankful.

About This Book

The MindShare Architecture Series

The MindShare Architecture book series includes: *ISA System Architecture, EISA System Architecture, 80486 System Architecture, PCI System Architecture, Pentium System Architecture, PCMCIA System Architecture, PowerPC System Architecture, Plug-and-Play System Architecture, CardBus System Architecture,* and *Protected Mode Software Architecture.* The book series is published by Addison-Wesley.

Rather than duplicating common information in each book, the series uses the building-block approach. *ISA System Architecture* is the core book upon which the others build. The figure below illustrates the relationship of the books to each other.

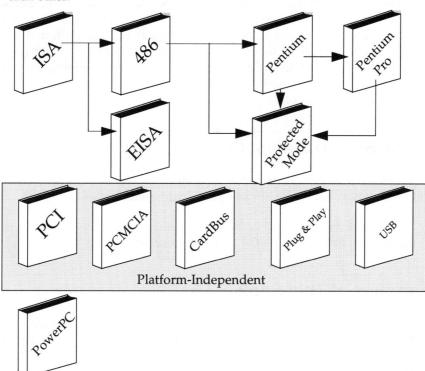

Protected Mode Software Architecture

Cautionary Note

The reader should keep in mind that MindShare's book series often deals with rapidly-evolving technologies. This being the case, it should be recognized that each book is a "snapshot" of the state of the targeted technology at the time that the book was completed. We attempt to update each book on a timely basis to reflect changes in the targeted technology, but, due to various factors (waiting for the next version of the spec to be "frozen," the time necessary to make the changes, and the time to produce the books and get them out to the distribution channels), there will always be a delay.

What This Book Covers

The purpose of this book is to provide a detailed description of x86 protected mode operation. However, real mode was the precursor to protected mode, so it is also necessary to understand real mode's capabilities and shortcomings. In order to understand why each component of both real and protected mode software architectures exist, the reader must first understand the problems that single-task and multitasking OSs must deal with. After providing the necessary background material, this book focuses on the protection mechanisms and multitasking capabilities of the post-286 processors.

What this Book Does not Cover

This book does not describe the x86 instruction repertoire. There are a host of books on the market that already provide this information.

Coverage of protected mode as implemented on the 286 processor has been minimized. The focus is on the post-286 processors.

Organization of This Book

Protected Mode Software Architecture extends MindShare's coverage of x86 processor architecture to the software environment. The author considers this book to be a companion to the MindShare books entitled *80486 System Architecture* and *Pentium Processor System Architecture* (both published by Addison-Wesley). The book is organized into three parts:

- **Part One—Background**
  - Chapter 1: Single-Task OS and Application
  - Chapter 2: Definition of Multitasking
  - Chapter 3: Multitasking Problems
- **Part Two—Register Set & Real Mode**
  - Chapter 4: The Control Registers
  - Chapter 5: Real Mode Operation
- **Part Three—Protected Mode**
  - Chapter 6: x86 Protected Mode Intro
  - Chapter 7: Intro to Segmentation
  - Chapter 8: Code Segments
  - Chapter 9: Data and Stack Segments
  - Chapter 10: Creating a Task
  - Chapter 11: Mechanics of a Task Switch
  - Chapter 12: Interrupt Sources and Handling
  - Chapter 13: Virtual Paging
  - Chapter 14: The Flat Model
  - Chapter 15: Virtual 8086 Mode

Who this Book is For

This book is intended for use by hardware and software design and support personnel. Due to the clear, concise explanatory methods used to describe each subject, personnel outside of the design field may also find the text useful.

Prerequisite Knowledge

It is highly recommended that the reader have a good knowledge of x86 processor architecture. Detailed descriptions of the 286 and 386 processors can be found in the MindShare book entitled *ISA System Architecture*. Detailed descriptions of the 486 and Pentium processors can be found in the MindShare books entitled *80486 System Architecture* and *Pentium Processor System Architecture*, respectively. All of these books are published by Addison-Wesley.

Documentation Conventions

This document utilizes the following documentation conventions for numeric values.

Hexadecimal Notation

All hex numbers are followed by an "h." Examples:

```
9A4Eh
0100h
```

Binary Notation

All binary numbers are followed by a "b." Examples:

```
0001 0101b
01b
```

Decimal Notation

Numbers without any suffix are decimal. When required for clarity, decimal numbers are followed by a "d." The following examples each represent a decimal number:

```
16
255
256d
128d
```

Signal Name Representation

Each signal that assumes the logic low state when asserted is followed by a pound sign (#). As an example, the CACHE# signal is asserted low when the processor wants to read a line from memory into its cache.

Signals that are not followed by a pound sign are asserted when they assume the logic high state. As an example, PCD is asserted high to indicate that the memory location(s) being accessed are not to be cached.

Identification of Bit Fields (logical groups of bits or signals)

All bit fields are designated in little-endian bit ordering as follows:

[X:Y],

where "X" is the most-significant bit and "Y" is the least-significant bit of the field. As an example, the IOPL field in the EFlags register consists of bits [13:12], where bit 13 is the most-significant and bit 12 the least-significant bit of the field.

Register Field References

Bit fields in registers are frequently referred to using the form **Reg[field name]**. As an example, the reference CR4[DE] refers to the Debug Extensions bit in Control Register 4.

Visit Our Web Page

Our Web site is now online at:

www.mindshare.com

As with most web pages, the content and therefore its value to you will increase over time.

Our publisher's web page contains a listing of our currently-available books and includes pricing and ordering information. Their home page is accessible at:

www.aw.com

We Want Your Feedback

MindShare values your comments and suggestions. You can contact us via mail, phone, fax or internet email.

Protected Mode Software Architecture

Phone: (214) 231-2216, and, in the U.S., (800) 633-1440
Fax: (214) 783-4715
E-mail: tshanley@interserv.com

To request information on MindShare seminars, email your request to:

tshanley@interserv.com.

Mailing Address:

MindShare, Inc.
2202 Buttercup Drive
Richardson, Texas 75082

Part One

Background

1 *Single-Task OS and Application*

This Chapter

This chapter describes the basic operational characteristics of a typical single-task OS and its relationship with applications programs designed to work with it.

The Next Chapter

The next chapter provides a basic description of a multitasking OS.

Operating System Overview

A single-task OS basically consists of the following components:

- The command line interpreter, or CLI
- The program loader
- OS services

Command Line Interpreter (CLI)

Once the OS has been loaded into memory by the startup firmware, control is passed to its initialization code. This sets up any necessary data structures (e.g., the interrupt table), loads and initializes device drivers, etc., and then passes control to the CLI.

The CLI issues a prompt to the user requesting that the user identify the program to be run. The exact form that the prompt takes and the method utilized to make a selection is OS-dependent. In the case of DOS's COMMAND.COM CLI, the prompt is not very user-friendly. In response, the user keys in the name of a program to be executed. In the case of DOS DOSSHELL, the user can use the mouse to point and click on a file name.

Program Loader

Once the user selects a file name, the OS reads the file's directory entry and ascertains the amount of RAM memory necessary to hold the program. The OS locates a block of free (i.e., unused) memory into which it can load the program. The OS either directly accesses the disk controller to initiate the read, or issues a disk read request to the disk BIOS routine in system memory or to the disk device driver. The BIOS routine or driver issues the request to the disk controller and, if the disk-to-memory transfer will be performed by the DMA controller, programs the disk controller's associated DMA channel to transfer the data into the target memory. The DMA controller transfers the block of information into memory and then instructs the disk controller to inform the BIOS routine (or driver) that the transfer has been completed. The disk controller generates its device-specific interrupt request, causing the processor to jump to the disk interrupt service routine. The service routine checks the disk controller's completion status to ensure that no errors were incurred during the transfer of the information into memory. It then returns a good completion to the BIOS routine (or driver), which returns with a good completion to the OS. Upon ascertaining that the program has been transferred into memory, the OS executes a far jump instruction to the program's entry point. The applications program then begins execution.

OS Services

In the course of accomplishing its task, the applications program may have to communicate with a number of devices in the system. It may have to read/write disk files, perform data communications, interface with the display and keyboard, etc.

Rather than force the author of every applications program to write routines to interface with these entities, the OS provides a variety of services to the applications program. When the programmer wishes to establish a communications channel that can be used to access a disk file, for instance, he or she issues a "file open" request to the OS. The OS performs this function for the programmer. When the programmer needs to change the appearance of the display, a request can be issued to the OS. In short, the OS provides a toolbox of services useful to

Chapter 1: Single-Task OS and Application

the applications program. This increases the productivity of the applications programmer by lessening the amount of code to be written. It also renders the applications program platform hardware-independent (because it doesn't communicate directly with the devices).

Direct IO Access

In order to achieve better performance, many applications programs access IO ports directly (rather than going through the OS services). As a side-effect, this renders the program much more platform design-dependent. In addition, the OS is left outside the loop, so it doesn't always "know" the current state of an IO device. In a single-task OS environment this usually will not cause problems because the OS only starts one applications program at a time and lets it run to completion before starting another. Because each applications program can manipulate IO ports directly, applications programs (and the OS) cannot make any assumptions about the current state of an IO device when they begin execution, but must always initialize all of the device's IO registers to a known state during each session.

Applications Program Memory Usage

Because a single-task OS only runs one program at a time, there is no need to protect applications programs from invading each other's memory space. As long as the applications program doesn't trash itself or the OS that gave birth to it and that nurtures it, everything should be fine.

Task Initiation, Execution and Termination

Figure 1-1 on page 12 illustrates the application program's dependence on the OS while it's executing. The OS loads the task into memory and executes it. While executing, the task may issue calls to the OS requesting performance of various functions. Upon completion, the task returns control back to the OS. The OS then deallocates the memory used by the program and prompts the user for another program name.

Protected Mode Software Architecture

Figure 1-1: *Task/OS Relationship*

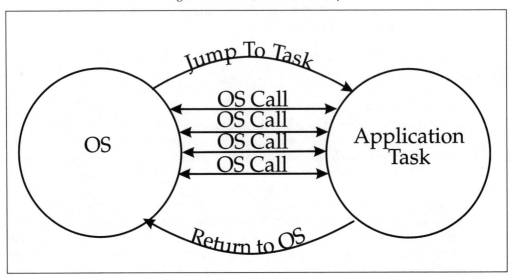

2 *Definition of Multitasking*

The Previous Chapter

The previous chapter provided a basic definition of the typical single-task OS and task. Once loaded and started by the OS, a task runs to completion and then returns control back to the OS. The OS then deallocates its memory and prompts the user for another program name.

This Chapter

This chapter provides a brief introduction to the concept of multitasking.

The Next Chapter

The next chapter defines the major problems that a multitasking OS must contend with.

Concept

It is incorrect to say that a multitasking OS runs multiple programs (i.e., tasks) simultaneously. In reality, it loads a task into memory, permits it to run for a while and then suspends it. It suspends the program by creating a snapshot, or image, of all of the processor's registers in memory. In the x86 architecture, the image is stored in a special segment referred to as a Task State Segment, or TSS. This is accomplished by performing a series of memory write transactions. In other words, the exact state of the processor at the point of suspension is saved in memory.

Having effectively saved a "bookmark" to indicate the point of suspension and the processor's complete state at that time, the processor then initiates another task by loading it into memory and jumping to its entry point. Based on some OS-specific criteria, the OS will at some point make the decision to suspend this task as well. As before, the state of the processor is saved in memory (in this task's TSS) as a "bookmark" for this task.

At some point, the OS makes the decision to resume a previously-suspended task. This is accomplished by reloading the processor's registers from the previously-saved register image (i.e., its TSS). This is accomplished by performing a series of memory read transactions. The processor then uses CS:EIP to fetch the next instruction, thereby resuming program execution at the point where it had been suspended earlier.

The criteria that an OS uses in making the decision to suspend a program is specific to that OS. It may simply use timeslicing—each program is permitted to execute for a fixed amount of time (e.g., 10ms). At the end of that period of time, it is suspended and the next task in the queue is started or resumed. The OS may assign priority levels to programs, thereby permitting a higher priority program to "preempt" a lower priority program that may currently be running.

An Example—Timeslicing

Prior to starting or resuming execution of a task, the OS would initialize a hardware timer to interrupt program execution after a defined period of time (e.g., 10ms). It then starts or resumes execution of a task. The task runs for 10ms unhindered. When the hardware timer expires, it generates an interrupt, causing the processor to suspend the task and jump to the OS's task scheduler. The OS determines which task to run next.

Another Example—Awaiting an Event

Task Issues Call to OS for Disk Read

The applications program calls the OS requesting that a block of data be read from a disk drive into memory. Once a disk read request is forwarded to the disk interface, the disk read/write head mechanism must be moved to the target cylinder. This is a lengthy process typically requiring ten or more milliseconds to complete. The disk interface must then wait for the start sector of the requested block to be presented under the read head. The duration of this delay is defined by the rotational speed of the disk drive. Once again, this is a lengthy delay that can be measured in milliseconds. Only then can the data transfer begin.

Rather than awaiting the completion of the disk read, the OS would better utilize the machine's resources by suspending the task that originated the request and transferring control to another program so work can be accomplished while the disk operation is in progress.

OS Suspends Task

As described earlier, the processor saves its current state, or register image, in a special area of memory set aside for this task (the application's TSS). Once this series of memory write transactions has completed, the task has been suspended.

OS Initiates Disk Read

The OS issues a disk read command to the fixed disk controller. The disk controller begins seek the heads to the target cylinder.

OS Makes Entry in Event Queue

The OS makes an entry in its event queue. This entry will be used to transfer control back to the suspended task when the disk interface completes the transfer.

OS Starts or Resumes Another Task

Rather than waiting for the completion of the disk read operation, the OS will start or resume another task.

Disk-Generated IRQ Causes Jump to OS

When the disk controller (or its associated DMA channel) completes the transfer of the requested information into system memory, it generates an interrupt request. This causes the processor to jump to the OS's disk interrupt service routine. The OS checks the completion status of the disk controller to ensure a good completion.

Task Queue Checked

The OS then scans the event queue to determine which suspended task is awaiting this completion notification.

OS Resumes Task

The OS reloads the suspended task's stored register image (its TSS) into the processor's registers. The processor then examines CS:EIP to determine what memory address to fetch its next instruction from. The resumed task then processes the data in memory that was read from the disk.

3 Multitasking Problems

The Previous Chapter

The previous chapter provided a brief introduction to the concept of multitasking.

This Chapter

This chapter defines the major problems that a multitasking OS must contend with.

The Next Chapter

The processor contains a number of registers, a subset of which contain bits that control the processor's operational characteristics. The next chapter introduces the processor characteristics controlled by each register. In addition, it defines the state of each of these registers immediately after reset is removed and the resultant startup operational characteristics of the processor.

OS Protects Territorial Integrity

The multitasking OS provides a method for loading multiple tasks into memory and permitting each to run for a slice of time. As described in an earlier chapter, it permits a task to run for a timeslice, suspends it, permits another task to run for a timeslice, suspends it, etc. If the OS is executing on a fast processor with fast access to memory, this task switching can be accomplished so quickly that all of the tasks *appear* to be executing simultaneously.

While the processor is executing a task, the OS and all of the other dormant tasks are resident in memory. When each of the tasks (and the OS) were suspended, the processor created a snapshot of the processor's register image in memory at the moment it was suspended. In the x86 environment, the OS sets up a separate Task State Segment (TSS) for each task to be used during task switches. When it's time to resume execution of a program, the processor can reload its register set from the task's TSS and pick up right where it left off.

Stay in Your Own Memory Area

It should be obvious that the currently-executing program utilizes certain areas of memory. Its program code resides in its code segment(s) within memory. Some of the data that it acts upon is stored within the processor's registers and much of it in the areas of memory designated as its data segments. When the program needs to store the information from a register briefly so that it can use the register for something else, it typically stores the data in the area of memory designated as its stack segment.

The currently-executing program is only aware of two entities—itself and the OS that created it. It is completely unaware of the existence of any other tasks that are currently suspended. The currently-executing program should only access its own memory. If permitted to perform memory writes anywhere in memory, it is entirely probable that it will corrupt the code, stack or data areas of programs that are currently suspended. Consider what would happen when the OS resumes execution of a task that had been corrupted while in suspension. Its program and/or data would have been corrupted, causing it to malfunction when it begins to run.

The OS must protect suspended tasks (including itself!) from the currently executing task. If it doesn't, multitasking will not work.

IO Port Anarchy

Assume that the currently-executing task needs to initiate a disk access. To do this, it must program the disk controller's IO registers with the information defining the disk command type (e.g., disk read), the cylinder number, the head (or surface) number, the start sector number and the number of sectors to be transferred. This is accomplished by executing a series of OUT instructions that cause the processor to perform a series of IO write transactions to transfer the command and associated parameters to the disk controller. Now assume that the task has programmed some, but not all of, the disk controller's registers when the task's timeslice expires. The OS suspends the current task and starts or resumes another task.

Chapter 3: Multitasking Problems

The new task, having no knowledge of the suspended tasks, may decide that it also wants to issue a command to the disk controller. Assume that it does so and that the operation completes without error. Eventually, the OS suspends this task and reawakens the other task. This task doesn't know that it was put to sleep when it resumes execution at the point of suspension. In other words, it completes the series of IO writes to transfer the remainder of the request parameters to the disk controller. It has no idea that the initial parameters that it sent to the disk controller (before it was suspended) were overwritten by the other task while it was asleep. The end result will be that this task's disk operation will not occur correctly.

Generally speaking, the system's IO devices should be considered a pool of shared resources to be managed by a central entity (the OS). Having one entity perform all communications with IO devices ensures that there will be no contention for IO devices between multiple tasks.

To accomplish this, the OS should not permit the tasks to talk directly to shared IO ports. In other words, any attempt to execute an IN or OUT instruction should cause the processor to trap (jump) to the OS. The OS then communicates with the IO device for the task.

The OS and/or processor could be configured to permit a task to access certain IO ports directly, but restrict access to other ports.

Unauthorized Use of OS's Tools

The OS maintains the integrity of the system. It manages all shared resources and decides what task will run next and for how long. It should be fairly obvious that the person in charge must have more authority (greater privileges) than the other tasks currently resident in memory. It would be ill-conceived to permit normal tasks to access certain processor control registers, system tables in memory, etc.

This can be accomplished in two ways: assignment of privilege levels to programs and assignment of ownership to areas of memory. The Intel x86 processors utilize both methods. There are four privilege levels:

- **Level zero**. Greatest amount of privilege. Assigned to the heart, or kernel, of the OS. It handles the task queues, memory management, etc.
- **Level one**. Typically assigned to OS services that provide services to the applications programs and device drivers.

Protected Mode Software Architecture

- **Level two**. Typically assigned to device drivers that the OS uses to communicate with peripheral devices.
- **Level three**. Assigned to applications programs.

The applications program operates at the lowest privilege level because its actions must be restricted. The OS has a very high privilege level so that it can accomplish its job of managing every aspect of the system. The integrity of the system would be compromised if an applications program could call highly-privileged parts of the OS code to accomplish things it shouldn't be able to do. This implies that the processor must have some way of comparing the privilege level of the calling program to that of the program being called. To gain entry into the called program, the calling program's privilege level (CPL, or current privilege level) must meet or beat the privilege level of the program it is calling. Intel x86 processors incorporate this feature.

No Interrupts, Please!

An applications program written to run under a single-tasking OS is master of all it surveys. It can communicate with any IO device, any memory location, disable interrupt recognition if it doesn't want to be interrupted, etc. In a single tasking environment, the programmer can disable recognition of interrupts if it will not adversely affect the operation of this, the only program executing in the system.

If this same program is run under the management of a multitasking OS, however, it can cause severe problems. If permitted to execute a CLI (Clear Interrupt enable) instruction, the processor will no longer recognize interrupt requests originated by IO devices throughout the system. This means that these devices may not receive the servicing they require on a timely basis. As a result, they may suffer from buffer overflow or underflow conditions. This can result in anything from poor performance of a subsystem to completely flawed operation (data may be lost due to insufficient temporary buffer space within the subsystem). It should be noted that an IO device may generate an interrupt request to signal an event to another program that is currently suspended. The correct action may be for the processor to recognize the request, perform a task switch to the other program, service the request, and return to the interrupted task.

To summarize, the processor and the OS should not permit the applications task to execute the CLI instruction. An attempt to execute a CLI should cause the processor to trap out to the OS. The OS would then set a bit indicating that this task prefers not to be interrupted. The EFlags[IF] bit would not really be cleared, so the processor would still be able to recognize interrupt requests. The OS then resumes execution of the task. If an interrupt request is detected while this task is still executing, the processor jumps to a special routine to determine if this particular interrupt request is deemed important enough to interrupt the currently executing program. If not, the OS marks this request for subsequent servicing and resumes the interrupted task. The request is serviced after the current task has been suspended. If the request is considered important enough to be serviced immediately, the OS executes the IO device's interrupt service routine and then resumes the interrupted task.

BIOS Calls

If an applications program that was originally written to run under a single-tasking OS needs to communicate with an IO device, it may do this in two fashions. It can communicate with the device directly by executing an `IN` or an `OUT` instruction or it can issue a request to the device's BIOS routine. The BIOS routine, in turn, performs the necessary series of `IN`s and `OUT`s to communicate the request to the IO device. The concept of trapping `IN`s and `OUT`s was discussed earlier.

DOS programs call BIOS routines by executing software interrupt instructions. An example would be `INT 13h` to call the disk BIOS routine. In response, the processor indexes into entry 13h in the interrupt table in memory and jumps to the start address of the disk BIOS routine indicated in this entry. Since all, or most, accesses to IO devices should be routed through the multitasking OS, the processor should trap to the OS whenever an attempt is made by an application program to execute an `INT` instruction. The OS can then use the IDT entry number specified by the `INT` instruction to determine what BIOS routine the task is calling. The OS can then execute its own device driver to communicate the request to the target IO device.

Part Two

Register Set
&
Real Mode

4 *The Control Registers*

The Previous Chapter

The previous chapter defined the major problems that a multitasking OS must contend with.

This Chapter

The processor contains a number of registers, a subset of which contain bits that control the processor's operational characteristics. This chapter introduces the processor characteristics controlled by each register. In addition, it defines the state of each of these registers immediately after reset is removed and the resultant startup operational characteristics of the processor.

The Next Chapter

After reset is removed, the processor begins operation in real mode. The next chapter provides a basic description of processor operation in real mode.

Control Register 0 (CR0)

CR0 Description

Refer to Figure 4-1 on page 28. Table 4-1 on page 26 tracks the evolution of CR0.

Protected Mode Software Architecture

Table 4-1: Evolution of CR0

Bit	Name	Description
[3:0]	TS, EM, MP, PE	The lower half of CR0 (bits [15:0]), also referred to as the Machine Status Word (MSW) register, was first implemented in the **286** processor. Only the lower four bits (bits [3:0]) were implemented, however.
[31] and [4]	PG, ET	The **386** processor expanded the register to 32 bits and renamed it Control Register 0 (CR0). Bits [4] (Extension Type, or ET) and [31] (Paging Enable, or PE) were added. As stated earlier, the lower half of the register is still referred to as the MSW register. The state of ET tells the 386 processor whether the attached x87 numeric coprocessor is a 287 or a 387 (so it knows which hardware communications protocol to use). Additional information on processor/coprocessor interaction can be found in the MindShare book entitled *ISA System Architecture*. The state of PG disables or enables the processor's paging capability. A detailed description of paging can be found in the chapter entitled "Virtual Paging" on page 219.
[4]	ET	The **486** processor hardwires bit [4], the Extension Type bit, to one (because processors beyond the 386 do not support the 287 numeric coprocessor).
[5]	NE	The **486** processor added bit [5], the Numeric Exception (NE) bit. The state of this bit tells the processor the action to take in the event of a floating-point exception—when cleared (zero), the processor asserts its FERR# output in the event of a floating-point error; when set (one), the processor generates an exception 16d in the event of an error. A detailed description of this bit can be found in the MindShare books entitled *80486 System Architecture* and *Pentium Processor System Architecture*.

Table 4-1: Evolution of CR0 (Continued)

Bit	Name	Description
[16]	WP	The **486** added bit [16], the Write-Protect (WP) bit. When set, denies the OS permission to write to pages marked read-only. The 386 processor permitted programs with privilege levels 0 through 2 (i.e., the OS) to write to read-only pages.
[18]	AM	The **486** added bit [18], the Alignment Mask (AM) bit. When set, the AC (Alignment Check) bit in the EFlags register controls whether or not an AC exception is generated when an attempt is made to perform a non-aligned memory access. When cleared, the processor cannot generate AC exceptions (even if the AC bit in the EFlags register is set). Detailed descriptions of misaligned transfers can be found in the MindShare books entitled *ISA System Architecture*, *80486 System Architecture* and *Pentium Processor System Architecture*.
[30:29]	CD, NW	The **486** added bits [30:29], Cache Disable (CD) and Not Write-through (NW) to control the internal cache. A detailed discussion of these two bits can be found in the MindShare books entitled *80486 System Architecture* and *Pentium Processor System Architecture* (published by Addison-Wesley).

CR0 State after Reset

CR0 contains 60000010h after reset, yielding the following results:

- Paging is disabled (PG = 0).
- The internal cache is disabled (CD and NW =11b).
- The Alignment Check exception is disabled (AM = 0).
- Pages marked read-only can be written to by the OS (WP = 0 and assuming that paging becomes enabled and the WP bit remains cleared).
- Protected mode is disabled (PE = 0; in other words, the processor is in real mode).
- The floating-point unit is disabled (MP and EM = 00b).
- No task switch has occurred (TS = 0).

Protected Mode Software Architecture

Figure 4-1: Control Register 0 (CR0)

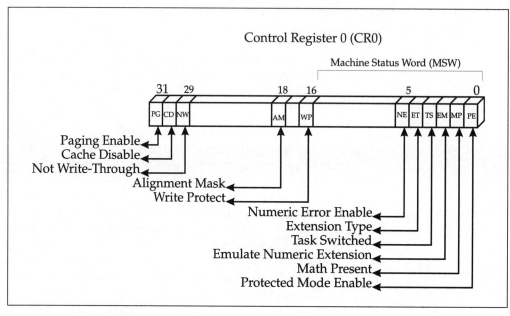

Control Register 1 (CR1)

CR1 Description

CR1 has not been implemented in any of the x86 processors through the Pentium processor.

CR1 State after Reset

Returns all zeros if read. This has no effect on the processor.Control Register 2 (CR2)

Control Register 2 (CR2)

CR2 Description

CR2 was first implemented in the 386 and is identical in all x86 processors through the Pentium processor (see Figure 4-2 on page 29). CR2 is only used if the processor is in protected mode and paging has been enabled. Assuming that this is the case, the processor uses CR2 to store the 32-bit linear address that caused a page fault exception. A detailed description of the paging mechanism can be found in the chapter entitled "Virtual Paging" on page 219.

CR2 State after Reset

CR2 contains 00000000h after reset. This has no effect on the processor's operation.

Figure 4-2: Control Register 2 (CR2)

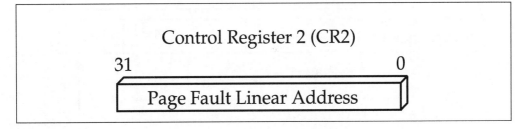

Control Register 3 (CR3)

CR3 Description

Also referred to as the Page Directory Base Address register, CR3 was first implemented in the 386 processor and is illustrated in Figure 4-3 on page 30. However, the PCD and PWT bits were not implemented until the 486 processor. CR3 has no effect unless the processor is in protected mode with paging enabled (CR0's PE and PG bits set).

CR3 contains the 4KB-aligned physical base address of the Page Directory in memory. The PWT and PCD bits were first implemented in the 486 processor (because, unlike the 386, it has an internal cache). These two bits define the cacheability and the cache policy to be used on memory writes (write-back or write-through) when the processor is reading an entry from or is updating one of the entries in the page directory.

A detailed description of paging can be found in the chapter entitled "Virtual Paging" on page 219. A detailed description of caching can be found in the MindShare books entitled *80486 System Architecture* and *Pentium Processor System Architecture* (published by Addison-Wesley).

CR3 State after Reset

CR3 is cleared after reset.

Figure 4-3: Control Register 3 (CR3)

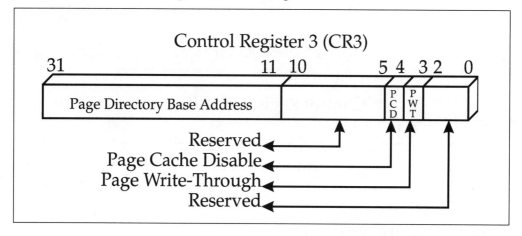

Control Register 4 (CR4)

CR4 Description

CR4 was first introduced in the initial version of the Pentium processor and was later included in the newer versions of the 486 processor. The bits in this register permit certain processor features to be enabled or disabled. The register is pictured in Figure 4-4 on page 34. The feature bits are described in Table 4-2 on page 31.

Table 4-2: CR4 Feature Bits

Bit	Name	Description
[0]	VME	Bit [0] is the **Virtual 8086 Mode Extension enable bit (VME)**. Intel has kept the description of this bit under non-disclosure. However, the author has taken the very small amount of information mentioned in the *Pentium Family User's Manual, Volume 3: Architecture and Programming Manual*, and has indulged in hopefully intelligent speculation regarding this feature bit. When cleared, the attempted execution of the interrupt-related instructions (CLI, STI, INT, PUSHF, POPF, and IRET) are handled in the same manner as the 386 processor. Assume that the processor is in protected mode, is currently executing a DOS program (8086 program), and it attempts to execute one of the instructions just mentioned (in other words, an instruction that may alter the state of the processor's external interrupt enable flag bit (IF) in the EFlags register). • If the VME bit is cleared, the processor generates an exception and traps to the Virtual Machine Monitor (VMM) program when one of these instructions is attempted. • If the VME bit is set, the processor permits these instructions to be executed and does not trap to the VMM. Instead of permitting the instruction to alter the state of IF bit, however, a copy of the bit is altered (the Virtual Interrupt Flag, or VIF, bit). Altering the VIF bit in the EFlags register does not affect the ability of the processor to recognize external interrupts. A detailed discussion of Virtual 8086 mode can be found in the chapter entitled "Virtual 8086 Mode" on page 265.

Table 4-2: CR4 Feature Bits (Continued)

Bit	Name	Description
[1]	PVI	Bit [1] is the **Protected Mode Virtual Interrupt (PVI) bit**. As with the VME bit, Intel continues to keep the PVI bit under non-disclosure. Once again, the author has indulged in hopefully intelligent speculation regarding the usage of the PVI bit. Assume that the processor is in VM86 mode executing an 8086 applications program (i.e., a DOS program at privilege level three) that attempts to execute an INT instruction (e.g., to call DOS). There are two possible cases: • the IOPL field in the EFlags register has been set to a value < three by the OS. In this case, the attempt to execute the INT instruction results in the processor switching to the VMM program. The VMM program must then determine the action to be taken (e.g., call MS-DOS, or call the protected mode OS to accomplish the desired function call). • the IOPL field has been set to a value of three by the OS. Processor switches to privilege level zero and executes the protected mode interrupt handler. In either case, there is a substantial amount of software overhead involved in servicing the INT call. If the PVI bit is set and the IOPL is set to three when the DOS task attempts to execute an INT instruction, the processor does not switch to privilege level zero. It just jumps to the indicated interrupt service routine (specified by the value *nn* in the INT *nn* instruction) using the pointer from the entry in the protected mode interrupt table. This eliminates much of the software overhead in servicing the interrupt, resulting in better performance.
[2]	TSD	Bit [2] is the **Time Stamp Disable (TSD) bit**. Intel has recently removed the description of some of the Pentium processor's performance monitoring features from non-disclosure, but a discussion of these features is outside the scope of this book.
[3]	DE	Bit [3] is the **Debug Extensions (DE) bit**. When cleared, the processor's debug features are compatible with those of the 386 processor. When the DE bit is set, IO breakpoint capability is enabled. This feature is described in the MindShare book entitled *Pentium Processor System Architecture* (published by Addison-Wesley).

Table 4-2: CR4 Feature Bits (Continued)

Bit	Name	Description
[4]	PSE	Bit [4] is the **Page Size Extension (PSE)** bit. As with the VME bit, Intel continues to keep the PSE bit under non-disclosure. Time for some hopefully intelligent speculation again. When this bit is set, the OS programmer may designate some pages as 4MB rather than 4KB in size. This capability is described in the chapter entitled "Virtual Paging" on page 219. When the PSE bit is cleared, all pages are 4KB in size.
[6]	MCE	Bit [6] is the **Machine Check Enable (MCE)** bit. Exception 18d is the machine check exception. It is processor-specific whether or not a processor implements the machine check exception and, if so, the conditions that cause the exception. On the Pentium processor, the exception is taken if MCE is set and one of the following conditions is detected: • BUSCHK# is asserted by external logic during a processor-initiated bus cycle. This indicates that the bus cycle cannot be completed for some reason. • On a read, the processor detects a data parity error, asserts PERR#, and, in response, external logic asserts PEN# to the processor. In both cases, the Pentium latches the address and the bus cycle (i.e., transaction) type into the Machine Check Address and Type registers, indicates (in the Machine Check Type register) whether the exception is the result of a bus check or a parity error, and generates an exception 18d. A more detailed discussion of BUSCHK#, PERR#, and Machine Check may be found in the MindShare book entitled *Pentium Processor System Architecture*.

CR4 State after Reset

After reset, CR4 is cleared to zero. This has the following effects:

- Virtual 8086 mode extensions are disabled (VME = 0).
- The Protected mode Virtual Interrupt (PVI) feature is disabled.
- The Time Stamp Disable (TSD) bit is cleared.
- Debug Extension bit (DE) is cleared, disabling processor's ability to monitor for IO breakpoints.
- The Page Size Extension bit (PSE) is cleared. All pages are 4KB in size.
- Machine Check Enable bit (MCE) is cleared, disabling ability of the processor to generate the Machine Check exception.

In other words, the processor is backward-compatible with the 386 processor.

Figure 4-4: Control Register 4 (CR4)

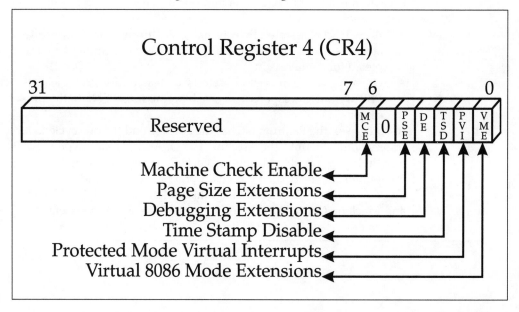

EFlags Register

EFlags Description

A subset of the bits in the Extended Flags register (EFlags) control certain aspects of the processor's operation. Table 4-3 on page 35 tracks the evolution of the EFlags register.

The bits within the EFlags register that control aspects of the processor's operation are defined in Table 4-4 on page 35.

Table 4-3: Evoluation of EFlags Register

Processor	Description
8088/8086	The lower 16 bits ([15:0]) is referred to as the Flag register and was first implemented in the 8088/8086 processor. However, those processors did not implement the IOPL and NT bit fields.
286	The 286 processor added the IOPL and NT bits.
386	The 386 processor extended the 16-bit Flags register into the 32-bit EFlags register. However, only the RF and VM bits were implemented in the upper 16-bits of the register.
486	The earlier versions of the 486 processor implemented the AC bit. Later versions also implement the VIF, VIP, and ID bits.
Pentium	The first (and all subsequent) versions of the Pentium processor implement the VIF, VIP, and ID bits.

Table 4-4: EFlag Register Control Bits

Bit	Name	Description
8	TF	**Trap Flag**. When set, places the processor in single-step mode. A debug exception is generated at the completion of each instruction. When cleared, program execution proceeds normally.

Table 4-4: EFlag Register Control Bits (Continued)

Bit	Name	Description
9	IF	**Interrupt Flag.** When set, the processor recognizes external interrupt requests detected on its INTR input. When cleared, requests for service are ignored.
10	DF	**Direction Flag.** When cleared, the processor auto-increments the address associated with string instructions. When set, the processor auto-decrements the address.
13:12	IOPL	**IO Privilege Level.** When the processor is operating in protected mode, the processor cannot successfully execute certain instructions (IN, INS, OUT, OUTS, CLI, STI) if the privilege level of the currently-executing program doesn't meet or beat the privilege level indicated the IOPL field. The contents of the IOPL field can only be changed by a task with the POPF or IRET instruction, but only if the current task is running at privilege level zero. Likewise, the state of the IF bit can only be changed by a task that meets or beats the IOPL value.
14	NT	**Nested Task.** Any interrupt that selects a task gate in the interrupt descriptor table (IDT) causes a task switch to the task that services the interrupt. In this case, the processor sets the NT bit. When the IRET instruction is executed at the end of the service task, the processor tests the state of the NT bit. If set, the processor performs a task switch to switch back to the interrupted task. Any interrupt that selects an interrupt or a trap gate in the IDT does not cause a task switch. The processor clears the NT bit and jumps to the interrupt service routine pointed to by the selected gate descriptor.
16	RF	**Resume Flag.** Whenever the processor is exiting the debugger to resume a program, the instruction used is the IRETD instruction. Upon executing this instruction, the processor sets the RF bit. This prevents the processor from immediately regenerating the same debug fault that originally caused the debug interrupt.

Table 4-4: EFlag Register Control Bits (Continued)

Bit	Name	Description
17	VM	**Virtual 8086 Mode**. This bit is set whenever a multitasking OS switches to a VM86 task. The OS ensures that the VM bit has been set in the EFlags field within the TSS associated with the VM86 program. The processor copies the register images (including that of the EFlags register) from the TSS into the processor's register set, thereby setting the VM bit. This places the processor in VM86 mode when the task starts. When the processor suspends the VM86 task, it saves the current contents of EFlags in the VM86 task's TSS and then copies the EFlags value from the next task's TSS into EFlags.
18	AC	**Alignment Check**. When the AM bit in CR0 is set, the AC (Alignment Check) bit in the EFlags register controls whether or not an AC exception is generated when an attempt is made to perform a non-aligned memory access. When AM is cleared, the processor cannot generate AC exceptions (even if the AC bit in the EFlags register is set).
19	VIF	**Virtual Interrupt Flag**. *It must be noted that this bit is still under non-disclosure. The following is based on hopefully intelligent speculation.* When the VME bit (CR4) is set and a DOS task is executing in VM86 mode, execution of a CLI or STI instruction affects the VIF bit rather than the IF bit. In other words, interrupts are not really disabled by execution of a CLI. Rather, the VIF bit is affected by the CLI and STI instructions, instead of the IF bit.

Table 4-4: EFlag Register Control Bits (Continued)

Bit	Name	Description
20	VIP	**Virtual Interrupt Pending**. *It must be noted that this bit is still under non-disclosure. The following is based on hopefully intelligent speculation.* If the VME bit (CR4) is set, a DOS task is executing in VM86 mode, and an interrupt is detected, one of two cases exists: • **The IF bit is set**. In this case, the processor recognizes the interrupt and jumps to the OS. The OS checks the state of the VIF bit to determine if the interrupted program prefers not to be interrupted. If VIF is set, the OS executes an interrupt handler to service the interrupt request now. If VIF is cleared, the OS determines whether the request is high priority. If not, the OS sets the VIP bit to record that an outstanding request must be serviced when the DOS program is suspended. If the request is considered important by the OS, it jumps to the appropriate interrupt handler and services the request immediately. • **The IF bit is cleared**. In this case, the processor will not service the interrupt at this time.
21	ID	**CPU Identification**. Before attempting execution of the CPUID instruction, the programmer must first determine if the processor implements the instruction. This is accomplished by attempting to change the state of the ID bit. If ID is hardwired to zero, the processor does not support the CPUID instruction. If ID is read/writable, CPUID is supported.

EFlags State after Reset

Reset forces the value 00000002h into the EFlags register. As a result, the control bits in this register are set as indicated in Table 4-5 on page 39.

Table 4-5: EFlags State after Reset

Bit	Name	Description
8	TF	Trap Flag cleared, disabling single-step operation.
9	IF	Interrupt Flag cleared, disabling external interrupt detection on the INTR input.
10	DF	Direction Flag cleared, causing processor to auto-increment the address during the execution of string instructions.
13:12	IOPL	IO Privilege Level set to zero, permitting only programs with privilege level zero to perform IO operations.
14	NT	Nested Task cleared, causing the IRET instruction to work normally (rather than causing a task switch).
16	RF	Resume Flag cleared, enabling Debug fault recognition on the instruction executed immediately after an IRETD instruction.
17	VM	Virtual 8086 Mode cleared, disabling the processor's "watchdog" logic that monitors the behavior of DOS programs.
18	AC	Alignment Check cleared, disabling the generation of the Alignment Check exception on misaligned transactions.
19	VIF	Virtual Interrupt Flag cleared. Has no effect on startup.
20	VIP	Virtual Interrupt Pending cleared. Has no effect on startup.
21	ID	CPU ID bit cleared. Has no effect on startup.

Protected Mode Software Architecture

Figure 4-5: The EFlags Register

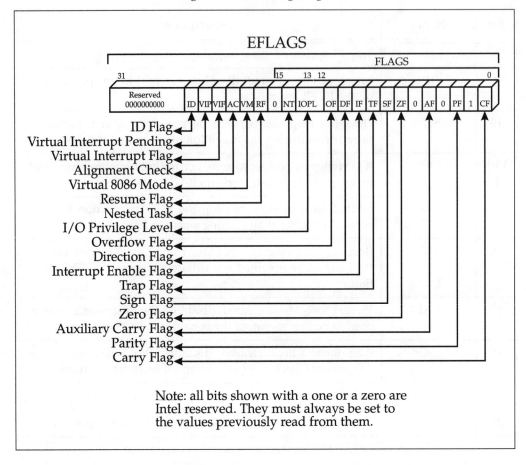

Note: all bits shown with a one or a zero are
Intel reserved. They must always be set to
the values previously read from them.

Interrupt Descriptor Table Register (IDTR)

Background

Whenever a maskable interrupt is detected on the processor's INTR input while
interrupt recognition is enabled (EFlags IF bit is set), the processor obtains the
interrupt vector from the external interrupt controller and uses it to index into
the IDT. Whenever a software interrupt instruction (INT nn) is executed, the *nn*
value supplies the vector.

In real mode, the IDT consists of a series of 256 four-byte entries, each of which specifies the start address of the interrupt service routine associated with that interrupt vector. When the processor obtains the 8-bit interrupt vector, it multiplies it by four (four bytes per IDT entry) to identify the start address of the IDT entry associated with the vector. It then reads the CS:IP value stored in that entry and jumps to the interrupt service routine entry point.

In protected mode, the IDT consists of a series of up to 256 eight-byte entries, each of which guards entry to the associated interrupt handler. When the processor obtains the 8-bit interrupt vector, it multiplies it by eight (eight bytes per IDT entry) to identify the start address of the IDT entry associated with the vector.

Detailed descriptions of interrupt handling can be found in the chapter on interrupts in the MindShare book entitled *ISA System Architecture*; in the APIC-related chapters in the MindShare book entitled *Pentium Processor System Architecture*; and in the chapter entitled "Interrupt Sources and Handling" on page 183 of this book.

IDTR Description

The IDTR is pictured in Figure 4-6 on page 42. In both real and protected mode, it identifies the base address and length of the IDT in memory. This register is accessible from real mode (using the Load IDT (LIDT) and Store IDT (SIDT) instructions), permitting the programmer to:

* set up a protected mode IDT anywhere in memory (while still in real mode)
* and then specify its base and size in the IDTR (using the LIDT instruction).

IDTR State after Reset

After reset, IDTR contains a base address of 00000000h and a limit of 03FFh. In other words, the real mode IDT starts at memory location 00000000h and is 1KB in length (256 entries of four bytes each). It should be noted that many of Intel's 486 and Pentium documents state that reset forces the length to FFFFh, rather than 03FFh. This is incorrect.

Protected Mode Software Architecture

Figure 4-6: Interrupt Descriptor Table Register (IDTR)

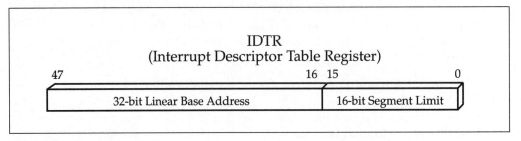

Debug Registers

Debug Registers Description

Figure 4-7 on page 43 illustrates the Debug registers. Note that the Debug Mode Control register was first implemented in the Pentium processor. These registers permit the processor to monitor for both memory and IO breakpoint conditions (note that only 486 and Pentium processors that implement the DE bit in CR4 can monitor for IO breakpoints). A detailed description of the Debug registers is outside the scope of this book.

Debug Registers State after Reset

After reset, DR7, the Debug Control register, contains 00000400h, disabling all breakpoint monitoring.

Figure 4-7: Debug Registers

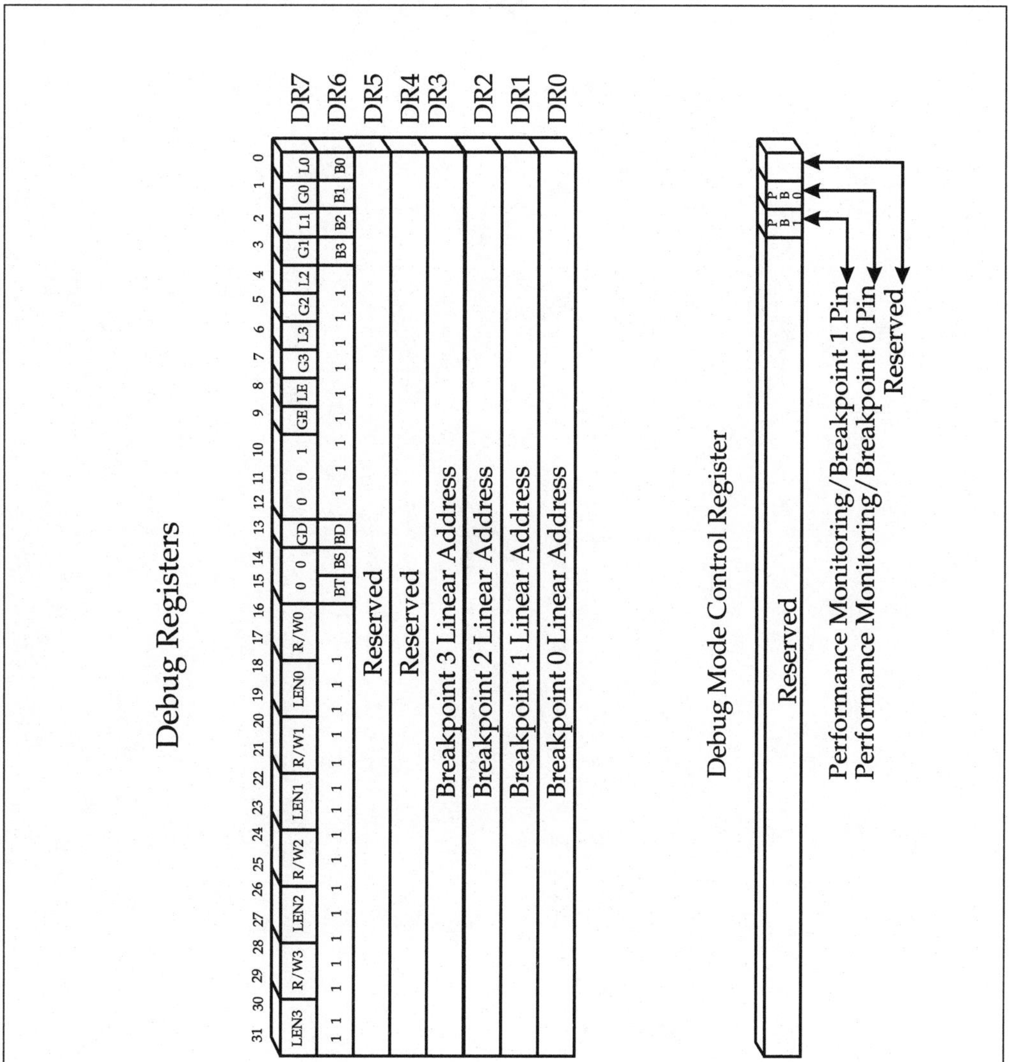

Debug Registers

31	30	29	28	27	26	25	24	23	22	21	20	19	18	17	16	15	14	13	12	11	10	9	8	7	6	5	4	3	2	1	0	
Control	LEN3	R/W3		LEN2	R/W2		LEN1	R/W1		LEN0	R/W0		0	0	GD	0	0	1	GE	LE	G3	L3	G2	L2	G1	L1	G0	L0	DR7
Status	1	1	1	1	1	1	1	1	1	1	1		BT	BS	BD	1	1	1	1	1	1	1	1	B3	B2	B1	B0	DR6

Reserved — DR5

Reserved — DR4

Breakpoint 3 Linear Address — DR3

Breakpoint 2 Linear Address — DR2

Breakpoint 1 Linear Address — DR1

Breakpoint 0 Linear Address — DR0

Debug Mode Control Register

| Reserved | PB1 | PB0 | |

Performance Monitoring/Breakpoint 1 Pin
Performance Monitoring/Breakpoint 0 Pin
Reserved

5 *Real Mode Operation*

The Previous Chapter

The previous chapter provided an introduction to the registers that control various aspects of the processor's operation.

This Chapter

This chapter provides an introduction to processor operation in real mode.

The Next Chapter

The next chapter provides a brief introduction to the Intel x86 protected mode environment and the facilities that it provides to solve the problems associated with multitasking.

Special Note

This chapter contains a number of references to protected mode operation and terminology. A detailed description of each is found in subsequent chapters. They are mentioned in this chapter in the interest of completeness.

286/386/486/Pentium Power-Up State

When the system is first powered up, the reset signal is asserted until the power supply output voltages have stabilized. Reset prevents the system from performing any actions until the power is stable. In addition, it presets many devices, including the processor, to a known state so that they always begin operation in the same manner.

Protected Mode Software Architecture

The assertion of reset on power up forces the values indicated in Table 5-1 on page 46 into the registers listed. This forces the processor to always come up in real mode with caching, paging and interrupts disabled. When reset is deasserted, the processor fetches its first instruction from memory.

Table 5-1: Registers after Reset

Register	State After Reset
CS	Contains **F000h**. As a result, the code segment starts at memory location 000F0000h. Actually, it starts at FFFF0000h (refer to the section entitled "Initial Memory Reads" on page 48). The invisible part of the CS register (referred to as the CS cache register) is loaded with values that define the code segment as having the following characteristics: • starts at FFFF0000h • length of 0FFFFh (64KB) • the segment is present in memory • read/write segment • segment has been accessed A description of the cache registers can be found in the section entitled "Segment Register—Selects Descriptor Table and Entry" on page 79.
EIP	Contains **0000FFF0h**. The first instruction is fetched from location 0000FFF0h in the code segment (see previous table entry) that starts at memory location FFFF0000h (in other words, location FFFFFFF0h).
DS, ES, FS, GS	All of the data segment registers contain **0000h**. The invisible part of the data segment registers (referred to as cache registers) are loaded with values that define the segments as having the following characteristics: • start at 00000000h • length of 0FFFFh (64KB) • the segment is present in memory • read/write segment • segment has been accessed A description of the cache registers can be found in the section entitled "Segment Register—Selects Descriptor Table and Entry" on page 79.

Table 5-1: Registers after Reset (Continued)

Register	State After Reset
SS	The stack segment register contains **0000h**. The invisible part of the stack segment register (referred to as a cache register) is loaded with values that define the segment as having the following characteristics: • starts at 00000000h • length of 0FFFFh (64KB) • the segment is present in memory • read/write segment • segment has been accessed • expand-up stack segment A description of the cache registers can be found in the section entitled "Segment Register—Selects Descriptor Table and Entry" on page 79.
CR0	Contains **60000010h**. As a result, the processor exhibits the following characteristics: • Real mode • Floating-point unit disabled • Do not emulate floating-point unit • Use DOS-compatible floating-point error reporting (assert FERR# output) • OS can write to read-only pages • Alignment Check exception disabled • Internal cache disabled • Paging disabled
EFlags	Contains **00000002h**. As a result, the processor exhibits the following characteristics: • Single-step disabled • Recognition of external interrupts (on INTR) disabled • String instructions auto-increment address • IOPL set to zero (no effect in real mode) • Debug fault checking enabled after execution of an IRETD instruction • Virtual 8086 mode disabled • Alignment Checking disabled
CR2	Contains Page Fault Linear Address of **00000000h**. No effect in real mode (because paging disabled).

Protected Mode Software Architecture

Table 5-1: Registers after Reset (Continued)

Register	State After Reset
CR3	Contains Page Directory start address of **00000000h** and page directory caching policy set to enabled and write-back. No effect (because paging disabled).
CR4	Contains **00000000h**. Processor extensions disabled. No effect in real mode.
ESP	Contains **00000000h**. Top-of-stack is set to memory location zero (same as base).
Caches	**Invalidated**. All memory reads and writes access external memory.
Debug	DR7 contains **00000400h**, disabling breakpoint recognition logic.
IDTR	IDT base set to **00000000h** with a size of 03FFh (256 entries, four bytes each).

Initial Memory Reads

x86 processors always starts up in real mode. All memory addresses are formed by adding the segment base address to the offset. Since the offset is a 16-bit value, all segments are restricted to a length of 64KB.

The CS register contains a segment start value of F000h and the EIP register contains an offset of 0000FFF0h. It would seem that the first instruction would be fetched from memory location 000FFFF0h. On power-up, however, the processor forms the memory addresses for the initial memory instruction reads differently than it does during normal real mode operation. The segment portion of the address is FFFF000h, not 0000F000h. When the IP offset of 0000FFF0h is added to the segment base address, the result is FFFFFFF0h. This is the address that the processor drives onto the address bus during the initial memory instruction read. The address for memory instruction reads is formed in this way until the programmer loads any value into the CS register (even if it's the same value that it already contains)—in other words, until a far jump (or call) is executed. Very typically, the first instruction found at the power-on restart address (FFFFFFF0h) is a far jump to the start of the system's power-on self-test (POST) program in ROM. The value loaded into the CS register becomes the 20-bit base address of the code segment. The upper 12 bits of the base address are always zero. From that point forward, the processor is only capable of addressing the first megabyte of memory space.

Chapter 5: Real Mode Operation

IO Port Addressing

The x86 processor family is restricted to a 64K range of IO addresses from 0000h through FFFFh. The programmer uses one of two instruction forms to identify the target IO location of a read or write operation. If the IO address is within the range from 0000h through 00FFh, the following form may be used:

```
IN   AL, nn          ;read data from IO port 00nnh into AL

MOV  AL, xx          ;set up data in AL
OUT  nn, AL          ;write data in AL to IO port 00nnh
```

where *nn* equals the target IO address. When the IO address is within the range from 0100h through FFFFh, the following form must be used:

```
MOV  DX, nnnn        ;set up the IO address in DX
IN   AL, DX          ;read data from address in DX into AL

MOV  DX, nnnn        ;set up the IO address in DX
MOV  AL, xx          ;set up the data in AL
OUT  DX, AL          ;write data from AL to IO port in DX
```

The IO address specified directly (as in the first form) or indirectly in DX (as in the second form) is used by the processor's bus unit when it starts the IO transaction and drives the IO address out onto the address bus (on A[15:0]; A[31:0] are set to zero).

Memory Addressing

General

The 8088/8086/286 processors contain a set of four segment registers—CS, DS, ES, and SS. The 386/486/Pentium processors contain a set of six segment registers—CS, DS, ES, FS, GS, and SS. In real mode, the programmer uses these registers to specify the start address of up to six different areas of memory space to be utilized by the currently-running program as data, code and stack areas. Figure 5-1 on page 50 illustrates the segment registers.

Protected Mode Software Architecture

Figure 5-1: Segment Registers

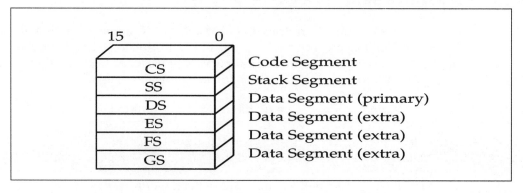

Each of the segment registers is only 16 bits in size. When the programmer loads a value into one of these registers in real mode, the processor automatically appends a least-significant digit (consisting of four bits of all zeros) to the lower end of the value contained in the segment register. As an example, if the following code is executed:

```
MOV AX, 1000
MOV DS, AX
```

the value 1000h is moved into the DS register and the processor appends a zero digit to the low end of the value, yielding a data segment start address of 10000h. The use of the six segment registers is defined in Table 5-2 on page 50.

Table 5-2: Segment Register Usage in Real Mode

Segment Register	Usage
CS	The **Code Segment** register indicates the start address in memory of the currently running program. It is loaded by performing a far jump or far call instruction.
SS	The **Stack Segment** register points to the start address of the area of memory used by the programmer and the processor to temporarily store data. It is loaded using a MOV or LSS instruction.
DS	The **Data Segment** register points to the start address of an area of memory that holds the data that the currently running program acts upon. It is loaded using a MOV or LDS instruction.

Table 5-2: Segment Register Usage in Real Mode (Continued)

Segment Register	Usage
ES	The **Extra Data Segment** register points to the start address of an area of memory that holds additional data that the currently running program acts upon. It is loaded using a `MOV` or `LES` instruction.
FS	The **F Data Segment** register points to the start address of an area of memory that holds additional data that the currently running program acts upon. It is loaded using a `MOV` or `LFS` instruction.
GS	The **G Data Segment** register points to the start address of an area of memory that holds additional data that the currently running program acts upon. It is loaded using a `MOV` or `LGS` instruction.

Accessing the Code Segment

The Code Segment (CS) and Instruction Pointer (IP) registers comprise a register pair. Together, they indicate the memory location the next instruction is to be fetched from. This is their only purpose. Figure 5-2 on page 51 illustrates the 16-bit IP register.

Figure 5-2: IP Register

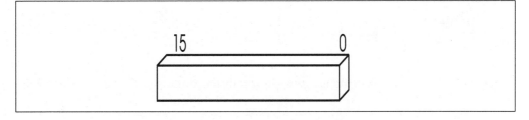

A far jump instruction tells the processor to fetch its next instruction from a location (offset) within a specific area of memory (the code segment). As an example, the following instruction,

```
JMP  2000:0005
```

tells the processor to fetch its next instruction from location five in the code segment that starts at memory location 20000h. In order to execute this instruction, the processor loads the segment start address, 2000h, into the CS register and the offset within the segment into the IP register. It appends the trailing zero (0000b) to the start address in the CS register and adds the offset to it, yielding the physical memory address of 20005h. This process is illustrated below:

```
CS value:20000h
IP value: 0005h
          20005h
```

The processor performs a read from this memory location to fetch the instruction that resides there. The instruction is then decoded and executed.

Unlike the far jump or far call, a near jump or call instruction only specifies an offset within the current code segment. As an example,

```
JMP   0009
```

instructs the processor to jump to location nine in the current code segment. The processor places the value 0009h into the IP register. If it is assumed that the CS register currently contains the value 2000h, the processor will fetch the next instruction from location 20009h.

Jumps and calls are two of the instructions that alter program flow. Each time that an instruction is fetched from memory, the processor automatically increments the IP register to point to the start address of the next instruction in the current code segment. Consider the following example:

```
MOV   AL,  33
OUT   63,  AL
ADD   AX,  BX
SUB   CX,  BX
JMP   3400
```

The first four instructions are not jump instructions and therefore do not load new values into CS or IP. The processor just auto-increments IP to point to the start of the next instruction. This is referred to as in-line code fetching. When the processor fetches the fifth instruction, however, it loads the value 3400h into the IP register, altering program flow. Because this is only a near jump, the CS register isn't altered.

It should be noted that the IP register is only 16-bits in size. This means that the greatest offset within the code segment would be FFFFh, or 64KB. The code segment's maximum size in real mode is therefore 64KB. *This is one of the most severe limitations imposed by real mode.* If a real mode program is greater than 64KB in size, the programmer must break it up into separate 64KB code segments. Whenever the programmer wishes to transfer execution to an instruction within another code segment, a far jump must be executed. This causes the start address of the new code segment to be loaded into the CS register and the new offset to be loaded into the IP register.

Accessing the Stack Segment

The area of memory designated as the stack is used as "scratch-pad memory" by the programmer and the processor. Sometimes, the programmer needs to save a value briefly and retrieve it later. The stack is frequently used for this purpose. The programmer doesn't need to specify a memory address when writing to or reading from stack memory. This makes it a very easy method for temporarily storing information.

The Stack Segment (SS) register points to the start address of the area of memory to be used as the stack. The Stack Pointer (SP) register provides the offset portion of the address and points to the exact location in the stack segment where the last item was stored. At the beginning of a program, the programmer places the base address of the program's stack segment in the SS register and the offset of the top of the stack in the SP register. Since the real mode SP register is only 16-bits in size, the stack cannot be greater than 64KB in size (an offset of FFFFh). *This is a real mode limitation.* As data items are stored in the program's stack, the stack grows downward (in protected mode, a stack can also be defined to grow downwards toward location 00000000h from its base address, but this is atypical) towards the stack segment start address specified in the SS register. The value placed in the SP register determines the start of (i.e., the top of) the stack.

Refer to Figure 5-3 on page 55. When the programmer wants to store a value on the stack, a PUSH instruction is executed. As an example, PUSH AX causes the contents of the AX register to be written into stack memory where SS:SP are currently pointing. Assume that the SS register contains 8000h, the SP register contains FFFFh and the stack is empty. Also assume that the AX register currently contains 1234h and BX contains AA55h. Now consider the following:

1. When the PUSH AX is executed, the processor first decrements the SP by two (FFFFh - 2 = FFFDh). It then writes the two bytes from AX, 12h and 34h, into memory starting at 8FFFDh (80000h + FFFDh). AL is stored in memory location 8FFFDh and AH is stored in 8FFFEh.
2. If BX were now pushed onto the stack (PUSH BX), the SP is again decremented by two and the two bytes from BX (AAh and 55h) are stored in memory starting at location 8FFFBh.

3. Each time the processor executes a subsequent PUSH operation, it first decrements the SP by two and then stores the data in stack memory.

The stack grows downward in memory from the highest memory location in the stack (i.e., the top) towards the segment base address specified in SS.

To read data back from the stack, the programmer uses the POP instruction. When the programmer executes a POP instruction, such as POP BX, the processor reads two bytes off the stack using the current value in SS:SP to form the memory address:

1. Continuing the example used earlier, a POP BX causes the processor to read the two bytes (AAh and 55h) from locations 8FFFBh and 8FFFCh and place them into the BX register.
2. The processor then increments SP by two, so SS:SP are now pointing at 8000:FFFD.
3. A POP AX causes the processor to read the two bytes (12h and 34h) from locations 8FFFDh and 8FFFEh and place them into the AX register.
4. The processor then increments SP by two, so SS:SP are now pointing at 8000:FFFF, the top of the stack. The stack is now empty.

As implemented by the x86 processors, the stack is a LIFO (Last In, First Out) buffer—the last object in is the first out.

If the programmer attempts to pop more data off the stack than was pushed onto it, the processor generates a special type of interrupt called a stack exception to indicate that the stack is empty. Conversely, if the programmer pushes data onto the stack until the entire segment is full and then attempts to push one more word onto the stack, the processor generates a stack exception.

In addition to the programmer using the stack for temporary storage, the processor also uses it. The following are some of the cases where the processor implicitly uses the stack:

- When an **INT instruction** is executed, the processor pushes the current CS, IP and EFlag values onto the stack before jumping to the target interrupt routine.
- When a **hardware interrupt** occurs, the processor pushes the current CS, IP and EFlag values onto the stack before jumping to the target interrupt service routine.
- When a **software exception** occurs, the processor pushes the current CS, IP and EFlag values onto the stack before jumping to the target exception handler.

- When the processor executes a **CALL instruction**, it pushes the current IP (for a near call) or CS:IP (for a far call) values onto the stack before jumping to the target routine.

Figure 5-3: Stack Segment

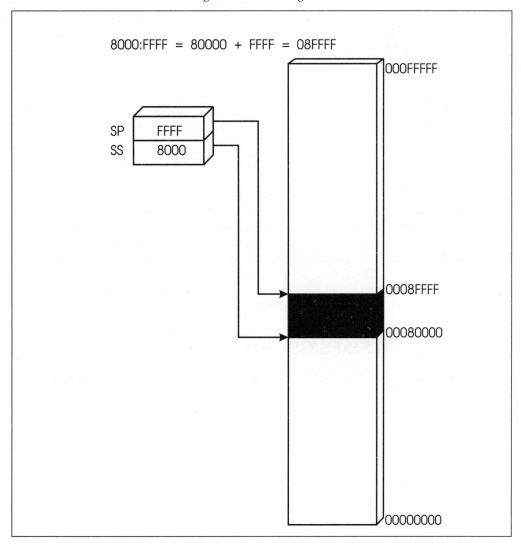

Protected Mode Software Architecture

Accessing DS Data Segment

Data is typically read from and written to the DS data segment using MOV instructions. The programmer first loads the DS register with the start address of the data segment in memory. This is accomplished using a MOV or LDS instruction, but the data must first be moved into another register and then copied into the DS register:

```
MOV  AX, 4500
MOV  DS, AX
```

The data segment now starts at location 45000h. The data segment pointed to by the DS register is the default data segment. In this example,

```
MOV  AX, 4500
MOV  DS, AX
MOV  AX, [0100]
```

the contents of locations 45100h and 45101h are moved into the AX register. The offset is enclosed within the brackets and the data segment to be used isn't explicitly specified in this instruction. The processor therefore uses the default data segment, DS, to calculate the physical memory address to be accessed. In real mode, it is illegal to specify an offset (portion within the brackets) greater than FFFFh. This means that the data segment is limited to 64KB in length in real mode. *This is one of the drawbacks to real mode.*

Accessing ES/FS/GS Data Segments

The following code is used to illustrate the process of accessing data segments other than DS:

```
MOV  AX, 1000
MOV  DS, AX
MOV  AX, 2000
MOV  ES, AX
MOV  AX, 3000
MOV  FS, AX
MOV  AX, 4000
MOV  GS, AX
MOV  BL, [0002]        ;move from DS data segment
MOV  BH, ES:[0002]     ;move from ES data segment
MOV  CL, FS:[0002]     ;move from FS data segment
MOV  CH, GS:[0002]     ;move from GS data segment
```

The first memory read moves one byte from location 10002h into the BL register. The second memory read moves one byte from location 20002h into the BH register. The third memory read moves one byte from location 30002h into the CL register. The fourth memory read moves one byte from memory location 40002h into the CH register. **ES:**, **FS:** and **GS:** are referred to as **segment overrides**. They instruct the processor to use the specified data segment rather than the default data segment (DS).

In all cases, the offset specified within the brackets may not exceed FFFFh when in real mode. *All segments are therefore restricted to 64KB in size when in real mode.*

An Example

Figure 5-4 on page 58 illustrates the use of the segment registers in real mode. The figure assumes that the following code has already been executed in real mode:

```
0600:0050  JMP  F000:0100    ;CS = F000, IP = 0100

F000:0100  MOV  AX, D000
           MOV  DS, AX       ;DS = D000
           MOV  AX, A320
           MOV  SS, AX       ;SS = A320
           MOV  AX, 7200
           MOV  ES, AX       ;ES = 7200
           MOV  AX, 3000
           MOV  FS, AX       ;FS = 3000
           MOV  AX, 1000
           MOV  GS, AX       ;GS = 1000
```

When the processor executes the far jump instruction fetched from memory location 0600:0050 (06050h), the code segment register is set to F000h and the IP register to 0100h. As a result, the processor fetches its next instruction from memory location 000F0100h. The series of instructions starting at this location causes the values indicated in the figure to be moved into the stack and data segment registers. The figure illustrates how the processor then uses the segment registers to identify the six segments of memory space.

Protected Mode Software Architecture

Figure 5-4: Example Usage of Segment Registers in Real Mode

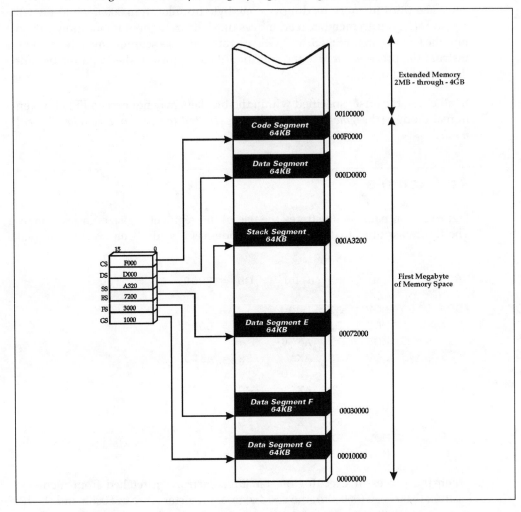

Accessing Extended Memory in Real Mode

It is possible to access a small amount of extended memory (memory above 1MB) while in real mode. Consider the following example:

```
MOV  AX,FFFF  ;FFFFh to AX
MOV  DS,AX    ;transfer FFFFh to DS
```

```
MOV  AL,[0010];transfer contents of memory
              ;location FFFF:0010 into AL
```

In order to form the physical memory address to place on the address bus when executing the third instruction, the processor appends the digit zero on the end of the DS data segment value (FFFFh) to point to the start address of the data segment (FFFF0h). It then adds the offset (0010h) to the data segment start address to create the physical memory address:

```
        DS + 0h=          FFFF0h
        OFFSET=             0010h
```

```
Physical memory address =100000h
```

The processor then performs a memory read transaction, driving the resultant physical memory address, 00100000h, onto the address bus. Notice that the 21st address bit, A[20], is a one. The processor is addressing the first memory location of the second megabyte of memory address space. This is extended memory and the processor is addressing it in real mode!

Now consider this example:

```
    MOV  AX,FFFF        ;FFFFh to AX
    MOV  DS,AX          ;transfer FFFFh to DS
    MOV  AL,[FFFF]      ;read byte from memory address
                       ;FFFF:FFFF into AL
```

As before, in order to form the physical memory address to place on the address bus when executing the third instruction, the processor places a 0h on the end of the DS data segment value (FFFFh) to point to the start address of the data segment (000FFFF0h). It then adds the offset (FFFFh) to the data segment start address to create the physical memory address:

```
        DS + 0h        =   FFFF0h
        OFFSET         =    FFFFh
```

```
Physical memory address =   10FFEFh
```

The processor then performs a memory read transaction, driving the resultant physical memory address, 0010FFEFh, onto the address bus. With the value FFFFh in the segment register and by supplying any offset in the range 0010h through FFFFh, any extended memory location from 00100000h through 0010FFEFh can be accessed. A total of 65520d extended memory locations can be accessed while still in real mode.

Protected Mode Software Architecture

This method is used by many DOS memory management programs to access extended memory while remaining in real mode. This memory area is usually referred to as the High Memory Area (HMA).

Notice that the code fragments shown earlier can be executed on an 8088/8086 processor. The results are different, however, when the code is executed on a post 8088/8086 processor. If an 8088/8086 processor executes the code, address bit A[20] will not be high (because the 8088/8086 processors do not implement address lines above A[19]. Therefore, the 8088/8086 produces an address that is between 00000000h and 0000FFEFh for the examples shown earlier. This is called address or segment wraparound. The address space of the segment wraps around from the highest physical addresses to the lowest physical addresses.

Some programs written for the 8088/8086 may depend on segment wraparound to access data in the low addresses, such as the interrupt table or the BIOS data area. If these programs are executed on a post-8088/8086 processor, they do not operate correctly because they aren't accessing the expected memory locations. In order for machines based on post-8088/8086 processors to be compatible with such old code, the processor's A[20] address output must be forced to zero to simulate the address generated by the 8088/8086.

Note that address bit A[20] was set to one when a segment value of FFFFh and offsets larger than 000Fh were used. Therefore, only A[20] needs to be masked. A[31:21] are not set to one when executing the old code.

This discussion assumes that the system is a PC-compatible and the processor is a 286 or 386. On the system board, external to the processor, A[20] is connected to one input of an AND gate. The other input of the AND gate is supplied by a signal called A20MASK#. The output of the AND gate becomes the A[20] address bit that is broadcast with the rest of the processor's address to the system. If A20MASK# is asserted (i.e., zero), the AND gate's output, the system's A[20] bit, is zero simulating an address generated by an 8088/8086. In a PC-compatible machine, the A20MASK# signal comes from the keyboard controller. Alternately, it can also be generated by intercept logic that watches for commands issued to the keyboard controller to raise or lower this line.

The Pentium and 486 processors incorporate the A20 gate into the processor itself and A20MASK# is an input to the processor.

Big Real Mode

Post-286 processors can address up to 4GB of memory space while in real mode, so long as they have at least once been switched to protected mode and back to real mode since the last reset. This is sometimes referred to as big real mode.

As an example, prior to switching back to real mode, the protected mode software sets up a segment descriptor table entry (see the chapter entitled "Intro to Segmentation" on page 77) that describes a segment as starting somewhere above 1MB and having a length of 64KB. The segment register is then loaded with a value that selects this descriptor, loading the invisible part of the segment register with the new start address and length. When the switch is made back to real mode, as long as the programmer doesn't load a new value into the segment register, the previous segment definition holds true. This permits the programmer to access any location within 64K of the segment's base address.

Note that the offset is still restricted to a maximum of FFFFh. A GP exception results when a larger offset is specified.

The 286 lacks this capability (because it cannot be switched from protected to real mode without resetting the processor, thus setting the contents of the invisible part of the segment register to values restricting the processor to accesses within the first meg of memory space).

Real Mode Instructions and Registers

Registers Accessible in Real Mode

The registers accessible in real mode include all of the 8088/8086-compatible registers plus many of the superset registers added by the 386 processor and 387 numeric coprocessor. This includes:

- FS and GS data segment registers
- the debug registers
- the control registers
- the test registers
- Global Descriptor Table register
- the Interrupt Descriptor Table (IDT) register
- the floating-point registers

Protected Mode Software Architecture

Registers Inaccessible in Real Mode

The following registers are not accessible in real mode:

- Local Descriptor Table register (LDTR)
- Task register (TR)

Instructions Usable in Real Mode

New instructions that permit access to the FS and GS registers are available and the programmer may use the FS and GS segment overrides. Programs can use applications-oriented instructions that were introduced for the 80186, 80188, 80286, 80386, 80486 and Pentium processors. The programmer may use operand size overrides to access 32-bit variables. The LIDT instruction can be used in real mode to change the base address of the interrupt table to somewhere other than the default base at memory location zero. The size of the interrupt table can also be changed using this instruction. *It should be noted that many real mode software packages assume that the interrupt table starts at location zero and do not examine the IDTR to see where it really resides.*

Instructions Unusable in Real Mode

The following instructions cause the invalid opcode exception when executed in real mode:

- **Verify Segment for Read (VERR)**. Tests the indicated segment descriptor's access rights byte to determine if the associated memory segment is accessible at the current privilege level and whether the segment can be read from without causing an exception.
- **Verify Segment for Write (VERW)**. Tests the indicated segment descriptor's access rights byte to determine if the associated memory segment is accessible at the current privilege level and whether the segment can be written to without causing an exception.
- **Load Access Rights (LAR)**. Loads the specified register with the access rights byte of the indicated code or data segment descriptor.
- **Load Segment Limit (LSL)**. Loads the specified register with the segment limit (i.e., its size) from the indicated segment descriptor.
- **Load Task Register (LTR)**. Loads the Task Register with a segment selector from the specified 16-bit register or from memory.

- **Store Task Register (STR).** Stores the segment selector currently in the Task Register into the specified 16-bit register or memory.
- **Load Local Descriptor Table Register (LLDT).** Loads the Local Descriptor Table register with a 16-bit selector (supplied from a 16-bit register or memory) that selects an entry in the Global Descriptor Table (GDT). The indicated GDT entry describes a Local Descriptor Table.
- **Store Local Descriptor Table Register (SLDT).** Stores the GDT selector currently in the Local Descriptor Table register into a 16-bit register or memory.

Real Mode Interrupt/Exception Handling

The 8088/8086 processor does not have an IDT register (IDTR), but all of the post 8088/8086 processors do. By definition, the 8088/8086 processor's interrupt table always starts at location 00000h and is 03FFh (1KB) in length, while the location and length of the interrupt table is programmable for all subsequent x86 processors. In the subsequent x86 processors, the assertion of reset at powerup presets the IDTR with an IDT base address of 00000000h and a table length of 03FFh (1KB; 256 entries of four bytes each). In real mode, the programmer can use the LIDT and SIDT instructions to access the IDTR. Refer to the warning under the heading "Registers Inaccessible in Real Mode" on page 62.

When a software (execution of INT *nn* instruction) or hardware (the assertion of the processor's INTR or NMI input) interrupt, or a software exception occurs in real mode, the processor takes the following actions:

1. The interrupt vector selects an entry in the IDT. The processor multiplies the vector by four and adds the result to the IDT base address (00000000h) to obtain the start memory address of the indicated table entry. It then reads the new CS and IP values (a total of four bytes) from the table entry, but does not yet place them into CS and IP.
2. Pushes the current contents of the CS, IP, and EFlags registers onto the stack. Saving CS and IP acts as a "bookmark" in the interrupted program. Saving EFlags saves the state of IF bit (and other control bits) at the point of interruption.
3. Clears the EFlags[IF] bit, disabling recognition of external interrupts.
4. Clears the EFlags[TF] bit, disabling the debug single-step mode (if it had been enabled).
5. Moves the values obtained from the IDT entry into the CS and IP registers.
6. Resumes program execution using CS:IP. These two registers now point to the first instruction of the interrupt/exception handler.

Protected Mode Software Architecture

The IRET instruction executed at the end of the handler reverses these steps, returning program execution to the interrupted program with EFlags restored to its original state.

Software exceptions do not return error codes in real mode (as some do in protected mode).

If the programmer uses the LIDT instruction to alter the length of the IDT and a subsequent interrupt vector indexes to an IDT entry beyond the length of the IDT, a double-fault exception is generated.

Table 5-3 on page 64 identifies the types of exceptions and interrupts that are recognized by an x86 processor. Exceptions 10, 11, 14, and 17 do not occur in real mode, but can occur while in VM86 mode.

Table 5-3: Exceptions and Interrupts

Type	Vector	Exception Source
Implemented in 8088/8086		
Divide Error	0	DIV and IDIV instructions.
Single-Step	1	Completion of any instruction while EFlags[TF} bit set.
NMI	2	Assertion of processor's NMI input pin.
Breakpoint	3	Execution of INT3 (breakpoint) instruction.
Overflow	4	Execution of INTO with EFlags[OF] bit set.
Implemented in 286 and subsequent processors		
Bounds Check	5	Execution of BOUND instruction where index not within specified array.
Invalid Opcode	6	Attempted execution of reserved opcodes or improper use of LOCK prefix.

Table 5-3: Exceptions and Interrupts (Continued)

Type	Vector	Exception Source
Processor Extension not Available	7	Occurs when the programmer wants ESC instructions to be handled by software (CR0[EM] is set), or when a WAIT or an ESC instruction is encountered and the context of the floating-point unit is different than that of the current task (EFlags[TS] is set).
Implemented in 386 and subsequent processors		
Double Fault	8	Generated when an exception is detected while the processor is attempting to call the handler for a prior exception and the two exceptions cannot be handled serially in a graceful fashion.
Coprocessor segment overrun abort	9	Only generated by the 386, not by the 486 or the Pentium (for the same condition, they generate an exception 13).
Invalid TSS	10d	Occurs if an attempt is made to switch to a task with an invalid TSS (something is wrong with its contents).
Segment not present	11d	Generated in protected mode if the selected segment descriptor has its Segment Present bit cleared to zero (indicating that the target segment is not currently present in memory).
Stack exception	12d	Occurs for stack overflow and underflow, and also when an attempt is made to load SS with a value that selects a segment descriptor that is valid except that the segment not present bit is zero.

Table 5-3: Exceptions and Interrupts (Continued)

Type	Vector	Exception Source
General Protection fault	13d	All protection violations that do not cause another exception generate this one.
Page fault	14d	Occurs when the selected page table or page is not present in memory, or when the current task does not have sufficient privilege to access the target page table or page.
Reserved	15d	Reserved.
Floating-point error	16d	Occurs if CR0[NE] is set and a floating-point error is detected.
Implemented in 486 and subsequent processors		
Alignment check	17d	Occurs if EFlags[AC] and CR0[AM] are set and an attempt is made to perform a misaligned access.
Implemented in Pentium and subsequent processors		
Machine check	18d	On the Pentium processor, occurs if CR4[ME] is set and either BUSCHK# or PERR# is sampled asserted during a bus transaction.
Intel Reserved	19-31d	Reserved.
Software Interrupts	0-255d	Occurs as a result of executing an INT *nn* instruction, where *nn* is any interrupt vector from 0 through 255.
Maskable external hardware interrupts	-	System design dependent. In a PC-compatible platform, the vectors associated with external hardware interrupts are 8 through 15d (Fh), and 112d (70h) through 119d (77h).

Chapter 5: Real Mode Operation

Protection in Real Mode

When operating in real mode, the x86 processor does not provide any mechanism to prevent one program from corrupting other programs or data that currently reside in memory. In addition, the currently-running program is permitted to access any IO port directly, rather than going through the OS. For these and other reasons, it would be very difficult to develop a multitasking OS that would run under real mode and provide bulletproof protection. Real mode is intended for use by a single task OS such as DOS. The next chapter describes the operational characteristics of a typical single-task OS and applications programs designed to run under its control.

Part Three

Protected Mode

6 x86 Protected Mode Intro

The Previous Chapter

The previous chapter provided an introduction to processor operation in real mode.

This Chapter

This chapter provides a basic introduction to the concept of protection as implemented in the Intel x86 processors.

The Next Chapter

The next chapter describes the usage of memory segmentation in isolating suspended tasks from the currently-executing task.

General

This chapter provides a brief introduction to the various types of protection offered in the x86 protected mode environment. The following topics are introduced:

- Memory Protection
- IO Protection
- Privilege Levels
- Virtual Memory Paging
- Virtual 8086 Mode (also referred to as VM86 mode, or VM mode)
- Task Switching
- Interrupt Handling

Protected Mode Software Architecture

Each of the topics introduced in this chapter are discussed in detail in subsequent chapters.

Memory Protection

Segmentation

Using segmentation, the OS programmer can define multiple areas of memory that may be accessed by the currently-executing program. In real mode, a segment has the following characteristics:

- Its start address must be in the first megabyte of memory space.
- The segment length is fixed at 64KB.
- The segment can be read from or written to by any program.

In a multitasking environment, the OS programmer must be able to define the following characteristics of a segment:

- A start address anywhere in the 4GB memory address space that can be addressed by the processor.
- A segment length ranging from one byte to 4GB.
- Program privilege level necessary to gain access to this segment of memory.
- Define the segment as read-only, execute-only or read/writable.
- Define the segment as a special segment used only by the OS or as a code or data segment to be used by a task.
- Whether or not the segment has been accessed since it was created.
- Whether or not the segment of information is currently resident in memory (it may be out on a mass storage device).

A detailed description of segmentation can be found in the chapters entitled:

- "Intro to Segmentation" on page 77
- "Code Segments" on page 99
- "Data and Stack Segments" on page 125
- "The Flat Model" on page 261

Virtual Memory Paging

When enabled and utilized by the OS, the processor's paging unit can redirect a memory access to either:

- an address in memory other than the address generated by the applications program, or
- a page of data on a mass storage device.

Two programs may attempt to use the same area of memory. When one of the programs is active, the paging unit can redirect accesses to one physical area of memory. When the other program becomes active, the paging unit can alter its redirection mechanism to redirect memory accesses to an area of physical memory separate from that used by the first program. This ensures isolated data areas for the two programs (so they don't interfere with each other). This process is transparent to the applications program.

It is especially useful when the OS is attempting to timeslice (i.e., multitask) multiple DOS tasks. Each will attempt accesses within the first megabyte of memory space. Paging can be used to direct each of their memory accesses to separate 1MB areas (other than the first megabyte). Also refer to the section entitled "Virtual 8086 Mode" on page 74. A detailed description of paging can be found in the chapter entitled "Virtual Paging" on page 219.

IO Protection

When operating in real mode, any program can execute IO-oriented instructions and communicate directly with IO devices. For reasons described in the previous chapter, it is dangerous to permit direct IO by tasks executing in a multitasking environment. To prevent this, the x86 processors implement the IO privilege level (IOPL). By setting this two-bit field in the EFlags register to the appropriate privilege level (a value between zero and three), the OS can ensure that only tasks with a privilege level equal to or greater than that indicated in the EFlags[IOPL] field are permitted to communicate directly with IO devices. An IO attempt by a task with a privilege level less than the IOPL results in a general protection exception. In other words, it's not permitted.

When a DOS task is executing in virtual 8086 (VM86) mode, the IOPL is not used. Rather, when the OS creates the task, it also creates an IO permission bit map (in the task's TSS in memory). Each bit in this map corresponds to one of the possible 64K IO ports. When the task attempts to access any IO port, the processor first checks the task's IO permission map to determine if the access is permitted. A general protection exception is generated if the access is prohibited.

Protected Mode Software Architecture

Privilege Levels

As discussed in an earlier chapter, the Intel x86 processors provide four privilege levels when executing in protected mode:

- **Level zero** is the **highest privilege** level. Typically, only the OS kernel will run with privilege level zero. This permits it to perform any operation.
- **Level one** is next privilege level. It is typically assigned to high-priority device drivers and OS services. It could also be assigned to debuggers to protect them from alteration by low-priority device drivers and applications programs.
- **Level two** is typically assigned to lower-priority device drivers.
- **Level three** is the **lowest priority** and is typically assigned to applications programs. This prevents them from performing actions that would be injurious to the OS, debuggers, device drivers, or each other.

Virtual 8086 Mode

Because programs written for DOS behave as if they own the entire machine, x86 processors (starting with the 386) implement a mode known as Virtual 8086 (VM86) Mode. When a task is executed with this processor feature enabled (via the EFlags[VM] being set to one), the processor enables "watchdog" logic to monitor the program's behavior on an instruction-by-instruction basis. When operating in VM86 mode, the processor traps out to a program referred to as a Virtual Machine Monitor (VMM) whenever the task attempts to perform an action inimical to the OS or the other currently-suspended programs. The VMM emulates the action required by the task in a fashion that is friendly to the OS and other programs. A detailed description of VM86 mode can be found in the chapter entitled "Virtual 8086 Mode" on page 265.

Task Switching

The x86 processors provide automated mechanisms to handle the suspension of one task and the initiation of another. The OS creates a task state segment (TSS) for each task to be run. In a task's TSS, the OS programmer defines the following characteristics of the task:

- The initial settings of the processor's registers
- The task's IO permission bit map

- The task's interrupt redirection bit map (feature available on some 486s and all Pentiums).

The task is launched by telling the processor the start address of its TSS. The processor then loads its register set from the TSS and begins execution of the program. When it's time to suspend the task and start or resume another task, the processor first stores the current state of all of its registers in the TSS of the task being suspended. It then loads its registers from the TSS associated with the next task and begins or resumes its execution. A detailed description of task switching can be found in the chapter entitled "Mechanics of a Task Switch" on page 157.

Interrupt Handling

In real mode, each entry in the interrupt table is four bytes long and represents the start address, in segment:offset format, of an interrupt handler. The handler is typically one of the following:

- a hardware interrupt service routine
- a software error exception handler routine
- a software interrupt handler (called via an INT nn instruction)
- a BIOS routine
- an OS request handler

In real mode, any program can use the INT instruction to call a BIOS routine or to make a request to the OS.

In protected mode, the OS must restrict entry to some routines that may be called using the INT nn instruction. In addition, the OS programmer may wish to handle some interrupts or exceptions by suspending the current task and switching to another task designed to handle the event (rather than just jumping to an interrupt or exception service routine within the same task).

To accommodate this added level of complexity, the structure of the interrupt table changes in protected mode. Each entry consists of eight rather than four bytes. In order to gain entry to a routine through an entry in the interrupt table, the calling program must have sufficient privilege.

In addition, a task's privilege level must meet or beat the privilege level specified in the EFlags[IOPL] field in order to successfully execute a CLI or STI instruction to disable or enable interrupt recognition. When a task is executing in VM86 mode, it is typically not permitted to execute CLI or STI. Any attempt

Protected Mode Software Architecture

to do so causes a trap to the OS which will then emulate the action in a manner "friendly" to the other elements of the system. For more information, see the section entitled "Attempted Execution of CLI Instruction" on page 292.

7 *Intro to Segmentation*

The Previous Chapter

The previous chapter provided an introduction to x86 protected mode.

This Chapter

This chapter introduces the following concepts:

- segment selector
- segment descriptor tables
- segment descriptor format

The Next Chapter

The next chapter provides a detailed description of code segments.

Special Note

Please note that the terms "program," "procedure," and "routine" are used interchangeably throughout the book.

Real Mode Limitations

In real mode, a segment has the following characteristics:

- Its start address must be in the first megabyte of memory space.
- The segment length is fixed at 64KB.
- The segment can read or written by any program.

Protected Mode Software Architecture

In order to have the maximum flexibility, the OS must be able to define a program's segments as residing anywhere within the 4GB memory address range. In real mode, segments may only be defined within the first megabyte of memory space. They cannot occupy extended memory (i.e., memory above the first megabyte).

Programs and the data they manipulate frequently occupy more than 64KB of memory space, but each segment has a fixed length of 64KB in real mode, neither shorter nor longer. If the OS only requires a very small segment for a program's code, data or stack area, the smallest (and largest size) is 64KB. This can waste memory space. If the code or data utilized by a particular program is larger than 64KB, the programmer must set up and jump back and forth between multiple code segments. This is a very wasteful use of the programmer's time and can be difficult to keep track of. It's one of the major things programmers dislike about segmentation.

In real mode, a segment can be accessed by any program. This is an invitation for one program to trash another's code, data or stack area. In addition, any program can call any other program. There is no concept of restricting access to certain programs.

Introduction to Segment Descriptor

In a multitasking environment, the OS programmer must be able to specify the following characteristics of each segment:

- The task that it belongs to.
- Its start address anywhere in the 4GB memory address range.
- Its length (anywhere from one to 4GB in length).
- How it may be accessed: read-only, execute-only, read/writable.
- The minimum privilege level a program must have to access the segment.
- Whether it's a code or data segment or a special segment that is only used by the OS.
- Whether the segment of information is currently present in memory or resides on a mass storage device.

Figure 7-1 on page 79 illustrates the manner in which the processor interprets the contents of a segment register while operating in real mode. The only thing it contains is the upper 16 bits of the 20-bit start address of the segment within the first megabyte of memory space. The processor automatically appends the lower four bits of the start address and always sets them to zero. As an example, if the programmer moved the value 1010h into the DS register

```
MOV AX, 1010
MOV DS, AX
```

this would set the start address of the data segment to 10100h.

Figure 7-1: Segment Register Contents in Real Mode

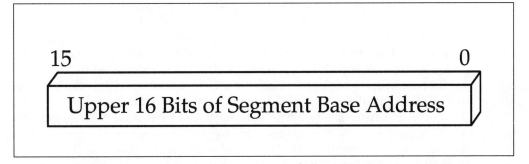

As stated earlier in this chapter, when in protected mode the OS programmer must be able to define many more properties of a segment in addition to its start memory address. It should be obvious that it would not be possible to define all of these characteristics in the 16-bit segment register.

In protected mode, it requires eight bytes of information to describe all of the characteristics associated with a particular segment of memory space. The protected mode OS must provide an eight byte descriptor for each memory segment to be used by each program (including those used by the OS itself). It would consume a great deal of processor real estate to keep descriptors for all segments used by all programs in registers on the processor chip itself. For this reason, the descriptors are stored in special tables in memory. The next section provides a description of the descriptor tables.

Segment Register—Selects Descriptor Table and Entry

When a programmer wishes to gain access to an area of memory, the respective segment register (the CS, SS, or one the data segment registers—DS, ES, FS, or GS) must be loaded with a 16-bit value. In real mode, the value loaded into the segment register represents the upper 16 bits of the 20 bit start address of the segment in memory. In protected mode, the value loaded into a segment register is referred to as the segment selector and is interpreted as illustrated in Figure 7-2 on page 80.

Protected Mode Software Architecture

- The Requestor Privilege Level (RPL) field is described in the chapters entitled "Code Segments" on page 99 and "Data and Stack Segments" on page 125.
- Bit [2] (the Table Indicator, or TI bit) of the segment register selects either the Global Descriptor Table (GDT) or the Local Descriptor Table (LDT). The descriptor tables are described in the sections following this one.
- The index field is used to select an entry in the indicated table.

Whenever a value is loaded into a segment register in protected mode, the processor multiples the index by eight to create the offset into the indicated table (because there are eight bytes per entry). It then adds this offset to the respective table's base address (supplied by either the GDT register, GDTR, or the LDT register, LDTR), yielding the start address of the selected segment descriptor in the table. The processor then performs a memory read to fetch the 8-byte descriptor from memory and places it into the invisible part of the specified segment register (see Figure 7-2 on page 80). The invisible part is referred to as the segment register's cache register. There is one segment cache register for each of the six segment registers.

Figure 7-3 on page 81 illustrates the segment register, the global and local descriptor tables, the GDTR and the LDTR. Note that although there is only one GDT, there may be more than one LDT.

Figure 7-2: Segment Selector

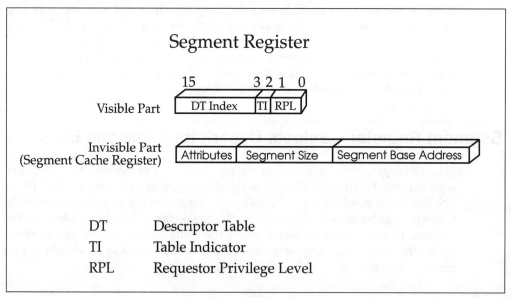

Figure 7-3: The Segment Register, GDT and LDTs

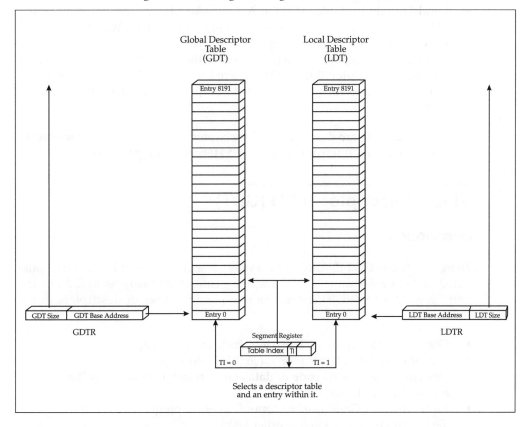

Introduction to Descriptor Tables

Segment Descriptors Reside in Memory

Whenever the programmer attempts to access a new memory segment (by loading a value into the respective segment register), the processor reads the indicated segment descriptor from memory into a special segment descriptor cache in the processor. From that point forward, the processor has instant access to the base address, length and other attributes related to that segment.

There are three types of descriptor tables:

Protected Mode Software Architecture

- **Global Descriptor Table (GDT).** Describes segments of memory that are global to all programs. There is only one GDT.
- **Local Descriptor Tables (LDTs).** A particular OS may not implement any LDTS, only one LDT for all tasks, or a separate LDT for each task. Ideally, the OS should implement a separate LDT for each task. The entries in the LDT describe segments of memory local to the currently-executing task.
- **Interrupt Descriptor Table (IDT).** There is only one IDT. The entries in the IDT describe interrupt and exception handlers and their respective access rights.

The GDT and LDTs are described in this chapter, while the IDT is described in the chapter entitled "Interrupt Sources and Handling" on page 183.

Global Descriptor Table (GDT)

Description

There is only one GDT defined in the system at a given instant in time. It is illustrated in Figure 7-4 on page 84, and may contain as many as 8192d entries. Entry zero is not used. There can be five possible types of descriptors in the GDT:

- One Task State Segment (**TSS**) descriptor for each task.
- One or more Local Descriptor Table (**LDT**) descriptors.
- Descriptors for shared **code or data/stack segments** of memory that may be accessed by multiple tasks.
- Procedure **Call Gates** used to control access to programs.
- **Task Gates** used to switch to other tasks.

TSSs and Task Gates are described in the chapter entitled "Creating a Task" on page 137. LDTs are described in the section entitled "Local Descriptor Tables (LDTs)" on page 85. Procedure Call Gates are described in the section entitled "Calling a Procedure in Current Task" on page 110. Code, data and stack segments are described in:

- the chapter entitled "Code Segments" on page 99.
- the section entitled "The Data Segments" on page 125.
- the section entitled "Selecting and Accessing Stack Segment" on page 131.

Setting GDT Base Address and Size

The OS programmer is responsible for creating and maintaining the GDT in memory. Once created in memory, the programmer must tell the processor the base address and size of the GDT. This is accomplished using the LGDT (Load GDT Register) instruction. When executed, six bytes of information are read from memory starting at the specified memory address and are placed in the processor's GTDR register. The GDTR is illustrated in Figure 7-4 on page 84. The information loaded into the GDTR consists of a 16-bit limit (i.e., size) plus a 32-bit base address for the table. At a maximum, the table can contain 8192d (minus one, because entry zero is unused) entries, each eight bytes long, for a total table length of 64KB.

GDT entry zero is unused for a good reason. This permits the programmer to place the null value of zero into any of the data segment registers without causing an exception (e.g., when initializing the register set). This selects entry zero in the GDT. The processor does not actually access GDT entry zero.

Figure 7-4: Global Descriptor Table (GDT)

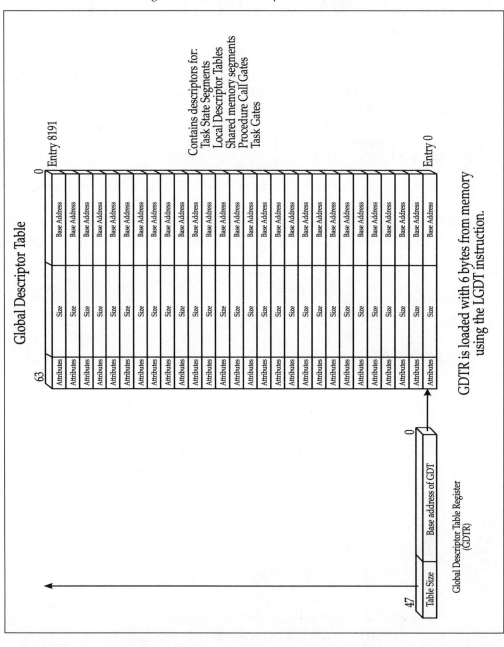

Local Descriptor Tables (LDTs)

Optimally, the OS programmer can define a set of segments for each separate task. The segments local to, or owned by, a task are defined in the task's LDT in memory. The GDT must contain an LDT descriptor for each LDT defined. An LDT descriptor in the GDT defines an LDT's base address and size. Figure 7-5 on page 86 illustrates the relationship of the GDT entries to the LDTs.

In order to select an LDT, the programmer must execute the LLDT instruction. The LLDT instruction loads a 16-bit value into the visible part of the processor's LDTR (Local Descriptor Table Register). The visible and invisible parts of the LDTR are pictured in Figure 7-6 on page 87. The Requestor Privilege Level (RPL) is discussed in the chapters entitled "Code Segments" on page 99 and "Data and Stack Segments" on page 125. Table Indicator (TI) = 0 tells the processor to access the GDT and the index in bits [15:3] tells the processor which of the 8192d entries in the GDT to read. To access the indicated entry, the processor performs the following series of actions:

1. Since each entry in a descriptor table is eight bytes long, the processor multiplies the index value by eight to create the proper offset into the GDT.
2. The offset is added to the GDT's base address supplied by the processor's GDTR to yield the start memory address of the LDT's descriptor in the GDT.
3. The processor reads the eight byte descriptor from memory into the invisible portion of the LDTR.

From this point forward, the processor has immediate on-chip access to the base address, size and attributes of the task's LDT. Figure 7-7 on page 88 illustrates the format of a Local Descriptor Table entry in the GDT. Since an LDT is considered to be an OS segment, the System bit must be set to zero. The remainder of the fields in the descriptor are defined later in this chapter (in the section entitled "General Segment Descriptor Format" on page 90).

An LDT may contain:

- Code, data and stack segment descriptors for memory segments local to this task.
- Procedure Call Gates that permit calls to procedures residing in code segments of a higher privilege level.
- Task Gates that permit the current task to execute another task.

Figure 7-5: The GDT and the LDTs

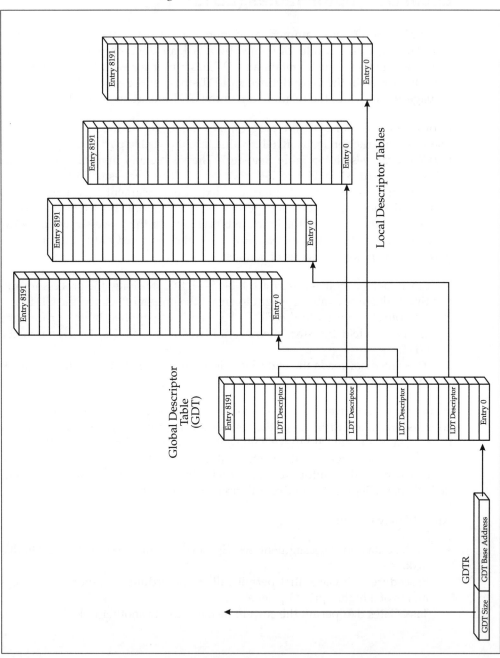

Figure 7-6: Local Descriptor Table Register

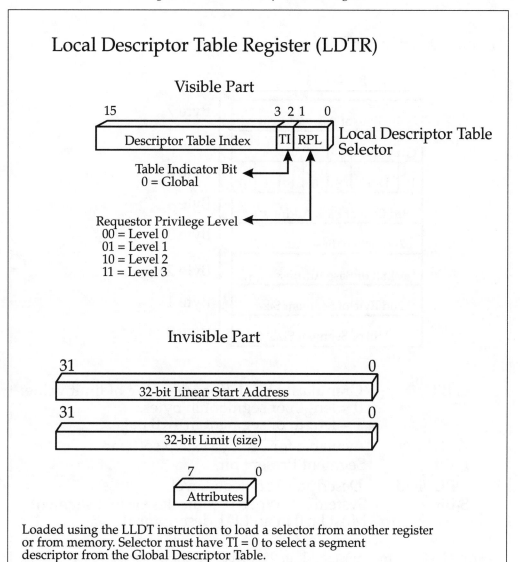

Loaded using the LLDT instruction to load a selector from another register or from memory. Selector must have TI = 0 to select a segment descriptor from the Global Descriptor Table.

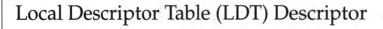

Figure 7-7: Format of LDT Entry in GDT

Local Descriptor Table (LDT) Descriptor

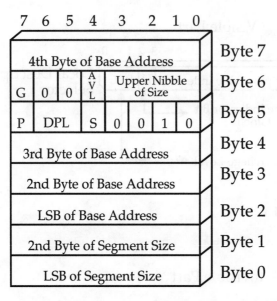

G Bit	Granularity bit defines meaning of limit value. 0 = length of segment in bytes. 1 = length of segment in 4KB pages.
AVL Bit	Available for use by system software
P Bit	Segment Present bit.
DPL Field	Descriptor Privilege Level.
S Bit	System bit. When 0, indicates system segment. Must be 0 in an LDT descriptor.

Note: All LDT entries must reside in the Global Descriptor Table (GDT).

Figure 7-8: LDT Structure

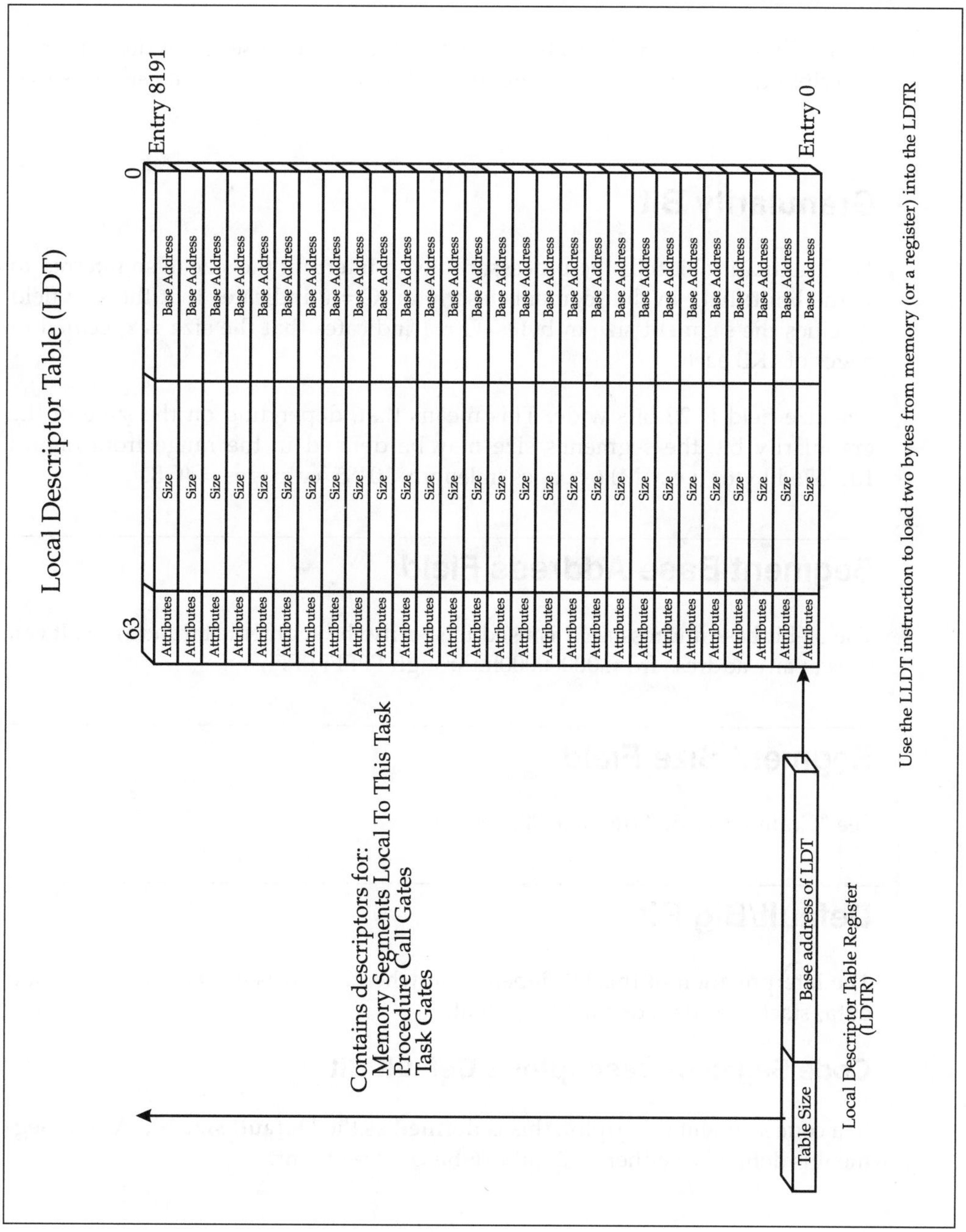
Local Descriptor Table (LDT)
63
0
Entry 8191
Entry 0
Attributes
Size
Base Address
Contains descriptors for:
Memory Segments Local To This Task
Procedure Call Gates
Task Gates
Table Size
Base address of LDT
Local Descriptor Table Register (LDTR)
Use the LLDT instruction to load two bytes from memory (or a register) into the LDTR

Protected Mode Software Architecture

General Segment Descriptor Format

Figure 7-9 on page 95 illustrates the general format of a segment descriptor. A description of each element of the descriptor can be found in the sections that follow.

Granularity Bit

The granularity bit tells the processor how to interpret the size (also referred to as the limit) field in the segment descriptor. $G = 0$ indicates that the size field specifies the segment size in bytes. $G = 1$ indicates that the size is specified in pages of 4KB each.

The size field is 20 bits wide. This means that, depending on the state of the granularity bit, the segment's size may be defined in the range from one to 1048576d bytes (i.e., 1M) or pages in length. 1048576d pages = 4GB.

Segment Base Address Field

The 32-bit base address field is used to specify the segment start address. It can start at any address from 00000000h through FFFFFFFFh.

Segment Size Field

See "Granularity Bit" on page 90.

Default/Big Bit

The interpretation of this bit depends on whether this is defined as a code or a data/stack (i.e., data or stack) segment.

Code Segment Descriptor's Default Bit

In a code segment descriptor, this is **defined as** the **Default size bit**. A code segment is defined as either a 32- or a 16-bit code segment:

- **D = 0** indicates that it is a **16-bit code segment**. Unless told otherwise (by the addition of one or two special instruction prefix bytes), the processor assumes the following when code from a 16-bit code segment is executed:
  - all memory operands are 16 bits in size
  - all memory addresses are 16 bits in size
- **D = 1** indicates that it is a **32-bit code segment**. Unless told otherwise (by the addition of one or two special instruction prefix bytes), the processor assumes the following when code from a 32-bit code segment is executed:
  - all memory operands are 32 bits in size
  - all memory addresses are 32 bits in size.

Programs that execute in real or VM86 mode use 16-bit addresses and 16-bit operand size by default.

Assume that the processor is executing code from a 32-bit code segment (D=1) and it fetches an instruction that uses 16-bit operands or addressing. In other words, the format of the bytes that comprise the instruction are not what the processor expects when operating in 32-bit mode. Unless the proper overrides are used (i.e., the address size and/or operand size prefixes), the processor will treat the instruction as a 32-bit instruction and will either execute it incorrectly or generate an error. On the other hand, if the proper override(s) are used, this warns the processor that the instruction that follows uses a different (pre-386) format and the fields that comprise the instruction are then interpreted correctly.

The opposite scenario is also true. If the processor is currently-executing code from a 16-bit code segment (D=0), it expects all instructions to adhere to the 16-bit instruction format. In the event that an instruction uses 32-bit addresses and/or data operands, it must be preceded by the appropriate overrides.

To override the processor's assumptions (address and/or operand size), the instruction must be preceded by the address size prefix (67h), the operand size prefix (66h), or both prefixes. When detected by a processor executing code from a 32-bit code segment (D=1), this instructs the processor to treat this as a 16-bit instruction (in interpreting the fields within the instruction that change meaning in 32- versus 16-bit mode). Conversely, when detected by a processor executing code from a 16-bit code segment (D=1), this instructs the processor to treat this as a 32-bit instruction.

Only post-286 x86 processors can execute 32-bit code segments. The address size and operand size prefixes were added in the 386 processor to permit it to execute both 16- and 32-bit code correctly.

Protected Mode Software Architecture

Stack Segment Descriptor's Big Bit

In a stack segment descriptor, this is **defined as** the **Big bit**. It defines the size of the stack pointer (SP) register and the upper bound of an expand-down stack.

- B = 1 indicates that the 32-bit ESP register is used as the stack pointer and the upper bound of the expand-down stack is FFFFFFFFh.
- B = 0 indicates that the 16-bit SP register is used as a stack pointer and the upper bound of the expand-down stack is 0000FFFFh.

For a description of both expand-up and expand-down stacks, refer to the section entitled "Selecting and Accessing Stack Segment" on page 131.

Segment Type Field

Introduction to Type Field

The four bit segment Type field defines what type of segment is defined by a descriptor. The state of the descriptor's System bit qualifies the meaning of the Type field:

- **S = 0** indicates that **segment is** a special OS **System segment** and the Type field defines the type of OS segment. This topic is covered under "System Bit" on page 96.
- **S = 1** indicates that **segment is either a code or a data/stack segment**. The Type field defines whether it is a code or a data/stack segment and some of the segment's access rights and its access history.

A detailed description of the Type field (for various types of non-system segments) can be found under the chapters entitled "Code Segments" on page 99, and "The Data Segments" on page 125. The following description of the Type field is general in nature and assumes that the System bit = 1 (non-system segment).

Non-System Segment Types

The segment Type field consists of bits [3:0] of byte five of the descriptor. Bit [3], the C/D (code or data) bit, defines whether it's a code or a data/stack segment (**C/D = 0** indicates that it is a **data/stack segment**, while **C/D = 1** indicates that it is a **code segment**). Table 7-1 on page 93 and Table 7-2 on page 94 define the various types of non-system segments. Note that the definition of bits [2:0] is different for code and data/stack segments.

Chapter 7: Intro to Segmentation

Stack segments must be designated as read/write. The subject of expand-up versus expand-down stacks is covered under the heading "Selecting and Accessing Stack Segment" on page 131.

The subject of conforming versus non-conforming code segments is covered under the heading "Conforming and Non-Conforming Code Segments" on page 108. Code segments that are marked "accessible for instruction fetch and data reads" may, in addition to instruction fetches, be read using MOV instructions. This would be necessary if the code segment contains data constants that would need to be read as data (using MOV instructions).

Table 7-1: Data/Stack Segment Types

Type Field Bits				Description
3	**2**	**1**	**0**	
C/D	E	W	A	**Data/Stack Segment Attributes & Access History**
0	0	0	0	Not yet accessed (A=0), read-only (W=0), data segment (stack segment must be read/writable).
0	0	0	1	Accessed (A=1), read-only (W=0), data segment (stack segment must be read/writable).
0	0	1	0	Not yet accessed (A=0), read/write (W=1), expand-up stack (E=0) or data segment.
0	0	1	1	Accessed (A=1), read/write (W=1), expand-up stack (E=0) or data segment.
0	1	0	0	Not yet accessed (A=0), read-only (W=0), data segment (stack segment must be read/writable).
0	1	0	1	Accessed (A=1), read-only (W=0), data segment (stack segment must be read/writable).
0	1	1	0	Not yet accessed (A=0), read/write (W=1), expand-down stack (E=1) or data segment.
0	1	1	1	Accessed (A=1), read/write (W=1), expand-down stack (E=1) or data segment.

Table 7-2: Code Segment Types

Type Field Bits				Description
3	**2**	**1**	**0**	
C/D	**C**	**R**	**A**	**Code Segment Attributes & Access History**
1	0	0	0	Not yet accessed (A=0), accessible for instruction fetch only (R=0), non-conforming (C=0).
1	0	0	1	Accessed (A=1), accessible for instruction fetch only (R=0), non-conforming (C=0).
1	0	1	0	Not yet accessed (A=0), accessible for instruction fetch and for data reads (R=1), non-conforming (C=0).
1	0	1	1	Accessed (A=1), accessible for instruction fetch and for data reads (R=1), non-conforming (C=0).
1	1	0	0	Not yet accessed (A=0), accessible for instruction fetch only (R=0), conforming (C=1).
1	1	0	1	Accessed (A=1), accessible for instruction fetch only (R=0), conforming (C=1).
1	1	1	0	Not yet accessed (A=0), accessible for instruction fetch and data reads (R=1), conforming (C=1).
1	1	1	1	Accessed (A=1), accessible for instruction fetch and data reads (R=1), conforming (C=1).

Figure 7-9: General Format of Segment Descriptor

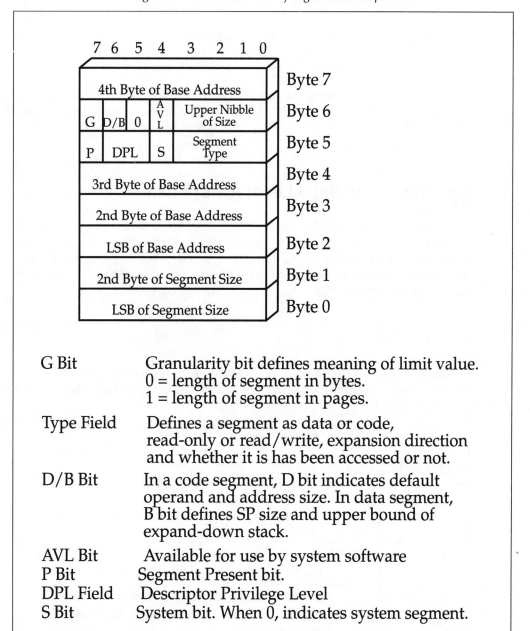

G Bit — Granularity bit defines meaning of limit value.
0 = length of segment in bytes.
1 = length of segment in pages.

Type Field — Defines a segment as data or code, read-only or read/write, expansion direction and whether it is has been accessed or not.

D/B Bit — In a code segment, D bit indicates default operand and address size. In data segment, B bit defines SP size and upper bound of expand-down stack.

AVL Bit — Available for use by system software

P Bit — Segment Present bit.

DPL Field — Descriptor Privilege Level

S Bit — System bit. When 0, indicates system segment.

Protected Mode Software Architecture

Segment Present Bit

The state of this bit indicates whether the segment of code or data is currently in memory. **P = 1** indicates that the **segment** of information is **present in memory** starting at the base address indicated in this descriptor.

P = 0 indicates that the **segment** of information is **not present in memory**. Bytes zero through four, six, and seven may be used by the OS (e.g., to store a mass storage address). Byte five is still the attribute byte and defines the privilege level and segment type.

Descriptor Privilege Level (DPL) Field

This two bit field defines the segment's privilege level. Generally speaking, the processor only permits a program to access this segment if the calling program's privilege level meets or beats the descriptor's privilege level. A detailed description of privilege checking can be found in the chapters entitled "Code Segments" on page 99 and "Data and Stack Segments" on page 125.

System Bit

A segment descriptor with the S = 0 defines a special segment used by the OS. System segments are defined in detail in later sections of this book. Table 7-3 on page 96 defines the system segment types.

Table 7-3: Types of System Segments

Type Field				Description
3	2	1	0	
0	0	0	0	Reserved.
0	0	0	1	Describes an **available 16-bit, 286 TSS** (Task State Segment). May only reside in the GDT.
0	0	1	0	Describes a **Local Descriptor Table** (LDT). An entry in the GDT (Global Descriptor Table) would select this descriptor.

Table 7-3: Types of System Segments (Continued)

Type Field				Description
3	**2**	**1**	**0**	
0	0	1	1	Describes a **busy 16-bit, 286 TSS**. May only reside in the GDT.
0	1	0	0	**16-bit, 286 Call Gate**. May reside in either the GDT or the LDT, but not in the IDT.
0	1	0	1	**Task Gate**. May reside in GDT, LDT, or IDT.
0	1	1	0	**16-bit, 286 Interrupt Gate**. May only reside in the IDT.
0	1	1	1	**16-bit, 286 Trap Gate**. May only reside in the IDT.
1	0	0	0	Reserved
1	0	0	1	**Describes an available 32-bit, post-286 TSS**. May only reside in the GDT.
1	0	1	0	Reserved
1	0	1	1	**Describes a busy 32-bit, post-286 TSS**. May only reside in the GDT.
1	1	0	0	**32-bit, post-286 Call Gate**. May reside in either the GDT or the LDT, but not in the IDT.
1	1	0	1	Reserved
1	1	1	0	**32-bit, post-286 Interrupt Gate.** May only reside in the IDT.
1	1	1	1	**32-bit, post-286 Trap Gate**. May only reside in the IDT.

Available Bit

This bit is not used by the processor and can be used by the OS programmer to describe an additional segment attribute.

8   *Code Segments*

The Previous Chapter

The previous chapter introduced the following concepts:

- segment selector
- segment descriptor tables
- segment descriptor format

This Chapter

This chapter provides a detailed description of code segments.

The Next Chapter

The next chapter provides a detailed description data and stack segments.

Selecting Code Segment to Execute

In order for it to fetch instructions from an area of memory, the programmer must inform the processor what code segment the instructions are to be fetched from. This is accomplished by loading a 16-bit value (a selector) into the Code Segment (CS) register. In real mode, this value represents the upper 16 bits of the 20 bit start address of the segment in memory. In protected mode, the value loaded into a segment register is interpreted as illustrated in Figure 8-1 on page 100.

Any of the following actions loads a value into the CS segment register, causing the processor to begin fetching instructions from the new code segment in memory:

- **Execution of a far jump instruction**. This loads both CS and EIP with new values.
- **Execution of a far call instruction**. This loads both CS and EIP with new values.
- A **hardware interrupt or a software exception**. In response, the processor reads values from the interrupt table into the CS and EIP registers.
- Execution of a **software interrupt instruction**. In response, the processor reads values from the interrupt table into the CS and EIP registers.
- **Initiation of a new task or resumption of a previously-suspended task**. During the task switch, the processor loads all of its registers, including CS and EIP, with the values from the TSS associated with the new task.
- Execution of a **far return instruction**. The return address is popped from the stack and placed in the CS and EIP registers.
- Execution of an **interrupt return instruction (IRET)**. The return address is popped from the stack and placed in the CS and EIP registers.

Figure 8-1: Segment Selector

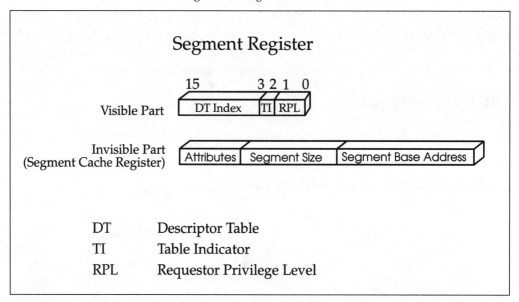

Chapter 8: Code Segments

Code Segment Descriptor Format

The value loaded into the visible part of CS (see Figure 8-1 on page 100) identifies:

- the descriptor table that contains the code segment descriptor. TI = 0 if the entry resides in the GDT, while TI = 1 indicates that the entry resides in the LDT.
- the entry in the specified descriptor table. The Index field identifies one of 8192d entries in the table.

The processor multiplies the index by eight (eight bytes per entry) to obtain the offset in the table. A check is performed to ensure that the offset is not beyond the indicated table's limit (supplied from the GDTR or LDTR register). An exception results if it is. The offset is then added to the table base address (supplied from the GDTR or LDTR register) to form the start address of the descriptor in memory.

The processor reads the code segment descriptor from the selected segment descriptor table and checks to ensure that the currently-executing program has sufficient privilege to access this code segment. If not, a general protection (GP) exception is generated. If the privilege test is passed, the processor saves the descriptor information in its internal code segment cache register (the invisible part of the CS register).

Figure 8-2 on page 103 and Table 8-1 on page 101 illustrate the format of a code segment descriptor.

Table 8-1: Code Segment Descriptor Format

Field	Value	Description
S	1	S = 1 because a code segment is not a special OS segment.
C/D	1	Code or Data bit = 1, indicating that the descriptor defines a code segment, rather than a data/stack segment.
Conforming bit	0 or 1	Refer to the section entitled "Conforming and Non-Conforming Code Segments" on page 108 for a description of conforming versus non-conforming code segments.

Table 8-1: Code Segment Descriptor Format (Continued)

Field	Value	Description
R	0 or 1	If R = 0, only the instruction prefetcher may access this code segment (in other words, the segment is execute-only). Any attempt to access the code segment using MOV instructions causes a GP exception. If R = 1, this segment may be read by both the instruction prefetcher and by using MOV instructions. This is necessary if the code segment contains data constants that must be read during the course of program execution.
Other fields		The remaining bit fields in the code segment descriptor are defined in the section entitled "General Segment Descriptor Format" on page 90.

Figure 8-2: Code Segment Descriptor Format

Code Segment Descriptor

```
      7  6  5  4  3  2  1  0
   ┌──────────────────────────┐
   │  4th Byte of Base Address │  Byte 7
   ├───┬───┬───┬─A─┬──────────┤
   │ G │ D │ 0 │ V │ Upper Nibble │  Byte 6
   │   │   │   │ L │   of Size    │
   ├───┬───────┬───┬D/C┬───┬───┬──┤
   │ P │  DPL  │ S │ 1 │ C │ R │ A│  Byte 5
   ├───┴───────┴───┴───┴───┴───┴──┤
   │  3rd Byte of Base Address    │  Byte 4
   ├──────────────────────────────┤
   │  2nd Byte of Base Address    │  Byte 3
   ├──────────────────────────────┤
   │  LSB of Base Address         │  Byte 2
   ├──────────────────────────────┤
   │  2nd Byte of Segment Size    │  Byte 1
   ├──────────────────────────────┤
   │  LSB of Segment Size         │  Byte 0
   └──────────────────────────────┘
```

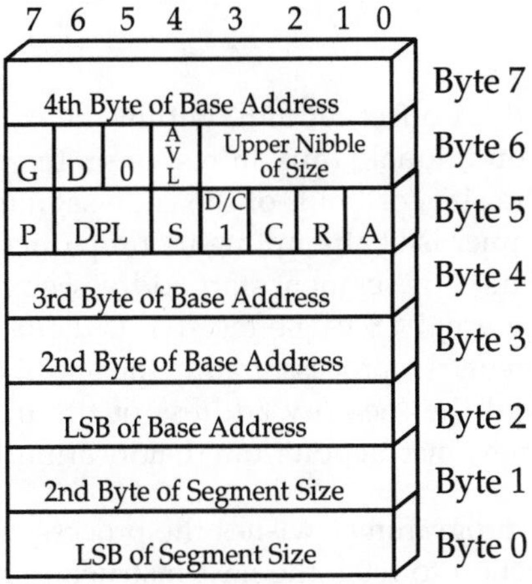

G Bit	Granularity bit defines meaning of limit value. 0 = length of segment in bytes. 1 = length of segment in 4KB pages.
D Bit	In code segment, Default bit defines default size of operands and effective addresses. 0 = 16-bit, 1 = 32-bit.
AVL Bit	Available for use by system software
P Bit	Segment Present bit (must be 1 if the code segment is present in memory).
DPL Field	Descriptor Privilege Level (0-3)
S Bit	System bit. When 0, indicates system segment. Must be 1 in a code segment descriptor.
D/C	This could be called the Data/Code bit. A 0 indicates a data segment and a 1 indicates a code segment.
C Bit	Conforming bit. Set to 1 if code segment is conforming. See text for a detailed description.
R Bit	Readable bit. A 0 indicates an execute-only segment, while a 1 indicates the segment may be read from by both the prefetcher and for data accesses.
A Bit	Accessed bit. Set to 1 by the processor when a code segment is accessed.

Protected Mode Software Architecture

Accessing Code Segment

The processor accesses the code segment whenever it has to fetch an instruction from memory. Consider the following unconditional near jump instruction:

```
JMP  0009
```

The programmer has specified an offset, 0009h, within the current code segment as the target of this unconditional jump. In response, the processor compares the specified offset to the size, or limit, of the code segment currently in use to ensure that the programmer isn't attempting to jump outside the bounds of the current code segment. The code segment start address, size and attributes are stored in the processor's internal CS cache register. If the target location is within the bounds of the segment, the processor adds the specified offset to the segment's base address to yield the memory address of the instruction to be jumped to. It then fetches the next instruction from that location.

In the following example, the programmer wishes the processor to perform an unconditional far jump instruction to fetch the next instruction from a location within a different code segment:

```
JMP  00D0:0003
```

Since this is an attempt to access a different code segment, the processor must first verify that the currently-executing program is permitted to access the location in the new code segment. To do this, it must read the new code segment descriptor from memory and check its descriptor privilege level. The value 00D0h is placed into the CS register and is interpreted as indicated in Figure 8-3 on page 105 (the index field is binarily-weighted). The processor reads the 26th entry from the GDT (TI = 0 selects the GDT). Figure 8-4 on page 106 illustrates the example code segment descriptor read from the GDT.

The processor verifies that the new segment is a code segment (System bit = 1, and C/D = 1) and is present in memory (P = 1). It must also determine if the currently-executing program is sufficiently privileged to call or jump to the targeted code segment. This subject is covered in the next section. It checks the specified offset, 0003h, to determine if it exceeds the limit (size) of the code segment (the segment size is 126525d bytes (Granularity bit = 0, indicating that the size is specified in bytes, not pages). If all tests are passed, it loads the new segment descriptor into its on-chip code segment cache register, adds the specified offset to the new code segment's base address (00131BCCh) and fetches the next instruction from the target address—00131BCFh.

Figure 8-3: Example Value in CS Register

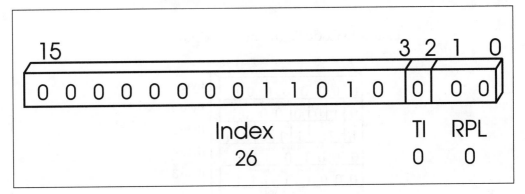

Figure 8-4: Sample Code Segment Descriptor

Example Code Segment Descriptor

```
 7  6  5  4  3  2  1  0
```

Upper byte of Base Address		
0 0 0 0 0 0 0 0	Byte 7	

G	D		Avl	Upper digit of Limit	
0	1	0	0	0 0 0 1	Byte 6

P	DPL	S	D/C	C	R	A	
1	11	1	1	0	0	1	Byte 5

3rd byte of Base Address
0 0 1 0 0 1 1 — Byte 4

2nd byte of Base Address
0 0 0 1 1 0 1 1 — Byte 3

1st byte of Base Address
1 1 0 0 1 1 0 0 — Byte 2

2nd byte of Limit
1 1 1 0 1 1 1 0 — Byte 1

1st byte of Limit
0 0 1 1 1 1 0 1 — Byte 0

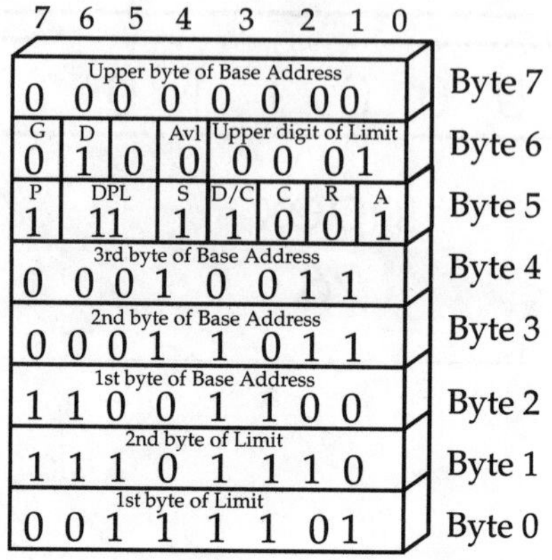

G Bit	Granularity bit defines meaning of limit value. 0 = length of segment in bytes.
D Bit	In code segment, Default bit defines default size of operands and effective addresses. 1 = 32-bit default operand and address length.
AVL Bit	Available for use by system software
P Bit	Segment Present bit (must be 1 if the code segment is present in memory).
DPL Field	Descriptor Privilege Level = 3
S Bit	System bit. When 0, indicates system segment. Must be 1 in a code segment descriptor.
D/C	This could be called the Data/Code bit. 1 indicates a code segment.
C Bit	Conforming bit. 0 = code segment is non-conforming. Can only be called by program at same level or through Call Gate.
R Bit	Readable bit. A 0 indicates an execute-only segment.
A Bit	Accessed bit. Set to 1 by the processor when a code segment is accessed.
Segment Base Address	Base address of the segment is 00131BCCh.
Segment Size	The size of the segment is 1EE3Dh, or 126,525d.

Privilege Checking

General

The goal of privilege checking is to ensure that the currently-executing program cannot access areas of memory unless permitted to do so. Any attempt to do so results in a General Protection (GP) exception.

Some Definitions

Before permitting access to a segment, the processor must verify that the currently-executing program has sufficient privilege to access the segment. The three components involved in this comparison are:

- the **CPL (current privilege level)** of the current program
- the **RPL (requestor privilege level)** in the segment register
- the **DPL (descriptor privilege level)** of the target code segment

Definition of a Task

The term "task" is used many times throughout this book. In a multitasking OS, the OS typically permits the processor to execute each program, or task, for a fixed period of time (e.g., 10ms). When the currently-executing task's timeslice has expired, a hardware timer is typically used to interrupt the task, forcing the processor to "jump" back to the OS. The OS suspends the current task by taking a "snapshot" of the processor's current state (in other words, it makes a complete copy of the processor's register set). This is referred to as the processor's current context, and it is saved in memory in the current task's TSS (task state segment). The current context is saved so that the task can be resumed at a later time at the point of suspension.

The processor determines the next task to be executed (or resumed at its point of previous suspension) and switches to the new task by reading the contents of the new task's TSS into the processor's register set. It then begins to fetch and execute from the location pointed to by CS:EIP. The timeslice hardware timer is initialized with the timeslice for the new task.

A task doesn't necessarily consist of just one set of code and data segments. At any time during task execution, the programmer can select a different code seg-

Protected Mode Software Architecture

ment and/or data segments (by placing a new 16-bit segment selector value in the appropriate segment register). A task can consist of a number of programs and data segments. Examples of tasks would be applications such as Lotus 123, Word for Windows, etc. We tend to think of each of these as a program, when in fact each consists of a group of programs that interact with each other to accomplish the overall task's job. The programs that comprise an application may reside in the same code segment, or may be distributed throughout a number of code segments in memory.

Definition of a Procedure

The term "procedure" is used a number of times in the book and refers to a program, or routine, within the current task.

CPL Definition

Normally, the current privilege level (CPL) is defined as the privilege level of the code segment (i.e., the DPL) from which instructions are currently being fetched. This is true unless the program currently executing resides in a conforming code segment (C = 1). Conforming and non-conforming code segments are defined in the section entitled "Conforming and Non-Conforming Code Segments" on page 108.

DPL Definition

Each code segment descriptor contains a two-bit descriptor privilege level (DPL) field and a bit (the C bit) that identifies the code segment as either a non-conforming (C = 0) or a conforming (C = 1) code segment. Together, these two fields define what privilege level a calling program must have in order to jump to or call code in the code segment defined by this descriptor.

Conforming and Non-Conforming Code Segments

Non-conforming code segments are far more common than conforming code segments. The definition of both follow:

- A code segment with **C = 0** is a **non-conforming code segment**. Code in a non-conforming code segment can only be jumped to or called by programs whose CPL matches the target code segment's DPL (i.e., CPL = DPL).
- A code segment with **C = 1** is a **conforming code segment**. Code in a conforming code segment can be jumped to or called by programs whose CPL is less privileged than the segment's DPL. Furthermore, the processor then executes the code in the conforming code segment at the same privilege

level as that of the program that called it. In other words, the code in the conforming code segment "conforms to," or assumes, the privilege level of the program that called it. The CPL remains the same as that of the calling program.

As an example, if the CPL of the currently-executing program is two, it may successfully call or jump to one of the following:

- a non-conforming code segment with a DPL that matches the CPL of the calling program (in other words, the DPL = 2)
- a conforming code segment with a privilege level of zero or one.

It cannot jump to or call code in the following without causing a GP exception:

- a non-conforming code segment with a DPL that doesn't match its CPL (in this case, privilege level two)
- a conforming code segment with a privilege level of two or three.

RPL Definition

The 16-bit value that is placed in the CS register during execution of a far jump or a far call instruction may have been created either by the program currently executing, or may have been passed to it by another program as a parameter. It was Intel's intention that the RPL portion of this value (bits [1:0]) represent the privilege level of the program that created the 16-bit value.

When the currently-executing program attempts to execute a far jump or a far call to another code segment, a privilege check must be performed to determine whether or not access permission will be granted. The privilege level value that is compared to the target code segment's DPL is the lesser-privileged of the CPL and RPL.

As an example, assume that the currently-executing program's **CPL = 2** and the CS register is loaded with a 16-bit value wherein the **RPL = 3** (because the 16-bit value was passed to it by a program with a privilege level of three). Also assume that the **target code segment** of the jump or call is a non-conforming code segment with a **DPL = 2**. The access attempt results in a **GP exception because** the **RPL** (3) is **not equal to** the **DPL** (2). RPL, rather than CPL, was used for the compare because it is the lesser privileged of the two (i.e., privilege level three, the RPL, is less privileged than privilege level two, the CPL).

Protected Mode Software Architecture

Calling a Procedure in Current Task

This section describes how to transfer control to another procedure in the currently-executing task. Table 8-2 on page 110 is a list of the possible scenarios and the method to be used.

Table 8-2: How to Transfer Control to another Procedure in Current Task

To Jump to or Call	Use
Procedure in the same code segment	The programmer uses a near jump or near call instruction.
Procedure in another code segment (assuming that the target code segment is non-conforming) with the same privilege level	The programmer uses a far jump or far call instruction. A Call Gate (described in the next section) could be used, but isn't necessary.
Procedure in another code segment with a higher privilege level	The programmer may use a far jump or far call instruction if the target code segment is a conforming code segment. A Call Gate could be used, but isn't necessary.
Procedure in another code segment with a higher privilege level	The programmer must use a far jump or a far call through a Call Gate if the target code segment is a non-conforming code segment. The Call Gate is described in the next section of this chapter.

Call Gate

The Problem

Assume that the OS includes a code segment residing at privilege level zero (the most privileged level) containing a number of procedures to handle requests from other programs. Some of the procedures within this code segment should only be accessible by lower-privileged OS programs residing at privilege levels one and two. Any attempt to call one of these procedures in this code segment by a program residing at privilege level three (an applications program) should be rejected (i.e., should cause a GP exception). Also assume that other procedures within the same OS code segment are designed to handle requests from applications programs (privilege level three).

The problem is that the code segment has one privilege level, zero, which means that all procedures within this code segment execute at privilege level zero. Ordinarily, any attempt to transfer control to (i.e., call or jump to) one of these routines from another privilege level would result in a GP exception. Making it a conforming code segment isn't the answer because all procedures within this code segment could then be successfully called by programs with lower privilege levels.

The Solution—Different Gateways

The solution is to define a separate gateway to control access to each procedure within the code segment. Each gateway would contain the entry point of its associated procedure and would limit access to the procedure based on the privilege level of the caller. It would reject access attempts by programs whose privilege level don't match its criteria and permit access attempts by programs that meet the criteria. These gateways are referred to as **Call Gates**.

A Call Gate is a special form of OS descriptor and may reside in either the GDT or LDT. It may not reside within the Interrupt Descriptor Table (IDT). A Call Gate is used to transfer control to a procedure whose privilege level is equal to or greater than that of the calling program.

- Only far call instructions can use Call Gates to transfer control to procedures with a higher privilege level than their own.
- Jump instructions can use Call Gates to transfer control to procedures with either the same privilege level or to a conforming code segment with a higher privilege level.

A Call Gate descriptor basically contains an indirect pointer to a code segment and an entry point (i.e., an offset) within it. To access a Call Gate, the programmer executes a far call or a far jump instruction, thereby loading a 16-bit value into the CS register. The CS value identifies the GDT or LDT entry containing the Call Gate descriptor. The offset portion of the called address is discarded. The format of a Call Gate descriptor is illustrated in Figure 8-5 on page 113. It consists of the elements described in Table 8-3 on page 112.

Protected Mode Software Architecture

Table 8-3: Call Gate Descriptor Elements

Field	Description
P	Segment Present bit. 0 = descriptor contents not valid, 1 = contents valid.
DPL	Descriptor Privilege Level.
S	S = 0 because a Call Gate is a System segment type.
X	0 = 16-bit Call Gate (formatted as defined for the 286 processor), while 1 = 32-bit Call Gate (formatted as defined for the post-286 processors). A 16-bit Call Gate descriptor exhibits the following differences from a 32-bit Call Gate descriptor: • Dword count field indicates words rather than dwords. • X = 0 • Bytes 6 and 7 are reserved (in other words, offset is 16 rather than 32 bits).
Byte 5, [2:0]	Contains 100b. Combined with S = 0, identifies this as a Call Gate descriptor. Bit [3] of byte 5 further identifies whether this is a 16- or a 32-bit Call Gate.
Dword Count	Tells processor how many dwords to copy from the caller's stack to the stack of the called procedure (see section entitled "Automatic Stack Switch" on page 122).
Selector	Identifies the code segment descriptor that contains the base address of the code segment that the called procedure resides within.
Offset	Identifies the offset of the called procedure within the target code segment (see previous row).

Figure 8-5: 32-bit Call Gate Descriptor Format

Call Gate Descriptor Format

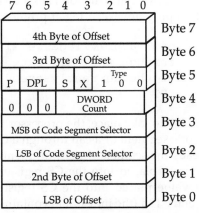

P Bit	Segment Present bit.
DPL Field	Descriptor Privilege Level.
S Bit	System bit. When 0, indicates system segment. Must be 0 in a Call Gate descriptor.

X Bit	This bit indicates whether this is a 16 or 32-bit Call Gate.
	    0 = 16-bit.
	    1 = 32-bit.

Type	Type = 100b indicates Call Gate descriptor.
Dword Count	Tells processor how many dwords (up to 31) to copy from the caller's stack to the stack of the called procedure.
Selector	Identifies the code segment descriptor that holds the base address of the code segment that contains the procedure being called.
Offset	The offset of the called procedure within the code segment identified by the selector (see above).

Note: All CALL GATE entries must reside in the Global Descriptor Table (GDT) or in a Local Descriptor Table (LDT).

Protected Mode Software Architecture

Call Gate Example

Execution Begins

Now assume that the following instruction is executed by an applications program (in other words, a program executing at privilege level three):

```
CALL 0067:0000  ;call a privilege level 0 procedure
                ;through the Call Gate in entry 12d
                ;of the currently-executing program's
                ;LDT
```

Before permitting the call to take place, the processor must determine if this is a far call directly to a code segment or a call through a Call Gate descriptor. To do this, the processor reads the segment descriptor identified by the segment portion of the target address placed into the CS register. Figure 8-6 on page 114 illustrates the 16-bit value placed into the CS register by the call instruction (0067h). This selects entry 12d (the index field contains Ch—12d) in the LDT (TI = 1).

Figure 8-6: CS Contents During Call through Example Call Gate

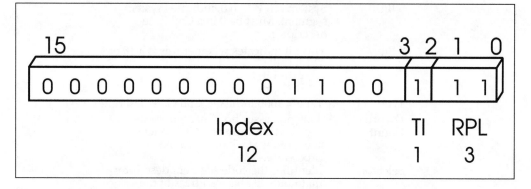

Call Gate Descriptor Read

The descriptor read from entry 12d in the LDT is pictured in Figure 8-7 on page 116. The processor examines the S bit and the segment Type field to determine the type of descriptor:

- **S = 0**, indicating that it is a special **system segment**.
- **Type = 1100b**, a **32-bit Call Gate** descriptor

Table 8-4 on page 115 provides a breakdown of the Call Gate descriptor's contents.

Table 8-4: Elements of the Example Call Gate (see Figure 8-7) Descriptor

Field	Location	Description
P	Byte 5, bit 7	P = 1 indicates that the descriptor is valid.
DPL	Byte 5, bits [6:5]	DPL = 11b, or 3. Defines the minimum privilege level the caller must have to use the gate. In this case, any program with a privilege level of 3 or higher (0, 1, or 2) can use the gate without causing an exception. The value compared to the DPL is the less-privileged of the caller's CPL and RPL. Read the section entitled "The Call Gate Privilege Check" on page 120 for more information.
S	Byte 5, bit 4	S = 0, indicating that this is a special, system segment (see the next row).
Type	Byte 5, bits [3:0]	S = 0 indicates that this is a special, system segment, and Type = 1100b indicates that it is a 32-bit Call Gate (formatted for the post-286 processors).
Dword Count	Byte 4, bits [4:0]	Dword Count = 00010b, indicating that 2 dwords are to be copied from the caller's stack to the called procedure's stack.
Selector	Bytes 2 and 3	Selector = 0150h, indicating target code segment's descriptor is entry 42d of the GDT. The RPL portion has no significance.
Offset	Bytes 0, 1, 6, 7	The offset = 00003400h, indicating that the procedure being called starts at location 00003400h in the target code segment.

Figure 8-7: Example Call Gate Descriptor

Example Call Gate Descriptor

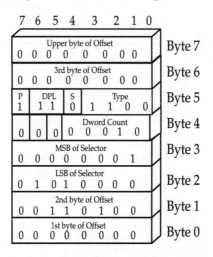

P Bit	Segment Present bit = 1.
DPL Field	Descriptor Privilege Level = 3.
S Bit	System bit. When 0, indicates system segment. Must be 0 in a Call Gate descriptor.
Type	This field indicates this is a 32-bit Call Gate.
Dword Count	Tells processor how many dwords (2) (up to 31) to copy from the caller's stack to the stack of the called procedure.
Selector	Identifies the code segment descriptor that holds the base address of the code segment containing the procedure being called (entry 42d in the GDT)
Offset	The offset of the called procedure within the code segment identified by the selector (00003400h).

Note: All CALL GATE entries must reside in the Global Descriptor Table (GDT) or in a Local Descriptor Table (LDT).

Call Gate Contains Code Segment Selector

Table 8-4 on page 115 and Figure 8-7 on page 116 illustrate the code segment selector found in the Call Gate descriptor. Figure 8-8 on page 117 shows the selector divided into its component fields. The descriptor for the code segment containing the target procedure is in entry 42d of the GDT.

Figure 8-8: Code Segment Selector Specified in Example Call Gate

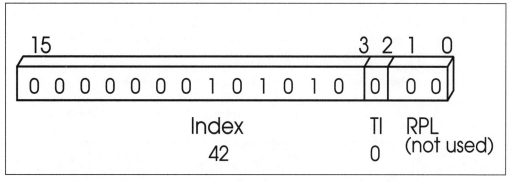

Code Segment Descriptor Read

The processor reads the descriptor from entry 42d in the GDT. The descriptor is pictured in Figure 8-9 on page 119 and its elements are identified in Table 8-5 on page 117.

Table 8-5: Example Code Segment Descriptor

Field	Location	Description
G	Byte 6, bit 7	G = 0 indicates that the 20-bit limit is expressed in bytes rather than pages.
D	Byte 6, bit 6	D = 1 indicates that this is a post-286, 32-bit code segment.
Avl	Byte 6, bit 5	Avl = 0. This is an OS-specific bit and has no meaning to the processor.
P	Byte 5, bit 7	P = 1, indicating that the descriptor is valid and the code segment is present in memory.

Table 8-5: Example Code Segment Descriptor (Continued)

Field	Location	Description
DPL	Byte 5, bits [6:5]	DPL of the code segment is 3 (the lowest privilege level). See the section entitled "The Call Gate Privilege Check" on page 120 for more information.
S	Byte 5, bit 4	S = 1, indicating that this is not a special, system segment.
D/C	Byte 5, bit 3	D/C = 1, indicating that this is a code rather than a data/stack segment.
C	Byte 5, bit 2	C = 0, indicating that this is a non-conforming code segment. See the section entitled "The Call Gate Privilege Check" on page 120 for more information.
R	Byte 5, bit 1	R = 0, indicating that this is an execute-only code segment.
A	Byte 5, bit 0	A = 1, indicating that the code segment has been accessed since it was placed in memory.
Base	Bytes 2, 3, 4, 7	32-bit base address of code segment = 00131BCCh.
Limit	Byte 0, 1, and bits [3:0] of byte 6	Segment length = 1EE3Dh (126525d bytes).

Figure 8-9: Example Code Segment Descriptor

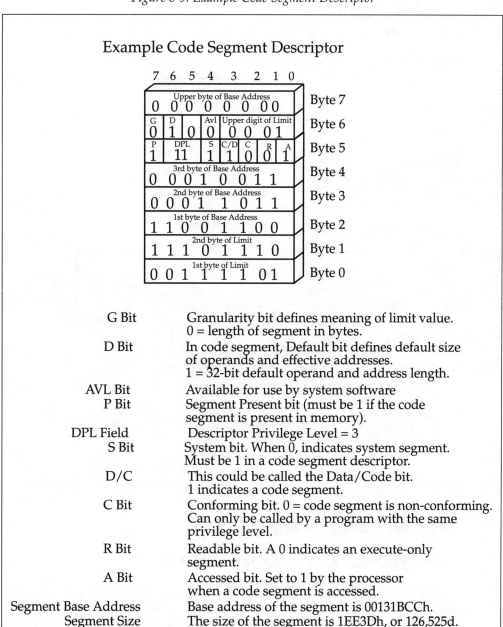

Example Code Segment Descriptor

G Bit	Granularity bit defines meaning of limit value. 0 = length of segment in bytes.
D Bit	In code segment, Default bit defines default size of operands and effective addresses. 1 = 32-bit default operand and address length.
AVL Bit	Available for use by system software
P Bit	Segment Present bit (must be 1 if the code segment is present in memory).
DPL Field	Descriptor Privilege Level = 3
S Bit	System bit. When 0, indicates system segment. Must be 1 in a code segment descriptor.
D/C	This could be called the Data/Code bit. 1 indicates a code segment.
C Bit	Conforming bit. 0 = code segment is non-conforming. Can only be called by a program with the same privilege level.
R Bit	Readable bit. A 0 indicates an execute-only segment.
A Bit	Accessed bit. Set to 1 by the processor when a code segment is accessed.
Segment Base Address	Base address of the segment is 00131BCCh.
Segment Size	The size of the segment is 1EE3Dh, or 126,525d.

Protected Mode Software Architecture

The Big Picture

Figure 8-10 on page 120 illustrates the overall relationship of the instruction, the Call Gate, the code segment descriptor and the called procedure.

Figure 8-10: Call Gate and CS Descriptors, Code Segment and Called Procedure

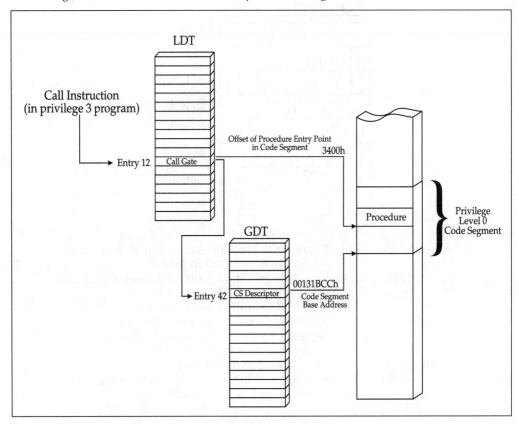

The Call Gate Privilege Check

Privilege Check for Call through Call Gate

A Call gate may be used to transfer execution to a more privileged code segment or a code segment with the same privilege level (although it's not necessary when transferring execution to a code segment with the same privilege level).

When executing a call through a Call Gate, a GP exception is generated unless **both** of the following tests are passed:

1. **Numerically greater of CPL and RPL ≤ call gate's DPL**. The Call Gate descriptor's DPL defines the minimum level of privilege a caller must have to use the gate. The value compared to the DPL is the lesser-privileged of the caller's RPL and CPL.

   As an example, a Call Gate descriptor with a DPL of two can be used by callers with privilege levels of zero, one, or two. Any attempt by a caller with a privilege level of three results in a GP exception.

2. **Destination code segment's DPL ≤ CPL**. The caller's CPL must be the same as or less-privileged than the target code segment descriptor's DPL. In other words, using the Call Gate, the code segment may be called by any program that doesn't have a higher privilege level than the target code segment's DPL.

   As an example, if the code segment descriptor's DPL is one, using a Call Gate, it can be called by programs with a privilege level of one, two, or three. An attempt by a program with a privilege level of zero to call this code segment using a Call Gate results in a GP exception.

Privilege Check for Jump through Call Gate

Unlike a call, a jump cannot use a Call Gate to jump to a code segment with a higher privilege level. The target of the jump may be in either a conforming or a non-conforming code segment. The following paragraphs define the access rules for both cases

When executing a **jump through a Call Gate to a non-conforming code segment**, a GP exception is generated unless **both** of the following tests are passed:

1. **Numerically greater of CPL and RPL ≤ call gate's DPL**. The Call Gate descriptor's DPL defines the minimum level of privilege the program executing the jump must have to use the gate. The value compared to the DPL is the lesser-privileged of the jumper's RPL and CPL. As an example, a Call Gate descriptor with a DPL of two can be used by jumpers with privilege levels of zero, one, or two. Any attempt by a jumper with a privilege level of three results in a GP exception.

2. **Destination code segment's DPL = CPL**. In other words, the program attempting to jump to the destination code segment must have the same privilege level as the destination code segment.

When executing a **jump through a Call Gate to a conforming code segment**, a GP exception is generated unless **both** of the following tests are passed:

Protected Mode Software Architecture

1. **Numerically greater of CPL and RPL ≤ call gate's DPL.** The Call Gate descriptor's DPL defines the minimum level of privilege a jumper must have to use the gate. The value compared to the DPL is the lesser-privileged of the jumper's RPL and CPL.

    As an example, a Call Gate descriptor with a DPL of two can be used by jumpers with privilege levels of zero, one, or two. Any attempt by a jumper with a privilege level of three results in a GP exception.

2. **Destination code segment's DPL ≤ CPL.** The jumper's CPL must be the same as or less-privileged than the target code segment descriptor's DPL. In other words, using the Call Gate the code segment may be jumped to by any program that doesn't have a higher privilege level than the target code segment's DPL.

    As an example, if the code segment descriptor's DPL is one, using a Call Gate it can be jumped to by programs with a privilege level of one, two, or three. An attempt by a program with a privilege level of zero to jump to this code segment using a Call Gate results in a GP exception.

Automatic Stack Switch

A call instruction automatically saves a pointer (CS and EIP are stored on the stack) to the instruction that follows the call instruction and then jumps to the called procedure. The called procedure executes. The last instruction in the called procedure should be a RET (Return). Execution of the RET instruction causes the processor to pop the previously-saved CS:EIP value off the stack, load it into CS:EIP, and fetch the instruction it points to. This is the instruction that follows the call instruction. Execution of the caller's program resumes at this point.

When calling a procedure that resides at a higher privilege level through a Call Gate, some additional steps are necessary because of a potential, stack-related problem. If the called procedure uses the same stack (pointed to by SS:ESP, or SS:SP) as the caller, the stack may prove to be too small to hold additional values that the called procedure may push onto the stack. This would cause a stack overflow exception. The processor addresses this problem by automatically switching to a new stack of sufficient size to hold CS:EIP (address to return to in the calling program), SS:ESP (pointer to the calling program's stack area) and any parameters that are passed by the caller (on the stack), as well as any local variables that the called procedure may subsequently need to push onto the stack.

When a procedure call (to a procedure on a higher privilege level) is made through a Call Gate, the processor creates a new stack to receive the CS:EIP,

SS:ESP and parameters from the caller. The Task State Segment (TSS) for the currently-executing task is consulted by the processor to get the stack segment selector and ESP pointer for the new stack. Figure 8-11 on page 124 illustrates the format of the TSS. In the example, the call is to a level zero procedure, so the processor uses SS0 to supply the base address of the new stack and ESP0 to supply the pointer to the top of its stack. These are loaded into SS:ESP and the caller's CS:EIP, parameters (if any), and the caller's SS:ESP values are copied to the new stack.

When calling a procedure (that resides at a higher privilege level) through a Call Gate, the following series of actions are performed in sequence:

1. The program that is about to make the call pushes any parameters onto its own stack that will be used by the procedure to be called.
2. The call instruction begins execution. The stack of the procedure being called is checked to ensure that it is large enough to hold the caller's SS:ESP, the parameters to be copied from the caller's stack, and the CS:EIP contents. A stack exception is generated if it isn't large enough.
3. The contents of SS:ESP are pushed onto the called procedure's stack as two, 32-bit values (the upper 16 bits of the value from the 16-bit SS register is filled with 16 bits of zero to form a 32-bit value).
4. The parameters are copied from the caller's to the called procedure's stack. A value of zero in the DWORD COUNT field of the Call Gate descriptor indicates that there are no parameters to be copied. In the example Call Gate descriptor (see Figure 8-7 on page 116), a parameter count of two is specified, so two doublewords are copied.
5. The contents of CS:EIP (pointer to the instruction after the call instruction) are pushed onto the called procedure's stack.
6. The processor then loads the CS cache register with the base address of the target code segment and EIP with the offset of the called procedure within the target code segment.
7. The called procedure executes. The parameters (if any) are read from the new stack and are used.
8. A RET instruction executes at the end of the called procedure, causing the processor to pop the CS:EIP and SS:ESP pointers off the called program's stack, and to adjust the caller's ESP to deallocate the stack doublewords used to store the passed parameters (the number of dwords to deallocate are stated with the RET instruction (e.g., RET 2).
9. The processor uses the restored CS:EIP to resume execution at the instruction after the call instruction.

Figure 8-11: Task State Segment Format

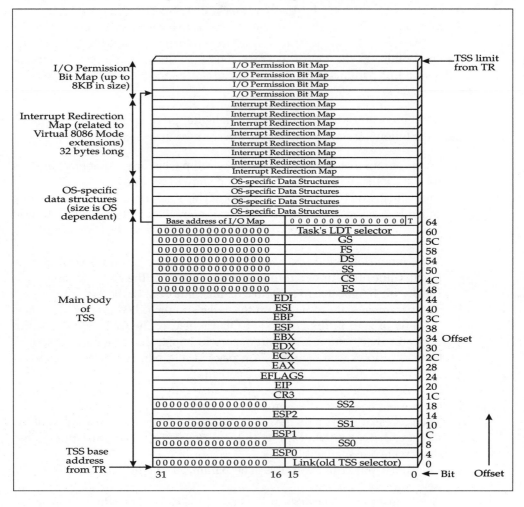

9   *Data and Stack Segments*

The Previous Chapter

The previous chapter provided a detailed description of code segments.

This Chapter

This chapter provides a detailed description of data and stack segments.

The Next Chapter

The next chapter discusses the creation of a task. It provides a detailed discussion of the TSS descriptor and the Task State Segment (TSS).

Introduction

Intel considers the stack segment to be a data segment. However, it is treated separately in this chapter because it is used differently than the average data segment.

The Data Segments

Selecting and Accessing a Data Segment

The post-286 processors have four data segment registers: DS, ES, FS and GS. They identify up to four separate data segments (in memory) that are accessed by the currently-executing program.

Protected Mode Software Architecture

To access data within one of the four data segments, the programmer must first load a 16-bit value into the respective data segment register. In real mode, the value in the data segment register specifies the upper 16 bits of the 20 bit memory start address of the data segment. In protected mode, the value selects a segment descriptor in either the GDT or LDT. Figure 9-1 on page 128 illustrates the format of a data segment descriptor. The example

```
MOV  AX, 4F36   ;load DS register
MOV  DS, AX     ;
MOV  AL, [0100] ;read from data segment into AL
MOV  [2100], AL ;write to data segment from AL
```

has the following effect. The value 4F36h is moved into the DS data segment register and is interpreted by the processor as indicated in Figure 9-2 on page 129. The RPL is two. The processor accesses entry 2534d in the LDT to obtain the data segment descriptor and perform an access rights check. Figure 9-3 on page 130 illustrates the example data segment descriptor fetched from the LDT. The segment is:

- a data segment (C/D = 0) 31550d bytes in length
- starting at memory location 00083EA0h
- with a DPL of two
- and is read\writable.

Assuming that the privilege check is successful, the eight byte segment descriptor is loaded into the DS register's invisible cache register on board the processor.

When the third instruction of the example (MOV AL, [0100]) is executed, the processor performs a limit check to ensure that the specified offset, 0100h, doesn't exceed the length of the DS data segment. 0100h is compared to the segment size in the DS cache register. Since 0100h is less than 07B3Eh, the access is within the segment's limit. The processor permits the access and the offset, 0100h, is added to the segment base address, 00083EA0h, yielding memory address 00083FA0h. One byte is read from this location and placed into the processor's AL register. The next MOV instruction involves a memory write into the DS data segment. Before permitting this, the processor checks the descriptor's W bit to ensure that this segment is marked as writable. Another limit check is performed to ensure that offset 2100h doesn't exceed the segment length. The offset, 2100h, is then added to the segment's base address, 00083EA0h, yielding memory address 00085FA0h. The byte in the AL register is written into this memory location.

The following code fragment is the same as the previous one except for the fact that it accesses the GS data segment instead of the DS data segment.

```
MOV  AX, 4F36      ;load GS register
MOV  GS, AX        ;
MOV  AL, GS:[0100] ;read from GS data segment
MOV  GS:[2100], AL ;write to GS data segment
```

Data Segment Privilege Check

The RPL, CPL and DPL are involved in the privilege check. The 16-bit value loaded into the respective data segment register is accepted if the lesser-privileged of the RPL and CPL has the same privilege level or is more privileged than the target data segment descriptor's DPL. Another way of stating it—a program can only access data in a segment with the same or a lesser privilege level.

Assuming that the currently-executing program's RPL and CPL are the same:

- a program with a CPL of zero can access data in a data segment with any DPL value.
- a program with a CPL of one can access data in data segments with a DPL of one, two, or three.
- a program with a CPL of two can access data in data segments with a DPL of two or three.
- a program with a CPL of three can only access data in data segments with a DPL of three.

Any violation of this criteria results in a GP exception.

Protected Mode Software Architecture

Figure 9-1: Data Segment Descriptor Format

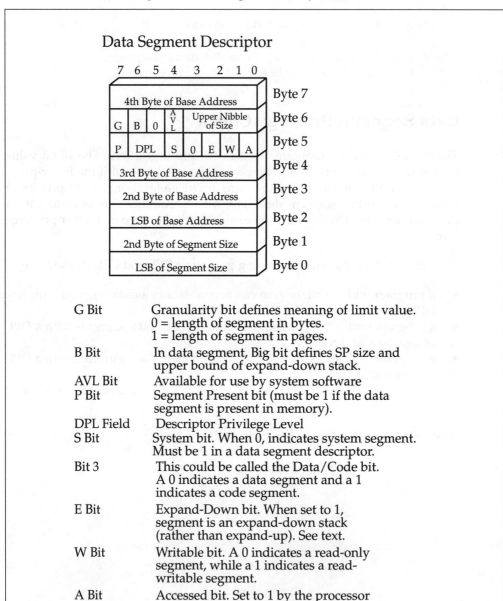

Data Segment Descriptor

G Bit	Granularity bit defines meaning of limit value. 0 = length of segment in bytes. 1 = length of segment in pages.
B Bit	In data segment, Big bit defines SP size and upper bound of expand-down stack.
AVL Bit	Available for use by system software
P Bit	Segment Present bit (must be 1 if the data segment is present in memory).
DPL Field	Descriptor Privilege Level
S Bit	System bit. When 0, indicates system segment. Must be 1 in a data segment descriptor.
Bit 3	This could be called the Data/Code bit. A 0 indicates a data segment and a 1 indicates a code segment.
E Bit	Expand-Down bit. When set to 1, segment is an expand-down stack (rather than expand-up). See text.
W Bit	Writable bit. A 0 indicates a read-only segment, while a 1 indicates a read-writable segment.
A Bit	Accessed bit. Set to 1 by the processor when a data segment is accessed.

Figure 9-2: Example Value in DS Register

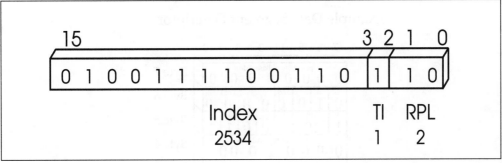

Figure 9-3: Example Data Segment Descriptor

Example Data Segment Descriptor

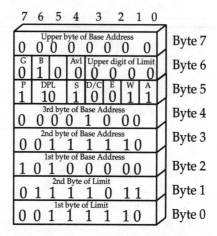

G Bit	Granularity bit defines meaning of limit value. 0 = length of segment in bytes.
B Bit	In stack segment, the B bit defines the SP size. It also identifies the upper boundary of an expand down stack segment. 1 = 32-bit SP (ESP) and upper limit of FFFFFFFFh.
AVL Bit	Available for use by system software
P Bit	Segment Present bit (must be 1 if the data segment is present in memory).
DPL Field	Descriptor Privilege Level = 2
S Bit	System bit. When 0, indicates system segment. Must be 1 in a data segment descriptor.
D/C	This could be called the Data/Code bit. 0 indicates a data segment.
E Bit	Expand down bit. Will be 0 in a data segment descriptor.
W Bit	Write-enable bit. A 1 indicates a read/writable segment.
A Bit	Accessed bit. Set to 1 by the processor when a data segment is accessed.
Segment Base Address	Base address of the segment is 00083EA0h.
Segment Size	The size of the segment is 07B3Eh, or 31,550d.

Chapter 9: Data and Stack Segments

Selecting and Accessing Stack Segment

Description

A stack segment is a form of data segment. Its descriptor must identify it as a read/writable segment so that the processor may perform both pushes (i.e., writes to the stack) and pops (i.e., reads from the stack). The descriptor also describes the stack's method of growth. Most often, a stack grows downwards from its upper limit towards its base as items are pushed onto the stack. Intel refers to this as an expand-up stack (sounds contradictory, doesn't it). A stack may also be designated as an expand-down stack, however. A description of the expand-down stack can be found in the section entitled "Expand-Down Stack" on page 134. It should be noted that most OSs implement expand-up stacks. The discussion that follows describes the operation of an expand-up stack.

Assume that the processor is in protected mode and the following series of instructions is executed:

```
MOV  AX, 02FF       ;put 02FFh in SS
MOV  SS, AX         ;
MOV  ESP, 00005FFE  ;set stack pointer initial value
PUSH BX             ;save BX in stack
MOV  BX, [0100]     ;read value from memory to BX
ADD  CX, BX         ;add BX to CX, result in CX
POP  BX             ;restore original value in BX
```

The first two instructions set SS to 02FFh. This value is interpreted as illustrated in Figure 9-4 on page 132. The processor reads the segment descriptor from entry 95d in the LDT (TI bit = 1, indicating LDT, and the index field contains 95d), performs privilege checking and ensures that the descriptor defines a read/write data segment (W = 1). The example stack segment descriptor is illustrated in Figure 9-5 on page 133, and has the following characteristics:

- The segment is a data/stack segment (System bit = 1 and C/D = 0)
- It can be read and written (W bit = 1)
- SS:ESP register (rather than the 16-bit SP register) is used to access it (B = 1)
- It can be accessed by a program with any privilege level (DPL = 3)
- The TOS (Top of Stack) equals the limit (07B3Eh, or 31550d)
- It is an expand-up stack that grows downward from the (base + limit) towards its base address (E bit = 0)
- Its base address is 00083EA0h.

When the PUSH instruction is executed, the processor decrements ESP by two and then writes the contents of the BX register (two bytes) into memory. Before performing the write, the processor performs a limit check to ensure that the new ESP value (00005FFEh - 2 = 00005FFCh) doesn't exceed the size of the stack specified in the descriptor (00005FFCh is < 00007B3Eh). It also checks to ensure that decrementing ESP by two doesn't decrement ESP past 00000000h. If this is the case, a stack exception is generated. The memory address is formed by adding the current contents of the ESP register (00005FFCh) to the segment's base address (00083EA0h), yielding memory address 00089E9Ch. The two bytes from BX are written into memory locations 00089E9Ch and 00089E9Dh. This example assumed that the code segment's default operand size is 16-bits (in other words, the code segment descriptor's D bit = 0, indicating that this is 16-bit, 286 code). When this is the case, the stack pointer is decremented by two during the execution of a PUSH. When executing 32-bit code (D = 1), it is decremented by four.

When the POP instruction is executed, the processor performs a two byte read from memory starting at the location currently pointed to by ESP + the stack segment's base address. The two bytes from memory locations 00089E9Ch and 00089E9Dh are read, with the byte from location 00089E9Ch (the lower location) placed in the lower half of BX (BL) and the byte from location 00089E9Dh placed in its upper half (BH). The processor then increments ESP by two.

Figure 9-4: Example Value in SS Register

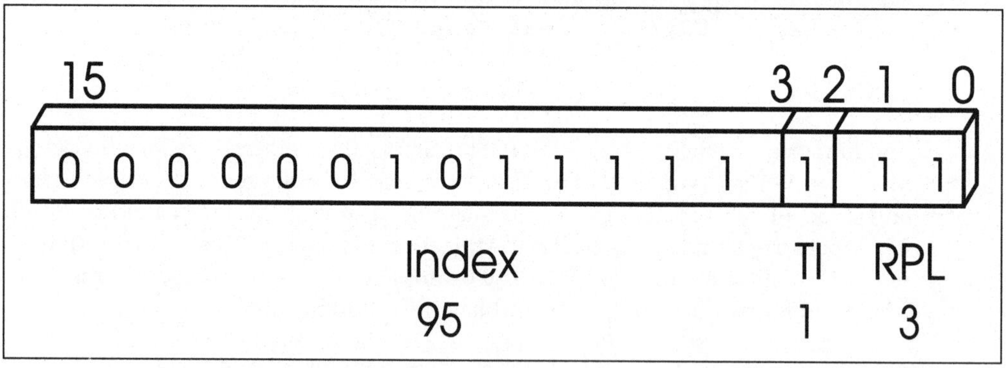

Figure 9-5: Example Stack Segment Descriptor

Example Stack Segment Descriptor

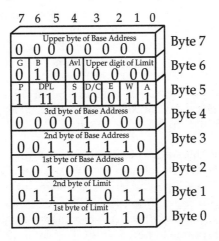

G Bit	Granularity bit defines meaning of limit value. 0 = length of segment in bytes.
B Bit	In stack segment, the B bit defines the SP size. It also identifies the upper boundary of an expand down segment. 1 = 32-bit SP (ESP) and upper limit of FFFFFFFFh.
AVL Bit	Available for use by system software
P Bit	Segment Present bit (must be 1 if the stack segment is present in memory).
DPL Field	Descriptor Privilege Level = 3
S Bit	System bit. When 0, indicates system segment. Must be 1 in a stack segment descriptor.
Bit 3	This could be called the Data/Code bit. 0 indicates a data segment.
E Bit	Expand down bit. Can be either 0 or 1. 0 indicates that the segment starts at the base address and extends upwards in memory to the limit.
W Bit	Write-enable bit. 1= read/writable segment. Stack segments must be writable.
A Bit	Accessed bit. Set to 1 by the processor when a stack segment is accessed.
Segment Base Address	Base address of the segment is 00083EA0h.
Segment Size	The size of the segment is 07B3Eh, or 31,550d.

Protected Mode Software Architecture

Expand-Down Stack

Problem

Assume that a programmer pushes a number of parameters onto the stack and that some of these values are pointers to other values that were pushed onto the stack. These pointers take the form of the offset from the BOS (bottom of stack). For example, assume that the value 1234h is pushed into the stack at position (i.e., offset) 00003000h (ESP = 00003000h) and that the programmer later pushes a pointer to that value into stack position 00002FF0h. The value 1234h is stored in the stack at offset 00003000h, while offset 00002FF0h contains the value 00003000h, the pointer to the value 1234h.

Now assume that the stack is approaching full (in other words, it has almost reached its base address). To make the stack larger, the programmer copies the current stack onto the top of a larger stack segment. Any pointers stored in the stack (such as the one at offset 00002FF0h in the older, smaller stack) are now wrong (because the base address has been changed relative to where the pointer and the location it points to now reside). The value 1234h now resides at an offset other than 00003000h.

The expand-down stack solves the problem.

Description

Most OSs implement expand-up stacks (discussed earlier). However, a stack segment with $E = 1$ in its descriptor is defined as an expand-down stack. When this is the case, the processor views the stack differently. **In an expand-up stack**, the lowest and highest stack addresses are defined as follows:

- **Lowest address** of the stack segment (i.e., the **BOS**, or bottom of stack) is **equal to** the **base address** specified in its stack segment descriptor.
- **highest address** of the stack segment (i.e., the **TOS**, or top of stack) is **equal to base + limit**.

In an expand-down stack, the lowest and highest stack addresses are defined as follows:

- **Lowest address** of the stack segment (i.e., the **BOS**, or bottom of stack) = **base + (limit-1)**. If the result > FFFFFFFFh, wrap around to lower memory.
- **Highest address** of the stack segment (i.e., the **TOS**, or top of stack) = **base + either FFFFh** (if B bit = 0) **or FFFFFFFFh** (if B bit = 1).

As an example, assume that the stack segment descriptor has the following characteristics:

- Expand-down (E = 1)
- Big bit (B = 1)
- Limit = FFFh
- Base address = 90000000h

This results in the following TOS and BOS values:

- **TOS** = base + FFFFFFFFh = 90000000h + FFFFFFFFh = 8FFFFFFFh.
- **BOS** = base + (limit - 1) = 90000000h + (FFFh - 1) = 90000FFEh.

Stack Segment Privilege Check

The privilege check performed when a value is loaded into the SS register is the same as that performed for a data segment (see "Data Segment Privilege Check" on page 127).

10 *Creating a Task*

The Previous Chapter

The previous chapter provided a detailed description of data and stack segments

This Chapter

This chapter describes how the OS creates and starts a task.

The Next Chapter

The next chapter describes the mechanisms the OS and processor use to switch from one task to another.

What Is a Task?

Each application consists of one more code segments, as well as a group of data segments. In the course of executing, the current application must be able to access one or more code and data segments in memory, as well as one or more stack areas. All of these elements taken together comprise a task in a multitasking OS environment. Examples would be Word for Windows, Corel Draw, etc.

Basics of Task Creation and Startup

The following sections describe the steps typically taken by the OS when it must start (or resume) a task.

Load All or Part of Task into Memory

The OS loads all or part of the task (i.e., at a minimum, the startup code for the task) into memory.

Create TSS for the Task

The OS creates a data structure in memory defining the context of the processor at the point when it first begins (or resumes) execution of the task. In other words, the data structure defines an exact image of the information that should be present in the processor's register set when the processor initiates (or resumes) execution of the task. This data structure is referred to as the Task State Segment (TSS), and the OS must set up a separate TSS for each task.

The OS creates a special TSS segment descriptor in the GDT defining the base address, length, and DPL of the TSS.

Start Timeslice Timer

A multitasking OS usually permits a task to execute for a predefined period of time, typically referred to as a timeslice. This is accomplished by starting a hardware timer prior to starting (or resuming) the task. The task is then started and continues to execute until a hardware interrupt is generated by the timeslice timer (unless the task is suspended by the OS prior to this for some other reason). This interrupt selects an IDT entry that contains a task gate that points to the OS's task scheduler. The task that was executing is suspended (by copying most of the processor's registers into the task's TSS). The new task (i.e., the OS task scheduler) is restarted by loading the processor's register set from the new task's TSS before resuming program execution.

Unlike many other processors (e.g., the PowerPC processor family), x86 processors do not incorporate a hardware "timeslice" timer to facilitate the timeslice approach to multitasking. Instead, the system designer must incorporate a hardware timer external to the processor. This timer is implemented as an IO device that can be programmed for the desired interval and then be enabled. It then initiates the timer and generates a maskable interrupt when the timer has expired.

Switch to the Task

The task is started by executing a far jump or a far call that selects the TSS descriptor in the GDT.

When the processor determines that a TSS descriptor has been selected, it suspends the current task (in this case, the OS) by copying the majority of the processor's registers in the OS's TSS. It then switches to the new task by loading the processor's register set from the new task's TSS. The processor uses the pointer placed in CS:EIP (from the new task's TSS) and begins fetching code from the new application.

TSS Structure

General

The 286 implemented a different TSS structure than that defined for the post-286 processors. This is referred to as a 16-bit TSS and is not covered in this book.

The post-286 processors implement the TSS structure illustrated in Figure 10-1 on page 141. This is referred to as a 32-bit TSS. Note that the 386 and the early 486 processors did not implement the Interrupt Redirection Map. This was first implemented in the Pentium processor and was later migrated to the new versions of the 486 processor, as well. It is described later in this chapter in the section entitled "Interrupt Redirection Bit Map" on page 146.

At a minimum, the TSS must include locations 00h through 67h (104d locations). This required portion consists of three type of fields:

- Those locations shown as zeros are **reserved** by Intel and must not be used.
- **Dynamic fields** are read by the processor whenever the task is started or resumed and are also updated by the processor whenever the task is suspended (hence the term "dynamic" because these fields change dynamically during system operation).
- **Static fields** are read by the processor but are not written to (in other words, they remain static).

Protected Mode Software Architecture

The **portion of** the **TSS** that resides **above location 67h** consists of three areas:

- The OS may utilize the optional area starting at location 68h for **OS-specific data** related to the task. The size of this area is OS-specific.
- The **interrupt redirection bit map** consists of 32 bytes (eight doublewords) and is only **necessary if** the OS supports the VM86 mode extensions that are enabled with the CR4[VME] bit.
- The **IO permission bit map** can be up to 8KB in size and is **necessary if** the OS supports IO protection.

The sections that follow describe each field in the TSS.

Figure 10-1: Task State Segment (TSS) Format

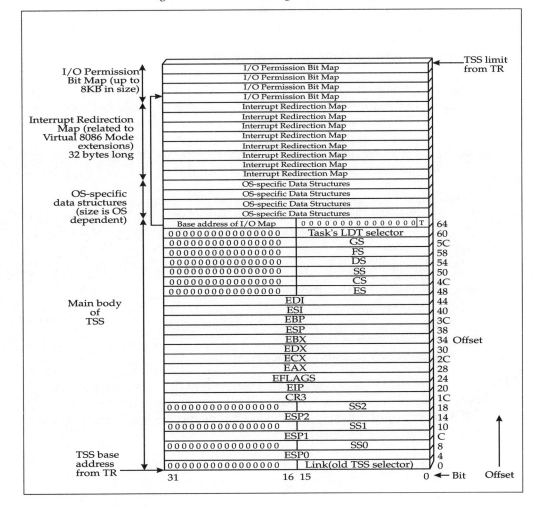

IO Port Access Protection

IO Protection in Real Mode

When the processor is operating in real mode, there isn't any IO protection. In other words, any program may execute the x86 processor's IO instructions at any time. As stated earlier in the section entitled "IO Port Anarchy" on page 18, the inability of the OS to restrict the ability of applications programs to talk directly to IO ports results in problems when multitasking. When operating in protected mode, the OS can place restraints on the ability of applications programs to communicate directly with IO ports. The manner in which this is done is discussed in the sections that follow.

Definition of IO Privilege Level (IOPL)

When the OS initially sets up the TSS for a task, it sets up the EFlags image in the task's TSS. A subset of this image is the EFlags[IOPL] field (see Figure 10-2 on page 143). Whenever a task is started (or resumed), the processor copies the register images from the task's TSS into the processor's register set. Thus, the processor's IOPL is automatically set to the value from the TSS whenever the task is started or resumed.

If the CPL of the currently-executing program is numerically ≤ IOPL (i.e., the program's privilege level is the same as or better than the IOPL), the processor permits the program to execute IOPL-sensitive instructions. The sensitive instructions are:

- **IN**. IO read instruction.
- **INS**. IO string read instruction.
- **OUT**. IO write instruction.
- **OUTS**. IO write string instruction.
- **CLI**. Clear interrupt enable instruction.
- **STI**. Set interrupt enable instruction.

If CPL > IOPL and the instruction is CLI or STI, a GP exception is generated. If the instruction is one of the IO instructions, the manner in which the privilege check is performed differs based on whether the processor is in VM86 mode or not. The differences are described in the next two sections.

Figure 10-2: The EFlags Register

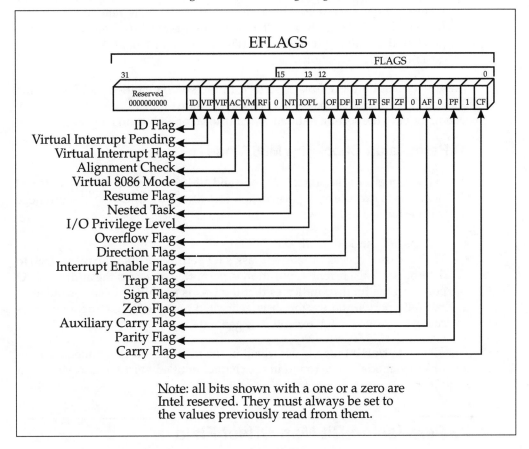

Note: all bits shown with a one or a zero are
Intel reserved. They must always be set to
the values previously read from them.

IO Permission Check in Protected Mode

When the processor is in protected mode but is not in VM86 mode (i.e., EFlags[VM] = 0) and attempts to execute an IOPL-sensitive instruction (see page 142), the privilege check is performed in the following manner:

- If the CPL is numerically ≤ IOPL (i.e., program's privilege level is the same as or better than the IOPL), no exception is generated and the IO instruction is executed.
- If the CPL is numerically > IOPL (i.e., the program's privilege level is not as good as the IOPL) and the instruction is one of the IO instructions (IN, OUT, INS, or OUTS), the processor checks the current task's IO permission bit map (in its TSS) to determine if the current application is permitted to

access the addressed IO port(s). If the bit map indicates that the task is permitted to access the indicated IO port(s), no exception is generated and the IO instruction is executed. Otherwise, a GP exception is generated.

- If the CPL is numerically > IOPL (i.e., the program's privilege level is not as good as the IOPL) and the instruction is either CLI or STI, the processor generates a GP exception.

The IO permission bit map is described in the section entitled "IO Permission Bit Map Offset Field" on page 144. For a discussion of memory-mapped IO protection, refer to the section entitled "Memory-Mapped IO" on page 275.

IO Permission Check in VM86 Mode

When the processor is in protected mode and VM86 mode (i.e., EFlags[VM] = 1) and attempts to execute an IO instruction (IN, INS, OUT, or OUTS), the privilege check is performed as follows.

- IOPL is not checked at all.
- The processor checks the current task's IO permission bit map (in its TSS) to determine if the current application is permitted to access the addressed IO port(s). If the bit map indicates that the task is permitted to access the indicated IO port(s), no exception is generated and the IO instruction is executed. Otherwise, a GP exception is generated.

The IO permission bit map is described in the next section. A detailed description of VM86 mode can be found in the chapter entitled "Virtual 8086 Mode" on page 265.

IO Permission Bit Map Offset Field

The two sections entitled "IO Permission Check in Protected Mode" on page 143 and "IO Permission Check in VM86 Mode" on page 144 referred to the IO permission bit map in the TSS (pictured in Figure 10-1 on page 141). Implementation of the IO permission **bit map is mandatory under the following circumstances**:

- The bit map is mandatory for **any VM86 task that accesses IO-mapped IO** ports.
- The bit map is mandatory for any non-VM86 protected mode task where the CPL of any part of the task that attempts IO is not as privileged as the IOPL.

In both of these cases, the processor interrogates the bit map in the TSS to determine whether or not to grant access to the addressed IO port(s).

The bit map is optional under the following circumstances:

- The bit map is optional if no code in the task ever attempts to execute an IO instruction (IN, OUT, INS, or OUTS). In other words, all IO devices are memory- rather than IO-mapped. This is true both in the case of a VM86 task or a non-VM86 protected mode task.
- The bit map is optional if no code (within the task) attempts to execute an IO instruction while executing with a CPL less-privileged than the IOPL field.

To determine if the current task has permission to access the IO port(s) addressed by the currently-executing IO instruction, the processor uses the IO port address to index into the IO permission bit map in the TSS. It checks the respective permission bit to determine whether or not to permit the access. If the bit = 0, the access is permitted. If the bit = 1, a GP exception is generated. If the IO instruction will access multiple locations, the permission bits corresponding to each port are tested.

Locations 66h and 67h of the TSS contain the 16-bit, byte-specific offset of the bit map start address from the TSS base address. Since the bit map resides at the end of the TSS, the end of the bit map is delineated by the size of the TSS itself (specified in the TSS descriptor in the GDT).

In order to designate the permission state for every possible IO port, 64K bits would be required (one bit for each of the possible 64K IO ports, 0000h through FFFFh). This would mean that the map would have to be 8KB in length (8KB * 8 bits/byte = 64K bits). In practice, however, the OS programmer only has to define the permission state for IO port zero through the highest IO port address the task attempts to access. As an example, if the task only attempts to access the first 80d IO ports (0000h through 004Fh), the map would be 10 bytes in length (10 bytes * 8 bits/byte = 80 bits).

IO ports are addressed at byte-specific addresses. In addition, an x86 processor may address a set of contiguous IO locations when executing an IO instruction. For example:

```
IN    AL,00h      ;reads contents of IO port 0000h
IN    AX,00h      ;reads contents of IO ports 0000h and 0001h
IN    EAX,00h     ;reads contents of IO ports 0000h through 0003h
```

In the preceding three examples, each of the addressed IO ports fall within the first eight IO port addresses. The permission bits for all of them are therefore found within the first location (consisting of eight bits) of the bit map. The processor would only have to read the bit map's first location to check the respective permission bits. The following example

```
IN   AX,07h      ;reads contents of IO ports 0007h and 0008h
```

reads the 8th and 9th IO locations. The permission bit for port 0007h is the last bit of the bit map's first location, while the permission bit for port 0008h is the first bit of the bit map's second location. Before permitting this IO instruction to execute, therefore, the processor would have to read the first two locations from the bit map to check the permission bits related to the addressed ports.

In reality, x86 processors are designed to always read two locations at a time when checking permission. This presents an interesting situation. Let's say the highest IO port that the task is permitted to access is 004Fh. This is the 80th IO port. The bit map would have to be 10 locations long—a total of 80d bits. Now assume that the following instruction is attempted:

```
IN   AL, 4Fh     ;read contents of IO port 004F
```

The processor would read the 10th and 11th bit map locations (remember that it **always** reads two bit map locations at a time). In other words, its reading one location beyond the end of the bit map. For this reason, the following must be true:

- The location immediately after the actual bit map must be present and its contents must be FFh (i.e., all bits = 1).
- The TSS descriptor's limit must be set to include this last location.

Interrupt Redirection Bit Map

If VM86 extensions have been enabled by the OS using CR4[VME], the TSS must include an interrupt redirection bit map (see Figure 10-1 on page 141). This map must be 256 bits (32 bytes) in length. Each bit corresponds to one of the 256 interrupt levels. The map's end address (plus one) is specified by the IO permission bit map base address specifier in the TSS (see "IO Permission Bit Map Offset Field" on page 144). For additional information, refer to the chapter entitled "Virtual 8086 Mode" on page 265.

OS-Specific Data Structures

The OS may use the TSS area between the IO base address field and the start address of the interrupt redirection bit map to store OS-specific data structures.

Debug Trap Bit (T)

The debug Trap bit (T) resides in bit zero of location 64h in the TSS. A debug exception occurs whenever a task switch occurs to a task with the T bit set. In other words, this provides a "breakpoint on task switch" capability.

LDT Selector Field

This 16-bit value is loaded into the processor's LDTR (LDT register), identifying the descriptor entry in the GDT that defines the start address and length of the task's LDT. This field permits the OS to define a separate LDT for each task, defining the memory segments that are "local" to the task.

Segment Register Fields

The OS stores the initial values for the data (DS, ES, FS and GS), stack (SS), and code segment (CS) registers in these TSS locations. When the task is started or resumed, these values are automatically read into their respective registers, automatically selecting the code, stack and data segments to be used at task initiation. When the task is suspended, the contents of the segment registers are stored here.

General Register Fields

The OS stores the initial values for the EDI, ESI, EAX, EBX, ECX, EDX and EBP registers in these TSS locations. When the task is started or resumed, these values are automatically read into the respective processor registers. When the task is suspended, the contents of the processor's general registers are stored here.

Extended Stack Pointer (ESP) Register Field

The OS stores the initial value for the extended stack pointer register (ESP) in this TSS location. When the task is started or resumed, this value is automatically read into the processor's ESP register. Together with the SS field, the ESP field tells the processor the base address and top-of-stack. When the task is suspended, the contents of the ESP register is stored here.

Extended Flags (EFlags) Register Field

The OS stores the initial value for the EFlags register in this TSS location. When the task is started or resumed, this value is automatically read into the processor's EFlags register. The EFlags register initial setting tells the processor:

- If interrupt recognition is enabled or disabled.
- If debug single-step interrupts are enabled or disabled.
- The direction to be used during string operations.
- The minimum privilege level at which to permit IO operations.
- If VM86 mode is enabled or disabled.
- If Alignment Checking is enabled or disabled.

When the task is suspended, the contents of the EFlags register is stored here.

Extended Instruction Pointer (EIP) Register Field

The OS stores the initial value for the extended instruction pointer register (EIP) in this TSS location. When the task is started or resumed, this value is automatically read into the processor's EIP register. Together with the CS field, the EIP field tells the processor the location to fetch its next instruction from. When the task is suspended, the contents of the EIP register is stored here.

Control Register 3 (CR3) Field

The OS stores the initial value for CR3 in this TSS location. When the task is started, this value is automatically read into the CR3 register (pictured in Figure 10-3 on page 149). CR3[31:11] contains the 4KB-aligned base address of the Page Directory. This permits the OS programmer to have a different Page Directory for each task (because CR3 is loaded with the task's page directory base address whenever the task is started or resumed). In this way, two tasks that both attempt to use the same memory space can have their memory accesses remapped to other areas of memory, isolating them from each other in a manner that is transparent to the tasks themselves. The chapter entitled "Virtual Paging" on page 219 provides a detailed discussion of paging. When the task is suspended, the contents of CR3 is stored here.

Figure 10-3: Control Register 3 (CR3)

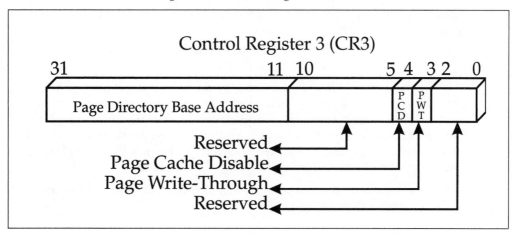

Privilege Level 0 - 2 Stack Definition Fields

When a program within the current task (i.e., application program) on a less-privileged level calls a more-privileged program (within the current task), the processor automatically creates a new stack and copies the following items to the newly-created stack:

- the pointer to the caller's stack
- the return address
- any parameters placed on the caller's stack

The following fields in the TSS define where these new stacks are created and how large they are:

- SS2:ESP2 fields define the base address and top-of-stack when a new stack must be created for a call to a level two procedure.
- SS1:ESP1 fields define the base address and top-of-stack when a new stack must be created for a call to a level one procedure.
- SS0:ESP0 fields define the base address and top-of-stack when a new stack must be created for a call to a level zero procedure.

Protected Mode Software Architecture

A more detailed description can be found in the section entitled "Automatic Stack Switch" on page 122.

Link Field (to Old TSS Selector)

When an interrupt or exception causes a task switch (because it selects a task gate in the IDT), the processor saves the processor's current context in the interrupted task's TSS and then switches to the interrupt handler task by loading the register set from the interrupt servicing task's TSS (pointed to by the Task Gate descriptor in the IDT). The EFlags[NT] (Nested Task) bit is set to a one. In performing the task switch, the processor stores the 16-bit selector for the interrupted task's TSS in the interrupt servicing task's Link field in its TSS.

At the conclusion of interrupt servicing by the interrupt servicing task, the last instruction in the interrupt servicing task is an IRET. When executed by the processor with EFlags[NT] set, the processor reloads the TR with the Link field's contents (the TSS selector for the task that was interrupted). This causes a task switch back to the interrupted task. Reloading EFlags with its original value (read from the interrupted task's TSS) turns off the NT bit.

The same sequence occurs when a far call selects a TSS descriptor in the GDT. As is the case for an interrupt, the called task must terminate with an IRET instruction.

A more detailed description can be found in the chapter entitled "Mechanics of a Task Switch" on page 157.

TSS Descriptor

The TSS descriptor is pictured in Figure 10-4 on page 151. A TSS descriptor may only reside in the GDT and describes the following characteristics of a task's TSS:

- **Base** address of the TSS.
- **Limit** (i.e., the size) of the TSS.
- The **DPL** of the TSS. A far call or a far jump instruction can cause a task switch if its CPL is at least as privileged as the TSS descriptor's DPL. The segment portion of the target address specified by the far call or far jump selects the entry in the GDT that contains the TSS descriptor.
- Whether the target **task** is currently **busy**.

The minimum size of a TSS is one 104 bytes, the size of the TSS main body. If the TSS limit is set to less than this value, an invalid TSS exception is generated. Loading a TSS descriptor into a segment register causes a GP exception.

Figure 10-4: The TSS Descriptor Format

Task State Segment (TSS) Descriptor

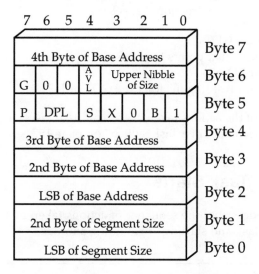

G Bit	Granularity bit defines meaning of limit value. 0 = length of segment in bytes. 1 = length of segment in pages.
AVL Bit	Available for use by system software
P Bit	Segment Present bit.
DPL Field	Descriptor Privilege Level.
S Bit	System bit. When 0, indicates system segment. Must be 0 in a TSS descriptor.
X Bit	This bit indicates whether this is a 16 or 32-bit TSS. 0 = 16-bit TSS. 1 = 32-bit TSS.
B Bit	Busy bit. 1 indicates task is busy.

Note: All TSS entries must reside in the Global Descriptor Table (GDT).

Protected Mode Software Architecture

How OS Starts Task

The OS builds an application's TSS in memory and creates a TSS descriptor in the GDT that points to the TSS. It can then select the task for initiation by executing a far jump or a far call instruction that selects:

- a TSS descriptor in the GDT
- a Call Gate descriptor (that points to a TSS descriptor in the GDT) residing in either the GDT or LDT
- a Task Gate descriptor residing in either the GDT or LDT

A detailed description of the actions taken in each of these cases can be found in the chapter entitled "Mechanics of a Task Switch" on page 157.

What Happens When Task Starts

The next chapter fully describes the sequence of actions taken by the processor when suspending one task and starting or resuming another.

Use of LTR and STR Instructions

General

The processor uses the TR (task register) to determine the base address and limit of the TSS associated with the current task. The TR is illustrated in Figure 10-5 on page 155.

If the TI bit is set to one, indicating that the target descriptor is in the current task's LDT, a GP exception is generated (because TSS descriptors may only reside in the GDT). Loading a new 16-bit value into the TR causes the processor to read the TSS descriptor from the GDT entry indicated by the TR index field into the invisible part of the TR. When initially loaded with a 16-bit value, it uses that value to select an entry in the GDT. This entry must contain a TSS descriptor. If it contains any other type of descriptor, or if the selected TSS descriptor has its Busy bit set to one, the processor generates a GP exception. A GP exception is also generated if the 16-bit value has TI = 1, selecting the LDT rather than the GDT.

The x86 instruction set provides two instructions that the programmer can use to place a new value in the TR or to read the current value from it. The LTR (load task register) and STR (store task register) instructions may only be executed when the processor is in protected mode (CR0[PE] = 1). Attempted execution of either in real mode results in an Invalid Opcode exception. The STR instruction can be executed at any privilege level, while the LTR instruction can only be executed by a program executing at privilege level zero. An attempt to execute the LTR instruction at any other privilege level results in a GP exception.

STR Instruction

At any privilege level, the programmer may use the STR instruction to obtain the selector for the currently-executing task's TSS descriptor in the GDT. The 16-bit value may be placed either into a 16-bit general purpose register or into memory. Using this value, the programmer can then read the TSS descriptor from the GDT to discover the base address and limit (i.e., the size of) the current task's TSS data structure.

LTR Instruction

At privilege level zero, the programmer may execute the LTR instruction to place a new 16-bit value into the TR. When executed, the processor performs the following actions:

- validates that the current program's CPL is sufficiently-privileged to perform a task switch (since the CPL of the program executing the LTR instruction is zero, this isn't a problem).
- generates a GP exception if the indicated GDT entry does not contain a TSS descriptor or if the descriptor's busy bit is set to one.
- generates a Segment Not Present exception if P = 0 in the TSS descriptor.
- generates a Page Fault exception if the page containing the TSS is not currently in memory.
- generates a GP exception if the CS selector in the TSS does not select a code segment.
- generates a GP exception if any of the data segment selectors in the TSS does not select a data segment.
- generates a Stack exception if the SS selector in the TSS doesn't select a stack segment.
- the invisible portion of the TR is loaded with the base address and limit of

the new TSS.
* the Busy bit in the TSS descriptor is set to one.

The LTR instruction does not cause a task switch. In other words, although the processor verifies the integrity of the new TSS and marks it busy, it does not reload its register set from the new TSS. The TR contents after reset is undefined. This instruction is typically used at startup time to identify the OS code's startup TSS for the processor. If the TR were not initialized in this manner, the first task switch would cause the processor to save its register set into memory within the TSS identified by the bogus TSS base address and limit defined by the junk in the TR. In other words, the register set would be stored into some undefined region of memory. This could have catastrophic results.

Figure 10-5: The Task Register

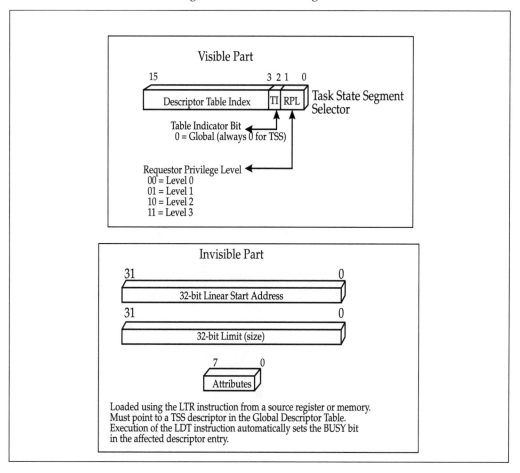

11 *Mechanics of a Task Switch*

The Previous Chapter

The previous chapter described how the OS creates and starts a task.

This Chapter

This chapter describes the events that can cause a task switch. It also details the sequence of actions taken by the processor when suspending the current task and starting or resuming another one.

The Next Chapter

The next chapter provides a detailed description of interrupt and exception generation and handling.

Events that Initiate a Task Switch

There are a number of events that can cause the processor to suspend the current task and start or resume another task. Table 11-1 on page 158 provides a description of each event. The sections that follow detail the sequence of actions taken by the processor when suspending the current task and starting or resuming another one.

Table 11-1: Events that Cause a Task Switch

Event	Description
Far call/jump to TSS descriptor	If the 16-bit segment address of a far jump or far call selects a TSS descriptor in the GDT, a task switch occurs. The offest portion of the target address is discarded. The processor loads the 16-bit segment selector into the visible portion of the TR and then loads the selected TSS descriptor from the GDT into the invisible part of the TR. A privilege check is performed and, if the currently-executing program has sufficient privilege (CPL ≤ DPL), the state of the current task is stored in its TSS and the new TSS (identified by the TSS descriptor) is loaded into the processor's register set. More detailed information can be found in the sections entitled "Switch as Result of Far Call" on page 168 and "Switch as Result of Far Jump" on page 171.
Far call/jump to task gate descriptor	All TSS descriptors must reside in the GDT. The DPL of a TSS descriptor is typically set to zero. This means that a program that resides at a less-privileged level could not switch to the task defined by the TSS. If the currently-executing program has access to a task gate in its LDT, it can switch to a task (if the less-privileged of the currently-executing program's CPL and RPL is at least as privileged as the task gate's DPL). The TSS DPL is ignored. The task gate has the format specified in Figure 11-1 on page 162 and is described in the section entitled "Task Gate Descriptor" on page 160. Also refer to the sections entitled "Switch as Result of Far Call" on page 168 and "Switch as Result of Far Jump" on page 171.

Table 11-1: Events that Cause a Task Switch (Continued)

Event	Description
INT execution that selects a task gate in IDT	When the processor executes an INT *nn* instruction, the value *nn* acts as an index into the IDT. If the selected IDT entry contains a task gate descriptor and the program executing the INT instruction has sufficient privilege, a task switch results. Additional information can be found in the sections entitled "Task Gate Descriptor" on page 160 and "Switch as Result of BOUND or INT Instruction" on page 173, and in the chapter entitled "Interrupt Sources and Handling" on page 183.
Hardware interrupt that selects a task gate in IDT	When a hardware interrupt request is detected by the processor, the interrupt vector obtained from the interrupt controller is used as an index into the IDT. If the selected IDT entry contains a task gate descriptor, a task switch results (exceptions, interrupts and IRET cause a task switch regardless of the task gate's DPL). Additional information can be found in the sections entitled "Task Gate Descriptor" on page 160 and "Switch as Result of Hardware Interrupt or Exception" on page 163, and in the chapter entitled "Interrupt Sources and Handling" on page 183. Also refer to "Start Timeslice Timer" on page 138.
Software exception that selects a task gate in IDT	When a software exception condition is detected by the processor, the exception condition type determines the index into the IDT. If the selected IDT entry contains a task gate descriptor, a task switch results (exceptions, interrupts and IRET cause a task switch regardless of the task gate's DPL). Additional information can be found in the sections entitled "Task Gate Descriptor" on page 160 and "Switch as Result of Hardware Interrupt or Exception" on page 163, and in the chapter entitled "Interrupt Sources and Handling" on page 183.

Table 11-1: Events that Cause a Task Switch (Continued)

Event	Description
IRET execution with EFlags[NT] bit set	Refer to the sections entitled "Link Field (to Old TSS Selector)" on page 150 and "Return to Interrupted Task or...There and Back Again!" on page 165 for a detailed description.

Switch Via TSS Descriptor

A far call or far jump can cause a task switch if the 16-bit segment portion of the target address selects a TSS descriptor in the GDT. However, a GP exception results if the following privilege check isn't passed:

The less-privileged of the RPL (lower two bits of the 16-bit segment address) or CPL must be at least as privileged as the TSS descriptor's DPL. Since TSS descriptors typically have a DPL of zero, this means that only privilege level zero programs can call or jump to another task using a TSS descriptor.

Task Gate Descriptor

TSS descriptors must reside in the GDT. Task Gate descriptors, on the other hand, may reside in the GDT, an LDT, or the IDT (Interrupt Descriptor Table). Figure 11-1 on page 162 illustrates the format of a Task Gate descriptor. It contains a 16-bit value that selects an entry in the GDT containing a TSS descriptor.

Task Gate Selected by Far Call/Jump

When a far call or a far jump selects a Task Gate descriptor, the DPL of the Task Gate, rather than the TSS descriptor, is checked during the privilege level check. The DPL of the TSS is ignored. A task switch occurs if the less-privileged of the RPL or CPL is at least as privileged as the Task Gate's DPL value. As examples,

- A Task Gate with a DPL of three permits any program to jump to or call the task pointed to by the TSS descriptor.
- A Task Gate with a DPL of two permits programs with privilege levels of zero through two to cause a task switch, while a program with a privilege level of three would cause a GP exception.

Task Gate Selected by Hardware Interrupt or Software Exception

When a Task Gate is placed in the IDT, any hardware interrupt or software exception that selects the IDT entry containing the Task Gate causes a task switch. Both the Task Gate's and the TSS descriptor's DPL are ignored. In other words, the privilege check isn't performed. More detail can be found in "Switch as Result of Hardware Interrupt or Exception" on page 163.

Task Gate Selected by INT Instruction

If an INT instruction selects an IDT entry containing a Task Gate, the privilege check is performed. The DPL of the Task Gate, rather than the TSS descriptor, is checked during the privilege level check. The DPL of the TSS is ignored. A task switch occurs if the less-privileged of the RPL or CPL is at least as privileged as the Task Gate's DPL value.

Figure 11-1: The Task Gate Format

Task Gate Descriptor Format

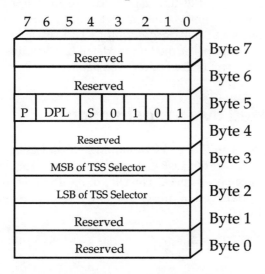

7 6 5 4 3 2 1 0					
Reserved					Byte 7
Reserved					Byte 6
P	DPL	S	0 1 0 1		Byte 5
Reserved					Byte 4
MSB of TSS Selector					Byte 3
LSB of TSS Selector					Byte 2
Reserved					Byte 1
Reserved					Byte 0

P Bit	Segment Present bit.
DPL Field	Descriptor Privilege Level.
S Bit	System bit. When 0, indicates system segment. Must be 0 in a Task Gate descriptor.
Byte 5[3:0]	With S = 0, 0101b indicates Task Gate descriptor.
TSS Selector	Identifies the TSS descriptor that holds the base address, limit and attributes of the TSS for the task being switched to.

Note: A Task Gate descriptor may reside in the Global, Local or Interrupt Descriptor Tables.

Chapter 11: Mechanics of a Task Switch

Switch as Result of Hardware Interrupt or Exception

General

A task switch results when a hardware interrupt or a software exception selects an entry in the IDT (Interrupt Descriptor Table, pictured in Figure 11-2 on page 167) that contains a valid Task Gate. A privilege check is not performed.

Suspension of Interrupted Task

In response to the interrupt or exception, the processor performs the following sequence of actions to suspend the current task:

1. Pushes CS, EIP and EFlags onto the stack.
2. Clears EFlags[IF] bit to mask further interrupts.
3. Checks that the TSS descriptor in the GDT that is pointed to by the Task Gate descriptor is valid (P = 1) and has a valid limit. At a minimum, the limit must be ≥ 67h (i.e., 103d). If P = 0, a Segment Not Present exception is generated, while an Invalid TSS exception results if the limit is less than 103d.
4. A GP exception is generated if the Busy bit (B) in the TSS descriptor is set to one. The busy bit is described in "The Busy Bit" on page 177.
5. Saves the state of the processor's register set in the interrupted (i.e., the current) task's TSS (pointed to by the base address in the TR register). This is accomplished by performing a series of memory write transactions.
6. This discussion continues in the next section.

Start Interrupt/Exception Handler Task

After suspending the interrupted task, the processor performs the following steps to start the interrupt/exception handler task:

1. The 16-bit TSS selector from the Task Gate descriptor is read by the processor, but is not placed in the TR register until the selector's integrity has been validated:
   - GP exception generated if TI = 1 (selecting LDT rather than GDT).
   - GP exception if selected GDT entry is not TSS descriptor.
   - Segment Not Present exception if P = 0 in TSS descriptor.

2. 16-bit GDT selector not placed in TR register until TSS data structure integrity is also validated:
   - Using the 16-bit selector to index into the GDT, the processor reads the base address and limit of the TSS from the TSS descriptor in the GDT.
   - Validates that the TSS limit ≥ 103d and generates Invalid TSS exception if < 103d (67h).

3. The processor reads new segment selector fields (CS, DS, ES, FS, GS, SS) from the interrupt/exception service task's TSS and validates each of them:
   - An Invalid TSS exception is generated if CS or SS DPL does not match CS or SS selectors' RPL.
   - An Invalid TSS exception is generated if a selector indexes to an inappropriate descriptor entry. As examples, if the CS selector selects a non-code segment descriptor; the SS selector selects a non-stack descriptor; or one of the data segment descriptors selects a non-data segment descriptor.
   - A Segment Not Present exception is generated if any of the selected segment descriptors (other than SS) have P = 0 (segment not present) in their respective segment descriptors.
   - A Stack exception is generated if the stack segment descriptor has P = 0 (segment not present).
   - An Invalid TSS exception is generated if the index portion of any of the segment selectors addresses an entry beyond the limit of the selected descriptor table (i.e., GDT or LDT).
   - An Invalid TSS exception is generated if any of the data segment selectors indexes to a descriptor entry that indicates the segment is non-readable.

4. An Invalid TSS exception is generated if the LDT selector (from the new TSS) does not select an LDT descriptor in the GDT, or if the LDT descriptor has P = 0 (table not present).

5. If any of the TSS integrity checks fail, the TR register is not loaded with the new TSS selector (the current TSS selector remains in it) and the exception generated as a result of the integrity failure is serviced in the context of the current task (in other words, the task switch does not occur).

6. When the integrity of the interrupt/exception service task's TSS has been verified, the task switch takes place. The TR register is loaded with the selector (from the task gate descriptor) for the interrupt/exception service task's TSS.

7. The processor sets the Busy bit in the interrupt/exception service task's TSS descriptor.

8. The processor sets the CR0[TS] bit to indicate that a task switch has occurred. This permits the OS programmer to compare the context of the floating-point unit vs. the integer execution unit to synchronize floating-

point exceptions with the task they are associated with.

9. The processor sets EFlags[NT] to indicate that this task was entered from another task that was interrupted and suspended. After the interrupt or exception is serviced, the processor must switch back to the interrupted task and resume execution at the point of interruption. The EFlags[NT] bit tells it to do this (for more information, see "Return to Interrupted Task or...There and Back Again!" on page 165.

10. The processor stores the old contents of TR register in the Link field of the new task. This is the selector to the interrupted task's TSS descriptor in the GDT.

11. The processor reads the register fields from the new TSS into its registers.

12. The processor then resumes normal operation. In other words, it uses the new values just placed in CS:EIP to fetch the first instruction. This is the first instruction of the interrupt/exception service task. The program executes at the privilege level indicated by the least-significant two bits of the CS field from the new task's TSS CS field (i.e., its RPL field). **The task switch is now complete**.

Return to Interrupted Task or...There and Back Again!

The body of the interrupt/exception service task services the interrupt request or the software exception condition. When it has completed execution, the last instruction in the task is an IRET instruction. When an IRET is executed with EFlags[NT] set to one, the processor recognizes that it is to resume the interrupted task at the point where it was interrupted. To do this, it takes the following actions:

1. Performs the following tests on the current task's TSS Link field (should point to GDT TSS descriptor for interrupted task):
    *   Generate Invalid TSS exception if TI = 1 (LDT) because TSS descriptor must be in GDT.
    *   Generate Invalid TSS exception if GDT Index exceeds GDT limit.
    *   Generate Invalid TSS exception if indicated descriptor in GDT isn't TSS descriptor.
    *   Generate Invalid TSS exception if Busy bit not set in TSS descriptor for interrupted task.
    *   Generate Segment Not Present exception if P = 0 in TSS descriptor for interrupted task.
2. Reload processor register set from interrupted task's TSS. At this point, the processor is ready to resume the interrupted task.

3. Clear the Busy bit in the TSS descriptor for the interrupt/exception service task.
4. Pop old CS, EIP and EFlags from stack into respective registers. This reenables interrupt recognition.
5. Generate GP exception if EIP exceeds code segment limit.
6. Resume execution of interrupted program.

Figure 11-2: The IDT (Interrupt Descriptor Table)

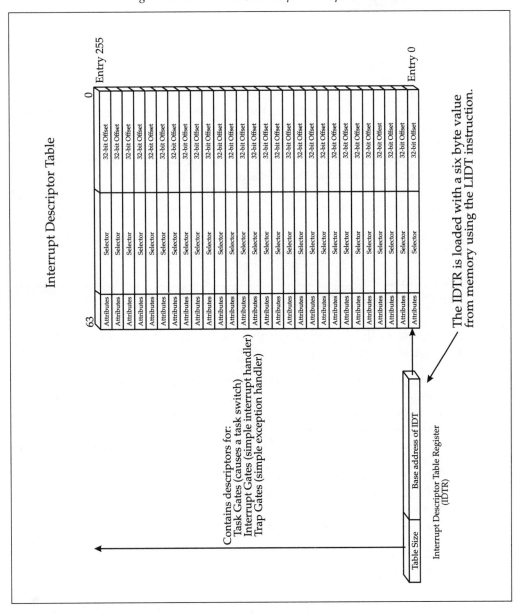

Protected Mode Software Architecture

Switch as Result of Far Call

A far call instruction causes a task switch under the following circumstances:

- it **selects a TSSdescriptor in the GDT**. In this case, the lesser-privileged of the selector RPL and the currently-executing program's CPL must meet or beat the privilege level indicated by the TSS descriptor's DPL. This is typically zero, severely restricting the programs that are successful in selecting the TSS descriptor.
- it **selects a Task Gate descriptor in either the GDT or LDT**. In this case, the lesser-privileged of the selector RPL and the currently-executing program's CPL must meet or beat the privilege level of the Task Gate descriptor's DPL (which can be different than the DPL of the TSS descriptor it points to in the GDT).

The difference between the two is in how the privilege check is performed. The sections that follow assume that the privilege check has been passed.

Suspension of Calling Task

In response to the far call instruction, the processor performs the following sequence of actions to suspend the current task:

1. Checks that the selected TSS descriptor in the GDT is valid (P = 1) and has a valid limit. At a minimum, the limit must be ≥ 67h (i.e., 103d). If P = 0, a Segment Not Present exception is generated, while an Invalid TSS exception results if the limit is less than 103d.
2. A GP exception is generated if the Busy bit (B) in the TSS descriptor is set to one.
3. Saves the state of the processor's register set in the caller's (i.e., the current task) TSS (pointed to by the base address in the TR register). This is accomplished by performing a series of memory write transactions.
4. This discussion continues in the next section.

Start Called Task

The offset portion of the target address is discarded. After suspending the calling task, the processor performs the following steps to start the called task:

Chapter 11: Mechanics of a Task Switch

1. The 16-bit TSS selector portion of the far call is not placed in the TR register until the selector's integrity has been validated:
   - GP exception generated if TI = 1 (selecting LDT rather than GDT).
   - GP exception if selected GDT entry is not TSS descriptor.
   - Segment Not Present exception if P = 0 in TSS descriptor.
2. 16-bit GDT selector not placed in TR register until TSS data structure integrity is also validated:
   - Using the 16-bit selector to index into the GDT, the processor reads the base address and limit of the TSS from the TSS descriptor in the GDT.
   - Validates that the TSS limit ≥ 103d and generates Invalid TSS exception if < 103d (67h).
3. The processor reads new segment selector fields (CS, DS, ES, FS, GS, SS) from the called task's TSS and validates each of them:
   - An Invalid TSS exception is generated if CS or SS DPL does not match CS or SS selectors' RPL.
   - An Invalid TSS exception is generated if SS DPL doesn't match CPL.
   - An Invalid TSS exception is generated if a selector indexes to an inappropriate descriptor entry. As examples, if the CS selector selects a non-code segment descriptor; the SS selector selects a non-stack descriptor; or one of the data segment descriptors selects a non-data segment descriptor.
   - A Segment Not Present exception is generated if any of the selected segment descriptors (other than SS) have P = 0 (segment not present) in their respective segment descriptors.
   - A Stack exception is generated if the stack segment descriptor has P = 0 (segment not present).
   - An Invalid TSS exception is generated if the index portion of any of the segment selectors addresses an entry beyond the limit of the selected descriptor table (i.e., GDT or LDT).
   - An Invalid TSS exception is generated if any of the data segment selectors indexes to a descriptor entry that indicates the segment is non-readable.
   - An Invalid TSS exception is generated if the CPL is not as privileged as the DPL of any of the data segment descriptors.
4. An Invalid TSS exception is generated if the LDT selector (from the new TSS) does not select an LDT descriptor in the GDT, or if the LDT descriptor has P = 0 (table not present).
5. If any of the TSS integrity checks fail, the TR register is not loaded with the new TSS selector (the current TSS selector remains in it) and the exception generated as a result of the integrity failure is serviced in the context of the current task (in other words, the task switch does not occur).
6. When the integrity of the called task's TSS has been verified, the task switch

takes place. The TR register is loaded with the selector (from the TSS descriptor) for the called task's TSS.

7. The processor sets the Busy bit in the called task's TSS descriptor.

8. The processor sets the CR0[TS] bit to indicate that a task switch has occurred. This permits the OS programmer to compare the context of the floating-point unit vs. the integer execution unit to synchronize floating-point exceptions with the task they are associated with.

9. The processor sets EFlags[NT] to indicate that this task was called from another task that was suspended. After the call is complete, the processor must switch back to the calling task and resume execution at the instruction that follows the far call. The EFlags[NT] bit tells it to do this (for more information, see "Return to Calling Task or...There and Back Again!" on page 170.

10. The processor stores the old contents of the TR register in the Link field of the called task. This is the selector for the calling task's TSS descriptor in the GDT.

11. The processor reads the register fields from the called task's TSS into its registers.

12. The processor then resumes normal operation. In other words, it uses the new values just placed in CS:EIP to fetch the first instruction. This is the first instruction of the called task. The program executes at the privilege level indicated by the least-significant two bits of the CS field from the new task's TSS CS field (i.e., its RPL field). **The task switch is now complete**.

Return to Calling Task or...There and Back Again!

The body of the called task is executed. When it has completed execution, the last instruction in the task is a IRET instruction. When an IRET is executed with EFlags[NT] set to one, the processor recognizes that it is to resume the calling task at the instruction that follows the far call. To do this, it takes the following actions:

1. Performs the following tests on the current task's TSS Link field (should point to GDT TSS descriptor for calling task):
   - Generate Invalid TSS exception if TI = 1 (LDT) because TSS descriptor must be in GDT.
   - Generate Invalid TSS exception if GDT Index exceeds GDT limit.
   - Generate Invalid TSS exception if indicated descriptor in GDT isn't TSS descriptor.
   - Generate Invalid TSS exception if Busy bit not set in TSS descriptor for calling task.

- Generate Segment Not Present exception if P = 0 in TSS descriptor for calling task.

2. Reload processor register set from calling task's TSS. At this point, the processor is ready to resume the calling task.

3. Clear the Busy bit in the TSS descriptor for the called task.

4. Pop CS and EIP from stack into respective registers.

5. Generate GP exception if EIP exceeds code segment limit.

6. Resume execution of calling program at the instruction immediately following the far call.

Switch as Result of Far Jump

A far jump instruction causes a task switch under the following circumstances:

- it **selects a TSS descriptor in the GDT**. In this case, the lesser-privileged of the selector RPL and the currently-executing program's CPL must meet or beat the privilege level indicated by the TSS descriptor's DPL. This is typically zero, severely restricting the programs that are successful in selecting the TSS descriptor.
- it **selects a Task Gate descriptor in either the GDT or LDT**. In this case, the lesser-privileged of the selector RPL and the currently-executing program's CPL must meet or beat the privilege level of the Task Gate descriptor's DPL (which can be different than the DPL of the TSS descriptor it points to in the GDT).

The difference between the two is in how the privilege check is performed. The sections that follow assume that the privilege check has been passed.

Suspension of Task Executing Jump

In response to the interrupt or exception, the processor performs the following sequence of actions to suspend the current task:

1. Checks that the TSS descriptor in the GDT that is pointed to by the Task Gate descriptor is valid (P = 1) and has a valid limit. At a minimum, the limit must be ≥ 67h (i.e., 103d). If P = 0, a Segment Not Present exception is generated, while an Invalid TSS exception results if the limit is less than 103d.

2. A GP exception is generated if the Busy bit (B) in the TSS descriptor is set to one.

3. Clears the Busy bit in the TSS descriptor associated with the task executing

the far jump.

4. Saves the state of the processor's register set in the current task's TSS (pointed to by the base address in the TR register). This is accomplished by performing a series of memory write transactions.

5. This discussion continues in the next section.

Start Target Task

After suspending the previous task, the processor performs the following steps to start the target task:

1. The 16-bit TSS selector from the Task Gate descriptor is read by the processor, but is not placed in the TR register until the selector's integrity has been validated:
    *   GP exception generated if TI = 1 (selecting LDT rather than GDT).
    *   GP exception if selected GDT entry is not TSS descriptor.
    *   Segment Not Present exception if P = 0 in TSS descriptor.

2. 16-bit GDT selector not placed in TR register until TSS data structure integrity is also validated:
    *   Using the 16-bit selector to index into the GDT, the processor reads the base address and limit of the TSS from the TSS descriptor in the GDT.
    *   Validates that the TSS limit ≥ 103d and generates Invalid TSS exception if < 103d (67h).

3. The processor reads new segment selector fields (CS, DS, ES, FS, GS, SS) from the target task's TSS and validates each of them:
    *   An Invalid TSS exception is generated if CS or SS DPL does not match CS or SS selectors' RPL.
    *   An Invalid TSS exception is generated if a selector indexes to an inappropriate descriptor entry. As examples, if the CS selector selects a non-code segment descriptor; the SS selector selects a non-stack descriptor; or one of the data segment descriptors selects a non-data segment descriptor.
    *   A Segment Not Present exception is generated if any of the selected segment descriptors (other than SS) have P = 0 (segment not present) in their respective segment descriptors.
    *   A Stack exception is generated if the stack segment descriptor has P = 0 (segment not present).
    *   An Invalid TSS exception is generated if the index portion of any of the segment selectors addresses an entry beyond the limit of the selected descriptor table (i.e., GDT or LDT).
    *   An Invalid TSS exception is generated if any of the data segment

selectors indexes to a descriptor entry that indicates the segment is non -readable.

- An Invalid TSS exception is generated if the CPL is not as privileged as the DPL of any of the data segment descriptors.
- An Invalid TSS exception is generated if SS DPL doesn't match CPL.

4. An Invalid TSS exception is generated if the LDT selector (from the new TSS) does not select an LDT descriptor in the GDT, or if the LDT descriptor has P = 0 (table not present).

5. If any of the TSS integrity checks fail, the TR register is not loaded with the new TSS selector (the current TSS selector remains in it) and the exception generated as a result of the integrity failure is serviced in the context of the current task (in other words, the task switch does not occur).

6. When the integrity of the target task's TSS has been verified, the task switch takes place. The TR register is loaded with the selector (from the TSS descriptor) for the target task's TSS.

7. The processor sets the Busy bit in the target task's TSS descriptor.

8. The processor sets the CR0[TS] bit to indicate that a task switch has occurred. This permits the OS programmer to compare the context of the floating-point unit vs. the integer execution unit to synchronize floating-point exceptions with the task they are associated with.

9. The processor reads the register fields from the new TSS into its registers.

10. The processor then resumes normal operation. In other words, it uses the new values just placed in CS:EIP to fetch the first instruction. This is the first instruction of the target task. The program executes at the privilege level indicated by the least-significant two bits of the CS field from the new task's TSS CS field (i.e., its RPL field). **The task switch is now complete**.

Switch as Result of BOUND or INT Instruction

A task switch occurs if any of the following instructions select a task gate in the IDT:

- The **BOUND instruction generates a Bound Range Exceeded exception** if the supplied array index is not within the bounds of the indicated memory array. This selects entry five in the IDT. If this entry contains a Task Gate descriptor, a task switch occurs. No privilege check is performed.
- The **INT nn instruction** selects entry nn in the IDT. If entry nn contains a Task Gate descriptor and the CPL of the currently-executing program meets or beats the DPL of the Task Gate descriptor, a task switch occurs.
- When the **INTO (interrupt on overflow) instruction** detects the EFlags[OF] bit set to one, it indexes to entry four in the IDT. If this entry contains a Task Gate descriptor, a task switch occurs. No privilege check is performed.

Protected Mode Software Architecture

If the instruction is BOUND, the resultant task switch and return is handled in the same manner as an exception (because it is one). The actions taken are detailed in the section entitled "Switch as Result of Hardware Interrupt or Exception" on page 163.

If the instruction is INT *nn* or INTO, the resultant task switch and return is handled in the same manner as a far call. The actions taken are detailed in the section entitled "Switch as Result of Far Call" on page 168.

Linked Tasks

Under the following circumstances, a task is linked to the task that transferred execution to it (because the old task must be resumed when the new task has completed execution):

- if the task is called via a far call
- if the task is executed as a result of a hardware interrupt
- if the task is executed as a result of a software exception
- if the task is executed as a result of the execution of an INT nn or INTO instruction

As part of the task switch, the processor takes the following actions:

- Updates the TSS Link field in the target TSS with the selector of the TSS for the task it must return to (i.e., link back to) when the task has completed execution.
- Sets the EFlags[NT] bit to one.
- Sets the Busy bit in the target task's TSS descriptor.

When the target task has completed execution, the execution of the final instruction (IRET) causes a task switch back to the interrupted or calling task. The task switch occurs because the processor detects EFlags[NT] set when the IRET is executed. The actions taken are:

- EFlags[NT] is cleared.
- Old TSS descriptor's Busy bit is cleared.
- Switch back to old task and resume (detailed in earlier sections of this chapter).

The called task may, in turn, call other tasks, or may be interrupted to another task. It may not, however, call a task that has already had the Busy bit set to one in its TSS descriptor (the fact that its Busy bit is already set indicates that the task is currently suspended and its TSS contains the register set contents at the point at which suspension occurred). This attempt results in a GP exception. It can, however, perform an interrupt return to a task with its Busy bit set (so the old task can be resumed). There is no limit (other than memory) to the task nesting depth. Figure 11-3 on page 176 illustrates an example where Task A has called task B, and task B has called task C. It's easy to see that a linked list has been created.

- The Busy bit is set to one in all three of their TSS descriptors.
- The EFlags[NT] bits in tasks B and C's TSS EFlag field are set to one.
- The EFlags[NT] bit in task A's TSS EFlags field is cleared to zero.
- The Link field in task A's TSS doesn't contain a valid link.
- The Link field in task B's TSS contains the selector for task A's TSS.
- The Link field in task C's TSS contains the selector for task B's TSS.
- The EFlags[NT] register bit is set to one.
- The TR contains the selector for the current task's (task C's) TSS descriptor.

Figure 11-3: Example of Linked Tasks

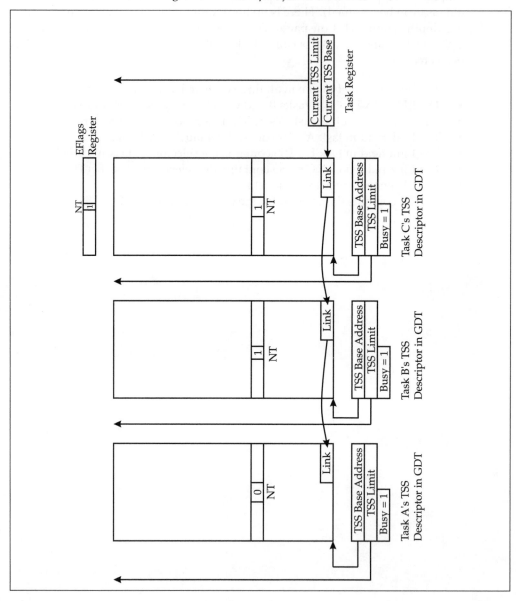

Chapter 11: Mechanics of a Task Switch

Linkage Modification

Refer to Figure 11-3 on page 176. Assume that task A called task B, and task B called task C. If an IRET instruction is executed at the end of task C, a task switch back to task B will result. Now assume that the programmer wants the IRET instruction at the end of task C to cause a task switch to task A, rather than to task B. This should be accomplished in the following manner:

1. Disable interrupts by executing a CLI instruction.
2. Replace the task C Link field (which currently contains the GDT selector for the task B TSS descriptor) with the selector for the task A TSS descriptor.
3. Clear Busy bit in task B's TSS descriptor.
4. Reenable interrupt recognition with an STI instruction.
5. Execute the IRET instruction.

The Busy Bit

Each TSS descriptor in the GDT has a Busy bit (see Figure 11-4 on page 179). Whenever control is first passed to the task, its Busy bit is set to one by the processor.

If the task is terminated with a far jump (performing an unconditional jump to another task implies that the current task has completed and is therefore not busy anymore) to another task, an IRET to return to a task that called it, or an IRET to return to an interrupted task, the task's Busy bit is cleared to zero.

If the task is exited via a far call to another task, or an interrupt/exception causes a task switch to an interrupt/exception service task, the task has not yet completed. Its Busy bit therefore remains set when control is passed to the other task.

The processor generates a GP exception if the target task is already busy. This is considered a serious error because busy implies that the target task saved a link back to another task in its TSS when it was entered earlier. The fact that its Busy bit is still set indicates it was originally entered via a call, or an interrupt/exception and has not yet returned to the task that originally passed control to it. If the processor permits another task to enter it, the link will be overwritten with a new one, thereby rendering it incapable of find its way back to the task that originally switched to it.

The processor automatically asserts its LOCK# output whenever it accesses the busy bit in a TSS descriptor. In a multiprocessor system, this ensures that two (or more) processors will not access the busy bit "simultaneously" and erroneously switch to the same task.

Figure 11-4: TSS Descriptor Format

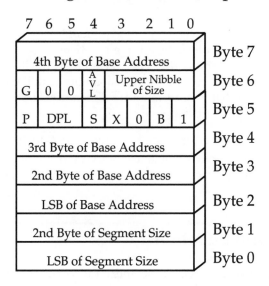

Task State Segment (TSS) Descriptor

G Bit   Granularity bit defines meaning of limit value.
0 = length of segment in bytes.
1 = length of segment in pages.

AVL Bit   Available for use by system software
P Bit   Segment Present bit.
DPL Field   Descriptor Privilege Level.
S Bit   System bit. When 0, indicates system segment.
Must be 0 in a TSS descriptor.
X Bit   This bit indicates whether this is a 16 or 32-bit TSS.
0 = 16-bit TSS.
1 = 32-bit TSS.

B Bit   Busy bit. 1 indicates task is busy.

Note: All TSS entries must reside in the Global Descriptor Table (GDT).

Protected Mode Software Architecture

Address Mapping

Linear vs. Physical Memory Address

As discussed in earlier chapters, when addressing memory the post-286 processor forms the 32-bit memory address by adding the 32-bit offset to the segment start address. The resultant 32-bit address is referred to as the linear address. If the OS has not enabled the processor's paging capability (CR0[PG] = 0), the linear address is the address that is used to address memory. In other words, the linear address and physical address are the same.

On the other hand, if the processor's paging capability is enabled (CR0[PG] = 1), the paging unit can convert, or map, the linear address to any physical memory address in the 4GB memory space. This is accomplished using the page directory and page tables.

GDT Purpose and Location

The GDTR (GDT register) contains the base linear address (and size) of the GDT in memory. The GDT entries define segments that are common to all applications. It's important to note that the contents of the GDTR does not change when a task switch occurs. This means that all tasks use the same GDT to access the pool of common segments.

CR3 contains the base physical memory address of the page directory. When a task switch occurs, CR3 is changed to point to the page directory for the current task (by copying the CR3 field from the new task's TSS). It is important that the page directory for every task be set up to map accesses to the GDT to the same range of locations in physical memory. The goal of a shared GDT would be defeated if each task mapped the GDT's linear address range to different physical memory ranges. They would be using different GDTs. For more information on paging, refer to the section entitled "Paging-Related Issues" on page 181 and the chapter entitled "Virtual Paging" on page 219.

LDT Purpose and Location

Whenever a task switch occurs, the processor updates the LDTR from the new task's LDT selector field. The memory segments that can be used by the new task consists of those defined by the GDT (which remains the same for all tasks) and those defined by the task's LDT as local for this task.

The OS sets up the LDT selector field of each task's TSS to point to that task's LDT descriptor in the GDT. Ideally, the OS sets up the TSS fields so that each task has its own, distinct LDT that defines the segments local to the task. However, the OS could set them up so all tasks shared one LDT, or so some tasks but not others shared an LDT.

Paging-Related Issues

Background

When paging is enabled, the processor's paging unit intercepts all linear memory addresses and converts them to physical memory addresses. The paging unit deals with two, distinct memory ranges: 4GB of linear memory space and 4GB of physical memory address space. It considers each space as being subdivided into 4KB pages of information.

When presented with a 32-bit linear memory address by the segmentation logic, the address naturally lies within some 4KB range of linear memory space (i.e., a linear memory page). The upper 20 bits of the linear address identify which of the one meg (1,048,576d) linear memory pages is being addressed. It then uses a directory lookup mechanism to find out which of the one meg physical memory pages the linear page (identified by the upper 20 bits of the linear address) should be mapped to. It replaces the linear page address (i.e., the upper 20 bits of the linear address) with the physical page address (the 20 bit field obtained from the page directories). The lower 12 bit portion of the linear address remains untouched—it identifies exactly which of the 4096d locations within the page is being addressed. In this manner, the paging unit converts the 32-bit linear address into a corresponding 32-bit physical memory address.

The directories the paging unit consults to make the address conversion are in memory and CR3 contains the start physical memory address of the top-level directory used for the lookup and address conversion.

Each Task Can Have Different Linear-to-Physical Mapping

Each time that a task switch occurs the processor updates CR3 with the physical start memory address of the new task's page directory. CR3 is also referred to as the Page Directory Base Register, or PDBR. In other words, by placing different addresses in the CR3 field of each TSS, each task can use a different set of directories to perform the linear-to-physical address conversion.

TSS Mapping Must Remain Same for All Tasks

The linear-to-physical mapping for the range of addresses associated with all TSS segments must remain constant for all tasks. In other words, these linear address ranges must be translated identically by all tasks. When a task switch occurs from task A to task B:

- The register set's current contents is saved in task A's TSS (using task A's page directory to perform the translation of the TSS's linear range to its physical range).
- The task switch then occurs and the register set is reloaded from task B's TSS segment.
- The Link field of task B's TSS is set to the GDT selector for task A's TSS descriptor.
- CR3 is loaded with the base address of task B's page directory.
- When task B has completed and its time to resume task A, the processor must restore its register set from task A's TSS. It uses task B's page directory to perform the translation of task A's TSS linear range to its physical range. If task B's page directory translates task A's TSS linear range to a different physical range than task A's page directory translated it when storing the register image, the processor would restore the wrong information to the processor's register set.

Placement of TSS Within Page(s)

An unrecoverable error results if a GP exception or a page fault occurs after the processor has started to read the TSS for the new task when performing a task switch. To prevent this, the following rules must be adhered to:

- If possible, place the entire first 104d bytes of the TSS (i.e., the part accessed during a task switch) within a single page. If necessary, the TSS can straddle a page boundary (i.e., an address divisible by 4KB), but both pages must be present in memory (P = 1 in both of their page table entries).
- The page or pages that contain the old and new TSSs must be present in memory and must be marked read/write (in the page table entry).

12 Interrupt Sources and Handling

The Previous Chapter

The previous two chapters provided a detailed description of task management, including task creation and switching.

This Chapter

This chapter provides a detailed description of interrupt and exception sources and handling in both real and protected mode. Sources and handling of interrupts or exceptions initiated by hardware interrupts, software interrupt instructions and software exceptions are covered.

The Next Chapter

The next chapter provides a detailed description of the processor's virtual paging mechanism.

Special Note

The program executed to service a hardware interrupt or a software exception is frequently referred to as a handler in this chapter. Alternately, it may be referred to as an interrupt service routine.

General

There are three types of interrupt-related events that can cause the currently-executing program to be interrupted:

Protected Mode Software Architecture

- an interrupt request from a hardware device external to the processor is recognized if recognition of external interrupts is enabled (EFlags[IF] = 1).
- execution of a software interrupt (INT) instruction.
- processor detection of a software exception error condition.

When any of these events occurs, the currently-executing program is interrupted. In other words, the processor must:

1. suspend execution of the program
2. mark its place for later resumption
3. determine the type of request
4. jump to an event-specific interrupt service routine (or task) to service the request.
5. return to the interrupted program and resume execution at the point of interruption.

Hardware Interrupts

There are two types of interrupt requests that can be initiated by hardware external to the processor:

- Maskable interrupt requests initiated by IO devices.
- Non-maskable interrupt requests.

For more detailed coverage of hardware interrupt generation and servicing in the PC-compatible environment, refer to the chapter on interrupts in the MindShare book entitled *ISA System Architecture* (published by Addison-Wesley). For a detailed discussion of the Pentium processor's Advanced Programmable Interrupt Controller (APIC), refer to the MindShare book entitled *Pentium Processor System Architecture* (published by Addison-Wesley).

Maskable Interrupt Requests

Some IO devices generate an interrupt request to signal that:

- an action is required on the part of the program in order to continue operation.
- a previously-initiated operation has been completed with no errors encountered
- a previously-initiated operation has encountered an error condition and cannot continue.

Chapter 12: Interrupt Sources and Handling

In any of these cases, the IO device asserts an IRQ (interrupt request) signal to the interrupt controller, which in turn asserts INTR (maskable interrupt request) to the processor.

An interrupt request may be temporarily ignored when an IO device is requesting service if the programmer has disabled recognition of requests from IO devices by executing a clear interrupt enable (CLI) instruction. This clears EFlags[IF], causing the processor to ignore its INTR input until a set interrupt enable (STI) instruction is executed. This feature must be used cautiously. Many IO devices are sensitive to lengthy delays while awaiting service and may suffer data overrun or underrun conditions if their interrupt requests are not serviced on a timely basis.

In protected mode, the CLI and STI (set interrupt enable) instructions are sensitive to the value in the EFlags[IOPL] field. They may only be successfully executed when the current program's CPL meets or beats the IOPL (IO privilege level). Any attempt to execute them with insufficient privilege results in a GP exception.

Other operations that affect EFlags[IF] are:

- Reset clears EFlags[IF], inhibiting recognition of maskable interrupts.
- The PUSHF (push flags) instruction copies EFlags to the stack and then clears the EFlags[IF] bit. The Eflags bits, including IF, can then be examined and modified in stack memory.
- The POPF instruction copies the EFlags image from stack memory into the EFlags register.
- A task switch modifies the EFlags register when it copies the EFlags field from the new TSS into EFlags. Task switching is covered in the chapter entitled "Mechanics of a Task Switch" on page 157.
- The IRET instruction copies the EFlags image from stack memory into the EFlags register.
- An interrupt that selects an IDT entry containing an interrupt gate descriptor clears EFlags[IF] after EFlags has been copied to stack memory.

Maskable Interrupt Servicing

Automatic Actions

If interrupt recognition is enabled and the INTR input is sampled asserted, the processor begins to service the hardware request upon completion of the currently-executing instruction. This discussion assumes that the system interrupt

Protected Mode Software Architecture

controller consists of either an 8259A programmable interrupt controller (PIC), or the Pentium's APIC is programmed for PIC-compatible mode. In response to the assertion of INTR, the following sequence of actions is performed by the processor:

1. Two, back-to-back interrupt acknowledge transactions are generated. The first one tells the 8259A interrupt controller to prioritize the currently-pending interrupt requests from IO devices. The second one is a request to the PIC for the interrupt vector number associated with the highest-priority request— an index into the interrupt descriptor table (IDT) in memory.
2. Using the vector to select an IDT entry, the processor reads the contents of the indicated IDT descriptor from memory.
3. The processor pushes the contents of its CS, EIP and EFlags registers onto the stack. This is necessary to save its place in the interrupted program.
4. EFlags[IF] is cleared to disable recognition of subsequent interrupt requests.
5. The processor jumps to the device-specific interrupt service routine indicated in the IDT entry. If the IDT entry contains a Task Gate descriptor, the processor performs a task switch and begins execution of the interrupt service task.

The actions just described are the ones that the processor performs automatically in order to start an interrupt service routine. The following discussion assumes that the IDT entry did not contain a Task Gate descriptor.

Handler Software Actions

Once in the interrupt service routine, the programmer must perform the following actions:

1. Save (in stack memory) the contents of any registers that will be altered in this routine. When control is returned to the interrupted program, all registers must be returned to their original states in order to ensure proper operation of the interrupted program.
2. Check the device's status and perform any device-specific servicing requested by the device.
3. Issue an end-of-interrupt (EOI) command to the 8259A interrupt controller to clear the request.
4. Execute an interrupt return (IRET) instruction. This causes the processor to pop the original CS, EIP and EFlags values (reenabling recognition of external, hardware interrupts) from the stack and load them into their respective registers.
5. The processor resumes execution of the interrupted program.

Chapter 12: Interrupt Sources and Handling

PC-Compatible Vector Assignment

Table 12-1 on page 187 defines the typical hardware interrupt request line assignment in a PC-compatible machine. It identifies the IDT entry number associated with each.

The table also highlights a particularly aberrant characteristic of the PC-compatible architecture. The original IBM PC was based on the Intel 8088 processor. As with any of the x86 processors, the 8088 generates software exceptions when certain special conditions are detected. Intel dedicated IDT entries 0 through 7 for these software exception conditions. The designers of the PC programmed the 8259A interrupt controller to associate IDT entries 8 through 15d (Fh) with the hardware interrupt lines IRQ0 through IRQ7. In order to be backward-compatible, the IBM PC-AT's interrupt controller was also programmed to use IDT entries 8 through 15d for these hardware interrupts. However, the PC-AT was designed around the 286 processor and that processor generates more type of software exceptions than the 8088. These new exceptions used IDT entries 8 through 13d. Later machines were based on the post-286 processors and they added additional exceptions using IDT entries 14d and 15d. In other words, IDT entries 8 through 15d can be selected when either hardware interrupt or software exception events occur. Table 12-1 on page 187 explains the actions software must take in order to ensure that all hardware and software events are serviced correctly.

Table 12-1: PC-Compatible IRQ Assignment

IRQ Line	IDT Entry	Typically Used By
0	08h	**System timer.** Same vector occurs on **double-fault exception**. This means that occurrence of either a system timer tick or a double-fault exception vectors to IDT entry 08. In a PC, the system timer interrupt handler hooks this entry prior to the OS boot. During OS initialization, the OS reads and saves the pointer to the timer handler and installs the pointer to its double-fault exception handler in IDT entry 08. If either event occurs during runtime, the processor jumps to the OS double-fault exception handler. The double-fault exception handler determines if external interrupts are enabled by testing for EFlags[IF] = 1 on the stack. If not enabled, execute exception handler to service double-fault condition. If enabled, polls bit 0 in the master 8259A interrupt controller's IRR (interrupt request register) to determine if system timer has ticked. If it has, jump to and execute the system timer interrupt handler. If it hasn't, execute the exception handler to service double-fault.

Table 12-1: PC-Compatible IRQ Assignment (Continued)

IRQ Line	IDT Entry	Typically Used By
1	09h	**Keyboard interface.** Same vector occurs on **Coprocessor segment overrun abort exception.** Occurrence of either keyboard request or overrun exception vectors to IDT entry 09. In PC, keyboard handler hooks this entry prior to OS boot. During OS initialization, OS reads and saves pointer to keyboard handler and installs pointer to its segment overrun exception handler in IDT entry 09. If either event occurs during run-time, the processor jumps to the OS's overrun exception handler. Exception handler determines if external interrupts are enabled by testing for EFlags[IF] = 1 on the stack. If not enabled, execute exception handler. If enabled, poll bit 1 in master 8259A interrupt controller's IRR (interrupt request register) to determine if keyboard has generated request. If it has, jump to and execute keyboard handler. If it hasn't, execute exception handler to service overrun exception.
2	0Ah (10d)	Requests from slave interrupt controller.
3	0Bh (11d)	**Serial port two.** Same vector occurs on **Segment Not Present exception.** Occurrence of either serial port 2 interrupt or segment not present exception vectors to IDT entry 11d. In PC, serial port handler hooks this entry prior to OS boot. During OS initialization, OS reads and saves pointer to serial port handler and installs pointer to its segment not present exception handler in IDT entry 11d. If either event occurs during run-time, the processor jumps to the OS segment not present exception handler. Exception handler determines if external interrupts are enabled by testing for EFlags[IF] = 1 on the stack. If not enabled, execute exception handler. If enabled, poll bit 3 in master 8259A interrupt controller's IRR (interrupt request register) to determine if serial port interrupt pending. If it is, jump to and execute serial port handler. If it isn't, execute the exception handler.
4	0Ch (12d)	**Serial port one.** Same vector occurs on **stack fault exception.** Occurrence of either serial port one request or stack exception vectors to IDT entry 12d. In PC, serial port one interrupt handler hooks this entry prior to OS boot. During OS initialization, OS reads and saves pointer to serial port handler and installs pointer to its stack exception handler in IDT entry 12d. If either event occurs during run-time, the processor jumps to the OS stack exception handler. Exception handler determines if external interrupts are enabled by testing for EFlags[IF] = 1 on the stack. If not enabled, execute exception handler. If enabled, poll bit 4 in master 8259A interrupt controller's IRR (interrupt request register) to determine if serial port one generating request. If it is, jump to and execute serial port handler. If it isn't, execute the exception handler.

Chapter 12: Interrupt Sources and Handling

Table 12-1: PC-Compatible IRQ Assignment (Continued)

IRQ Line	IDT Entry	Typically Used By
5	0Dh (13d)	**Parallel port two.** Same vector occurs on **GP exception**. Occurrence of either parallel port 2 interrupt or GP exception vectors to IDT entry 13d. In PC, parallel port handler hooks this entry prior to OS boot. During OS initialization, OS reads and saves pointer to parallel port handler and installs pointer to its GP exception handler in IDT entry 13d. If either event occurs during run-time, the processor jumps to the OS GP exception handler. Exception handler determines if external interrupts are enabled by testing for EFlags[IF] = 1 on the stack. If not enabled, execute exception handler. If enabled, poll bit 5 in master 8259A interrupt controller's IRR (interrupt request register) to determine if parallel port 2 generating interrupt. If it is, jump to and execute parallel port handler. If it isn't, execute the exception handler.
6	0Eh (14d)	**Floppy interface.** Same vector occurs on **page fault exception**. Occurrence of either floppy interrupt or page fault exception vectors to IDT entry 14d. In PC, the floppy interrupt handler hooks this entry prior to OS boot. During OS initialization, OS reads and saves pointer to floppy handler and installs pointer to its page fault exception handler in IDT entry 14d. If either event occurs during run-time, processor jumps to OS page fault exception handler. Exception handler determines if external interrupts are enabled by testing for EFlags[IF] = 1 on the stack. If not enabled, execute exception handler. If enabled, poll bit 6 in master 8259A interrupt controller's IRR (interrupt request register) to determine if floppy generating request. If it is, jump to and execute the floppy handler. If it isn't, execute exception handler.
7	0Fh (15d)	**Parallel port one.**
8	70h (112d)	Alarm output of the real-time clock chip.
9	71h (113d)	VGA vertical retrace interrupt.
10	72h (114d)	Available for use by expansion cards.
11	73h (115d)	Available for use by expansion cards.
12	74h (116d)	Mouse interface.
13	75h (117d)	Error output of the numeric coprocessor.
14	76h (118d)	Hard drive interface.
15	77h (119d)	Available for use by expansion cards.

Non-Maskable Interrupt Requests

In the PC-compatible world, the processor's non-maskable interrupt request input (NMI) is used to report catastrophic hardware failures (such as a system board DRAM parity check) to the OS. The programmer may mask out the external hardware's ability to generate NMI by writing a one to bit seven of IO port 70h. Caution should be exercised, however, because bits [6:0] of this same IO port are assigned to the real-time clock chip's address port. Although bit seven of IO port 70h can be used to block the assertion of NMI, the programmer has no way of commanding the processor not to service an NMI request when it detects it active.

When an NMI request is detected, the processor saves its place on the stack and jumps to the NMI interrupt service routine pointed to by IDT entry 2. The processor automatically disables recognition of additional NMI interrupts until the IRET instruction is executed at the end of the NMI interrupt service routine. In this routine, the programmer polls the various external hardware devices that are capable of generating an NMI in order to discover the type of failure. Upon discovering the source of the failure, a failure-specific message is typically output to the display, maskable interrupts are disabled, and a HALT instruction is executed. In response to the HALT instruction, the processor broadcasts a halt message (to inform external logic of its intention to stop fetching and executing instructions) using its special cycle transaction and ceases to fetch and execute instructions.

Software-Generated Exceptions

General

Software-generated exceptions fall into two categories:

- Software **exceptions** generated **as** a **result of** an **error condition** detected while attempting execution of an instruction. The type of error condition defines the IDT entry that is vectored to.
- Software **exceptions deliberately generated by execution of special instruction types** (INT and BOUND). Generated by the INT *nn*, INTO, and INT3 instructions. Execution of an INT *nn* instruction vectors to entry *nn* in the IDT. Execution of an INTO instruction vectors to IDT entry four if EFlags[OF] = 1. Execution of the INT3 instruction (the breakpoint instruc-

tion) vectors to IDT entry three. Conditionally generated by the BOUND instruction if the indicated array index is not within the bounds of the indicated memory array (causes processor to vector to IDT entry five).

Faults, Traps, and Aborts

Prior to executing each instruction, the processor pre-evaluates the instruction to determine if it can be safely executed without adverse effects. Problems of this nature are referred to as software exception conditions. When such a problem is detected, the processor invokes a special exception handler routine designed to attempt a graceful recovery from the respective exception condition. The pointer to the various exception handlers are stored in dedicated slots in the IDT. Software exceptions are categorized as faults, traps, or aborts. These terms are defined in Table 12-2 on page 191. Table 12-3 on page 192 defines each software exception and identifies it as a fault, trap, or abort.

Table 12-2: Software Exception Types

Type	Definition
Fault	An exception reported at the start of the instruction that caused the exception. The fault is reported with the processor restored to a state that permits the instruction to be restarted (i.e., all registers are restored to their original state). The **return address** stored in the stack **points to** the **instruction that caused** the **fault**, rather than to the next instruction.
Trap	A trap is reported after the instruction that caused it has completed. The **return address** in the stack **points to** the **instruction that follows** the **one that caused** the **exception**. If the trap occurs during execution of an instruction that alters program flow (e.g., a jump instruction), the return address points to the address that is the target of the instruction (e.g., the address being jumped to). When the instruction has a repeat prefix and the count has not been exhausted, the return address points to the same instruction and the values in the other registers related to the instruction contain the values for the next iteration.

Table 12-2: Software Exception Types (Continued)

Type	Definition
Abort	An abort does not always reliably supply the address of the instruction that caused the exception. This makes it **impossible** for the exception handler **to** fix the problem and **resume program execution**.

Table 12-3: Exception Categories

Level	Description	Type
0	Divide-by-zero attempt can be generated during execution of the DIV or IDIV instruction.	fault
1	**Debug exception** caused by instruction address breakpoint.	fault
	Debug exception caused by data address breakpoint.	trap
	Debug exception caused by General Detect. This occurs when an attempt is made to use the processor's debug registers when they are already in use by an in-circuit emulator (ICE).	fault
	Debug exception caused by single-step.	trap
	Debug exception caused by task-switch breakpoint.	trap
2	**NMI** is not a software exception.	trap
3	The INT3 instruction is also referred to as the **Breakpoint** instruction. Unlike the two-byte INT *nn* instruction, it is one byte long.	trap
4	Generated by execution of the **INTO** instruction if the EFlags[OF] is set to one. Useful because the signed and unsigned arithmetic instructions cannot detect an overflow of the result.	trap
5	Generated by the **BOUNDS** instruction if the specified array index is not within the bounds of the specified memory array.	fault

Table 12-3: Exception Categories (Continued)

Level	Description	Type
6	Generated when an **invalid opcode** is detected upon attempted execution of the instruction (instruction prefetch cannot cause this exception). Also generated when an invalid operand is used with an instruction (e.g., specifying a register as the target of a jump). Use of the LOCK prefix with instructions for which locking is not supported also causes this exception.	fault
7	**Device Not Available** exception is generated under two circumstances: • CR0[EM] = 1 (indicating that FPU is not present) and ESC instruction encountered (i.e., a FP instruction). This exception handler can be used to emulate floating-point instruction. • CR0[TS] = 1, CR0[MP] = 1, and WAIT or ESC instruction encountered. The floating-point unit is about to execute an instruction associated with another task and a task switch has occurred.	fault
8	**Double-fault encountered**. The processor has encountered a fault while attempting to call an exception handler for a previously-encountered fault. Most of the time this can be handled by servicing the two exceptions serially, but some combinations are unrecoverable. These result in a double-fault exception. If a third exception occurs while the processor is attempting to call the double-fault handler, the processor generates a special cycle transaction to broadcast a shutdown message and then enters the shutdown state.	abort
9	**Coprocessor segment overrun abort** is reserved in post-386 processors. Only generated by the 386/387 when a page or segment violation is detected during the transfer of an operand to or from memory. The Pentium and i486 processors generate exception 13h instead (general protection)	abort
10 *	**Invalid TSS fault**. Generated if a task switch is attempted to a task with an invalid TSS.	fault

Table 12-3: Exception Categories (Continued)

Level	Description	Type
11 *	**Segment Not Present**. Generated when selected segment descriptor (CS, DS, ES, FS, GS) has P = 0. An SS descriptor with P = 0 results in a stack exception (number 12).	fault
12	**Stack exception** occurs for two reasons: • Stack underflow or overflow error (in other words, too many pops or pushes). • Attempt to load SS with selector for a descriptor marked not present (P = 0).	fault
13	**General Protection (GP)** exception. All protection violations that don't cause another exception cause a GP exception.	fault or trap
14 *	**Page fault** exception. Occurs for one the following reasons: • Page table or page is not present in memory (page directory entry's P = 0, or page table entry's P = 0). • Current program's CPL has insufficient privilege to access the page.	fault
15	Reserved	n/a
16	**Floating-point error** exception. Error generated by attempted execution of a floating-point math instruction. Can only occur when CR0[NE] = 1.	fault
17 *	**Alignment Check** exception. Occurs if processor attempts a misaligned transfer and alignment checking is enabled. Alignment checking is enabled if all of the following are true: • CR0[AM] = 1 • EFlags[AC] = 1 • CPL = 3 (applications program executing)	fault
18	**Machine Check** exception. May or may not be implemented on a processor. If implemented, cause is processor model-specific. On the Pentium processor, occurs if the machine check exception is enabled (CR4[MCE] = 1) and either BUSCHK# (bus check) or PEN# (parity enable) is sampled asserted.	abort

Table 12-3: Exception Categories (Continued)

Level	Description	Type
19-31	**Intel reserved**. Do not use.	n/a
32-255	Available for use by maskable hardware interrupts and the INT *nn* instruction.	traps

* *Note*: These exceptions do not occur in real mode, but may occur in VM86 mode.

Instruction Restart

When the processor generates any of the fault exceptions, it restores all of its registers to the state that they were in prior to the attempted execution of the instruction. The return address pushed onto the stack by the exception is therefore the CS:EIP value that points to the instruction that caused the fault. This permits the fault handler to examine the instruction in question and determine whether or not it can correct the problem and then re-execute the instruction successfully.

A classic example would be a page fault exception. This occurs because the target page of information is not currently present in memory. In the exception handler, the programmer could take the following actions:

1. Read the page from mass storage into a physical page in memory
2. Create a page table entry mapping any access within the linear page to that physical page
3. Resume execution of the interrupted program at the instruction that caused the page fault exception.

When the instruction is re-executed, the access takes place successfully because the target page is now present in memory.

Software Interrupt Instructions

The software interrupt instruction emulates the hardware interrupt mechanism. Consider the following example instruction (assume that the system is a PC running DOS):

```
INT  13h          ;call disk BIOS routine
```

When executed by the processor, the following events take place:

1. The processor uses the immediate operand, 13h, as an index into the IDT.
2. The processor reads the contents of IDT entry 13h (19d) from memory.
3. The processor pushes the contents of its CS, EIP and EFlags registers onto the stack. This is necessary to save its place in the interrupted program.
4. The processor jumps to the device-specific interrupt service routine indicated in the IDT entry.
5. At the end of the routine, an interrupt return (IRET) instruction is executed, causing the processor to pop the original CS, EIP and EFlags values from the stack and into their respective registers.
6. The processor resumes execution of the interrupted program.

Interrupt/Exception Priority

It should be fairly obvious that the processor can only execute one program at a time. This being the case, if multiple interrupts and/or exception conditions occurred simultaneously, the processor can only execute one handler at a time. This means that servicing of the other conditions will have to wait. This raises the question of how the processor selects which interrupt or exception to service first when more than one condition occurs simultaneously. It also raises the question of the fate of the interrupts and/or exceptions that aren't chosen for immediate servicing.

The x86 processor family divides the possible types of interrupts and exceptions into five classes (listed in Table 12-4 on page 197). Class one is the highest priority group, while class five is the lowest. The processor services the exception or interrupt from the highest class first. Lower priority exceptions are discarded, while lower priority interrupts are held in the pending state. Discarded exception conditions are generated again when the current handler returns execution to the point of interruption.

Chapter 12: Interrupt Sources and Handling

Table 12-4: Interrupt/Exception Priority

Priority	Class	Description

Highest	1	**Traps on previous instruction**:
		• breakpoint caused by execution of INT3 breakpoint instruction.
		• debug trap exceptions caused by:
		   • single-step enabled (EFLags[TF] = 1).
		   • task breakpoint encountered (TSS T bit = 1).
		   • Hardware breakpoint detected using debug registers.

	2	External **maskable or non-maskable interrupts**.
	3	**Faults caused by fetch of next instruction**: • Code breakpoint fault via debug registers. • Code segment limit violation (EIP exceeds segment limit). • Page fault on prefetch.
	4	**Faults on decode of next instruction**: • Illegal opcode. • Instruction length > 15 bytes (includes prefixes). • Coprocessor not available.
Lowest	5	**Faults on execution of an instruction**: • General detection • Floating-point error on previous floating-point instruction. • Interrupt on overflow. • Bounds check. • Invalid TSS. • Segment Not Present. • Stack exception. • GP exception. • Data Page fault. • Alignment check.

Protected Mode Software Architecture

Real Mode Interrupt/Exception Handling

Interrupt Descriptor Table (IDT) Structure

In real mode, the interrupt table resides in memory starting at location zero. This is true because the power-on assertion of reset forces the following values into the IDTR (IDT register):

- Base address = 00000000h. IDT starts at location zero.
- Limit = 03FFh. IDT size is 1KB.

Each IDT entry (the IDT has a fixed length of 256 entries) contains four bytes of information (hence the length of 1KB):

- The first two bytes of the selected IDT entry are loaded into the lower part of the EIP register when the related interrupt or exception occurs. The upper 16 bits of EIP is set to zero.
- The second two bytes of the selected IDT entry are loaded into the CS register.

Figure 12-1 on page 199 illustrates the structure of the IDT in real mode. It is 1KB (1024d) in length. The default start address of the IDT in memory is location zero. In real mode, the LIDT instruction to specify a different start address and length for the table, but this is not advisable in a PC-compatible environment. Most PC software assumes that the interrupt table starts at location zero and expects it to be there. Execution of the LIDT instruction is permitted in real mode so that the programmer can set up a protected mode IDT and set its start address in the IDTR.

Figure 12-1: Structure of Real Mode Interrupt Table

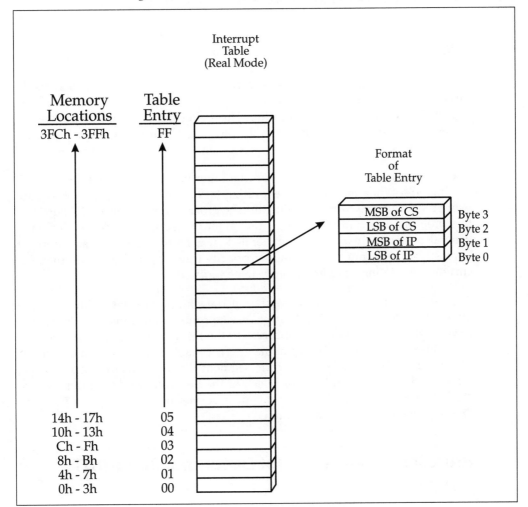

Real Mode Interrupt/Exception Handling

Refer to the descriptions under the earlier headings, "Maskable Interrupt Requests" on page 184, "Software Interrupt Instructions" on page 195, and "Faults, Traps, and Aborts" on page 191.

Protected Mode Software Architecture

Protected Mode Interrupt/Exception Handling

General

In real mode, a single program is executing, rather than multiple programs. In this case, all BIOS and disk services and interrupt service routines exist solely to support the program that is executing. This being the case, there is no need to restrict access to these services when the program executes a software interrupt instruction.

The protected mode environment, on the other hand, exists to support multi-tasking OSs. When the currently-executing task attempts to access a procedure using the software interrupt instruction, the processor must check to ensure that this program is permitted to access the target procedure. If access is denied, a general protection exception is generated. If a hardware event (an interrupt request) occurs, it must have a higher priority (higher privilege level) than the currently-executing program in order to be serviced.

This implies that the processor must not only know the start address of the interrupt table and of each interrupt service routine, but must also know the access rights necessary to permit access to the respective interrupt service routine. This means that each entry in the interrupt table must contain a descriptor defining the start address of the code segment that contains the interrupt service routine; the start address, or offset, of the interrupt service routine within the code segment; and the DPL that must be met or beaten in order to gain access to the interrupt service routine.

Protected Mode Interrupt Descriptor Table (IDT) Structure

Figure 12-2 on page 202 illustrates the protected mode Interrupt Descriptor Table, or IDT. The OS programmer specifies its start memory address using the LIDT instruction. A six byte value is loaded into the IDTR (Interrupt Descriptor Table Register) by the LIDT instruction (can only be executed at privilege level zero when in protected mode; but can also be executed in real mode). This consists of a 32-bit base address and a 16-bit IDT size. The value in the IDTR may also be copied to memory using the SIDT (store IDT) instruction. The IDTR format is illustrated in Figure 12-3 on page 203.

Chapter 12: Interrupt Sources and Handling

Although the IDT can contain up to 256d entries (one for each interrupt and exception type), it doesn't have to (if the system doesn't use all of the vectors). The limit field in the IDTR must reflect the actual length of the IDT (in other words, if the system only uses entries 0 through 149d, the table length should be set to 150d * 8). In protected mode, each entry in the IDT contains an eight byte segment descriptor. When an interrupt or exception occurs, the processor creates the offset into the table by multiplying the interrupt vector (entry number) by eight. The resulting offset is then added to the table's base address (supplied by the IDTR) to form the start address of the descriptor entry. If the offset exceeds the table's size (specified in the IDTR), the processor ceases to fetch instructions, executes a shutdown transaction, and stops. If the address is within the table's limits, the processor then reads the eight byte descriptor from memory. Three types of descriptors may be found in the IDT:

- interrupt gate descriptor
- trap gate descriptor
- task gate descriptor

The following sections defined the purpose, format and use of each of the three descriptor types.

Figure 12-2: Interrupt Descriptor Table (IDT)

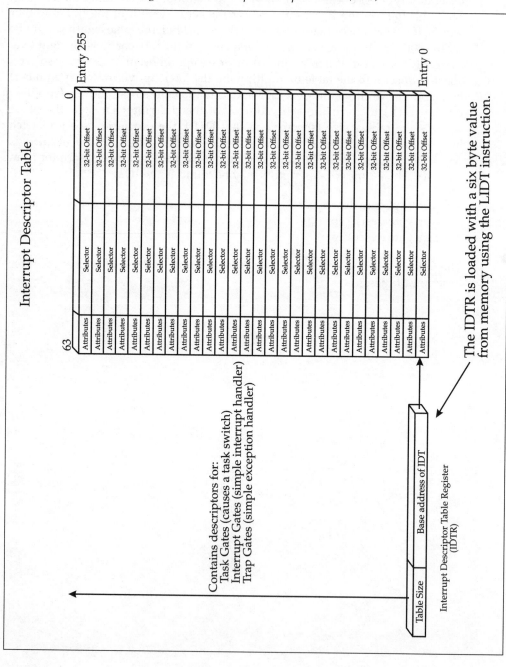

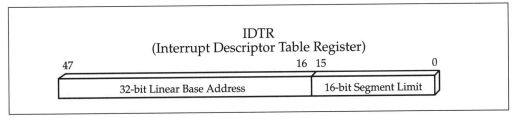

Figure 12-3: Interrupt Descriptor Table Register (IDTR)

Interrupt Gates

General

The processor does not permit an interrupt to transfer control to a procedure in a code segment less-privileged than the current program. To state this more succinctly, the currently-executing program cannot be interrupted by an event with a lesser privilege level. An attempt to do so results in a general protection exception.

An interrupt gate descriptor permits more flexibility—a program can transfer control to an interrupt service routine if the following rules are obeyed:

- In the first part of the privilege check, the processor compares the gate's DPL to the currently-executing program's CPL—the CPL must be equal to or less privileged than the DPL of the interrupt gate descriptor.
- In the second part of the privilege check, the DPL of the code segment that contains the interrupt service routine must indicate that the destination code segment is more privileged or the same privilege as the CPL of the currently-executing program. In other words, you can invoke an interrupt service routine in a code segment with the same or greater level of privilege, but not a lesser level of privilege.

Figure 12-4 on page 206 illustrates the format of an interrupt gate descriptor. The elements are discussed in Table 12-5 on page 203.

Table 12-5: Elements of Interrupt Gate Descriptor

Element	Description
Offset	32-bit **offset** of the interrupt service routine within the target code segment.

Protected Mode Software Architecture

Table 12-5: Elements of Interrupt Gate Descriptor (Continued)

Element	Description
Code segment selector	The 16-bit **segment selector** identifies the code segment descriptor (in either the GDT or LDT) that describes the code segment containing the interrupt service routine.
X bit	The **X bit** defines this as a 16- (X = 0) or 32-bit (X = 1) interrupt gate descriptor.
S bit	The **System bit** must be set to zero, indicating that this descriptor defines a special system segment.
Byte 5[2:0]	In combination with S = 0, 110b indicates that this is an interrupt gate descriptor. The X bit further defines this as a 16- or 32-bit interrupt gate descriptor. The format shown in Figure 12-4 on page 206 is that of a 32-bit descriptor. Bytes 6 and 7 are reserved in a 16-bit (i.e., a 286) interrupt gate descriptor.
DPL	The CPL of the currently-executing program must meet or beat the gate's **DPL** (descriptor privilege level) and must reside at a lower privilege level than the target code segment.
P bit	The **segment Present bit** must be set to one or a segment not present exception is generated.

Actions Taken when Interrupt Selects Interrupt Gate

When either a hardware interrupt occurs or a software interrupt instruction is executed and an IDT entry containing an interrupt gate is selected, the following sequence of events takes place:

1. The processor reads the interrupt vector supplied either by the 8259A interrupt controller (if a hardware interrupt) or as an operand of the software interrupt instruction.
2. The processor multiplies the vector by eight to create the offset into the IDT. If the offset exceeds the limits of the IDT specified in the IDTR, a general protection exception results.
3. The processor reads the eight byte descriptor from the respective IDT entry.
4. The processor compares the gate's DPL to the currently-executing program's CPL. The CPL must be equal to or less privileged than the DPL of the interrupt gate descriptor.
5. To obtain the start address and length of the code segment that contains the

interrupt or exception handler, the processor reads the eight byte descriptor from the table entry (in either the LDT or the GDT) indicated by the code segment selector field of the interrupt gate descriptor.

6. The processor performs the second part of the privilege check. The target code segment's DPL must indicate that the destination code segment is more privileged or the same privilege as that of the CPL of the interrupted program.

7. The jump to the interrupt service routine is permitted if both privilege level tests were passed. The contents of the EFlags, CS and EIP registers are pushed onto the stack to save a pointer to the interrupted program.

8. The processor clears EFlags[IF]. This blocks recognition of hardware-initiated, maskable interrupts requests. In addition, the processor clears EFlags[TF]. This disables a debugger's ability to single-step through an interrupt service routine (so single-step interrupts will not interfere with the timeliness of interrupt servicing).

9. The processor moves the start address of the target code segment into the invisible part of the code segment cache register. It moves the offset of the interrupt service routine into the EIP register.

10. The processor fetches its next instruction from the address pointed to by CS:EIP—the first instruction of the target interrupt service routine.

11. The body of the interrupt service routine is executed to service the request.

12. If this is a hardware interrupt service routine, an end-of-interrupt (EOI) command is issued to the 8259A interrupt controller by the programmer. If servicing an interrupt request in the range for IRQ8 through IRQ15, an EOI must be issued to both the master and the slave interrupt controllers.

13. The IRET instruction is executed at the end of the routine, causing the original values of the CS, EIP and EFlags registers to be reloaded from the stack.

14. The interrupted program resumes at the point of interruption.

Figure 12-4: 32-bit Interrupt Gate Descriptor Format

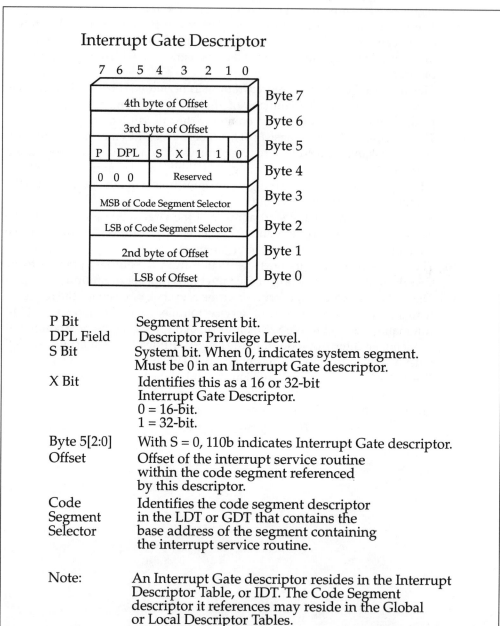

P Bit	Segment Present bit.
DPL Field	Descriptor Privilege Level.
S Bit	System bit. When 0, indicates system segment. Must be 0 in an Interrupt Gate descriptor.
X Bit	Identifies this as a 16 or 32-bit Interrupt Gate Descriptor. 0 = 16-bit. 1 = 32-bit.
Byte 5[2:0]	With S = 0, 110b indicates Interrupt Gate descriptor.
Offset	Offset of the interrupt service routine within the code segment referenced by this descriptor.
Code Segment Selector	Identifies the code segment descriptor in the LDT or GDT that contains the base address of the segment containing the interrupt service routine.
Note:	An Interrupt Gate descriptor resides in the Interrupt Descriptor Table, or IDT. The Code Segment descriptor it references may reside in the Global or Local Descriptor Tables.

Trap Gates

The difference between an interrupt gate and a trap gate is the treatment of EFLags[IF]:

- When an interrupt or exception selects an IDT entry containing an **interrupt gate, EFlags[IF] is cleared** after EFlags is pushed onto the stack. This prevents the interrupt/exception handler from being interrupted by a maskable interrupt.
- When an interrupt or exception selects an IDT entry containing a **trap gate, EFlags[IF] is not cleared** after EFlags is pushed onto the stack. If EFlags[IF] was set when the interrupt or exception is detected, the interrupt/exception handler will continue to recognize maskable interrupts.

The trap gate format is illustrated in Figure 12-5 on page 208.

Figure 12-5: Trap Gate Format

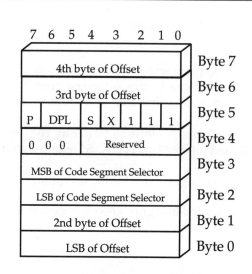

P Bit	Segment Present bit.
DPL Field	Descriptor Privilege Level.
S Bit	System bit. When 0, indicates system segment. Must be 0 in a Trap Gate descriptor.
X Bit	Identifies this as a 16 or 32-bit Trap Gate Descriptor. 0 = 16-bit. 1 = 32-bit.
Byte 5[2:0]	With S = 0, 111b indicates Trap Gate descriptor.
Offset	Offset of the interrupt service routine within the code segment referenced by this descriptor.
Code Segment Selector	Identifies the code segment descriptor in the LDT or GDT that contains the base address of the segment containing the interrupt service routine.
Note:	A Trap Gate descriptor resides in the Interrupt Descriptor Table, or IDT. The Code Segment descriptor it references may reside in the Global or Local Descriptor Tables.

Using Procedure as Interrupt/Exception Handler

When an interrupt or exception selects an IDT entry that contains an interrupt or a trap gate descriptor, the interrupt/exception handler pointed to by the descriptor is called as if a CALL instruction had been used. This section defines the processor actions taken in calling the handler and in returning to the interrupted program.

State Save

Before jumping to the interrupt/exception handler, the processor saves state information on the stack. At a minimum, this state information consists of the return address (in the form of the CS:EIP contents) and the processor's operational status (contents of EFlags register). Other factors include whether the handler resides at a higher privilege level than the interrupted program and whether or not the exception pushes an error code (see "Exception Error Codes" on page 215) onto the stack. The four possible cases are listed in Table 12-6 on page 209.

Table 12-6: Interrupt/Exception Handler State Save Cases

Case	Description
Same privilege level without error code	The only items pushed onto the stack are the EFlags, CS and EIP register contents (see Figure 12-6 on page 210). The target handler resides at the same privilege level as the interrupted program, so the interrupted program's stack contents aren't copied to the handler's stack (i.e., the current stack is used). In this case, the interrupt/exception does not supply an error code to the handler.
Privilege level switch without error code	The items pushed onto the stack are SS, ESP, EFlags, CS and EIP. The interrupt handler resides at a higher privilege level than the interrupted program (DPL < CPL), so the processor uses the stack for the handler's privilege level (rather than the interrupted program's stack) to save the pointer to the old stack (SS:ESP), EFlags, CS and EIP. The pointer to the new stack is obtained from the current TSS. Depending on the privilege level of the handler, it consists of either SS0:ESP0, SS1:ESP1, or SS2:ESP2. The stack switch process is described in the section entitled "Automatic Stack Switch" on page 122. Figure 12-7 on page 211 illustrates the contents of the handler's stack upon entry to the handler.

Protected Mode Software Architecture

Table 12-6: Interrupt/Exception Handler State Save Cases (Continued)

Case	Description
Same privilege level with error code	The items pushed onto the stack are the EFlags, CS and EIP register contents (see Figure 12-8 on page 211). In addition, the 32-bit, exception-specific error code is pushed onto the stack. The target handler resides at the same privilege level as the interrupted program, so there is no need to copy the interrupted program's stack contents to the handler's stack (i.e., the current stack is used). In this case, the interrupt/exception does supply an error code to the handler.
Privilege level switch with error code	The items pushed onto the stack are SS, ESP, EFlags, CS and EIP. In addition, the 32-bit, exception-specific error code is pushed onto the stack. The interrupt handler resides at a higher privilege level than the interrupted program (DPL < CPL), so the processor must use the stack for the handler's privilege level (rather than the interrupted program's stack) to save the pointer to the old stack (SS:ESP), EFlags, CS, EIP and the error code. The pointer to the new stack is obtained from the current TSS. Depending on the privilege level of the handler, it consists of either SS0:ESP0, SS1:ESP1, or SS2:ESP2. The stack switch process is described in the section entitled "Automatic Stack Switch" on page 122. Figure 12-9 on page 211 illustrates the contents of the handler's stack upon entry to the handler.

Figure 12-6: Same Privilege Level and No Error Code

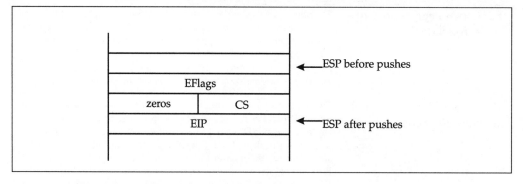

Figure 12-7: Privilege Level Switch without Error Code

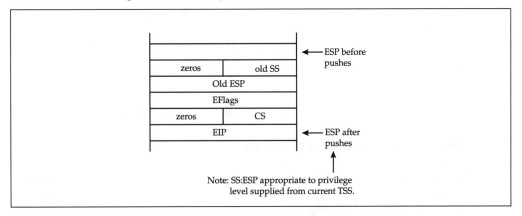

Figure 12-8: Same Privilege Level with Error Code

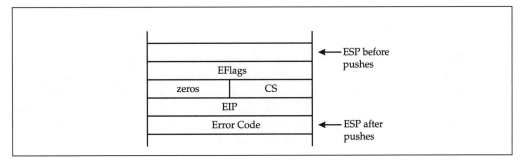

Figure 12-9: Privilege Level Switch with Error Code

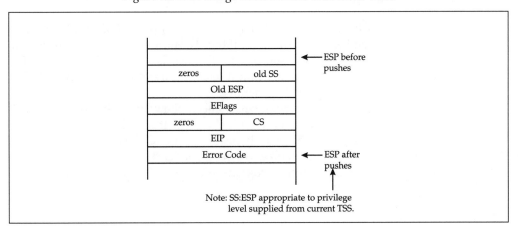

Protected Mode Software Architecture

Jump to Handler

Instruction execution is transferred to the handler. The target address is formed as follows:

- The offset supplied by the descriptor in the IDT is placed into EIP.
- The code segment selector supplied from the interrupt or trap gate descriptor is placed into CS.

The processor begins fetching and executing the handler.

Return to Interrupted Program

At the conclusion of the handler, the last instruction must be an IRET (interrupt return). When executed, it returns program execution to the interrupted program at the point of interruption. Depending on whether the interrupt/exception was a fault or a trap, execution of the interrupted program resumes by either re-executing the instruction that caused the exception (in the case of a fault), or executing the next instruction (in the case of a hardware interrupt or a trap).

Returning to Same Privilege Level. If there wasn't a privilege level change, the IRET causes the old CS, EIP and EFlags to be popped from the stack back into their respective registers. The processor then resumes execution of the interrupted program using the original CS:EIP values. It should be noted that the EFlags[IOPL] register field is only restored if the CPL is zero, and the IF bit is only changed if the CPL meets or beats the IOPL.

Returning to Different Privilege Level. If there was a privilege level change, the IRET causes the processor to take the following actions:

1. Before restoring the original contents of the CS, EIP, SS, ESP and EFlags registers from the handler's stack, an integrity check is performed on the values to ensure they make sense (e.g., CS selects valid code segment, EIP wouldn't exceed code segment limit, etc.). If any of the integrity tests fail, the appropriate exception is generated.
2. Assuming that they pass the integrity check, the values are copied into their respective registers from the handler's stack. It should be noted that the EFlags[IOPL] register field is only restored if the CPL is zero, and the IF bit is only changed if the CPL meets or beats the IOPL.
3. Execution of the interrupted program resumes.

Chapter 12: Interrupt Sources and Handling

Using Task as Interrupt/Exception Handler

The OS programmer may wish to use a separate task (rather than a handler within the same task) to service an interrupt or exception. This is accomplished by supplying a task gate in the IDT entry that corresponds to the interrupt or exception. The task gate takes the form illustrated in Figure 12-10 on page 214. When the interrupt or exception event occurs, the processor indexes into the IDT and reads the descriptor. If it is a task gate descriptor, the processor executes a task switch. Task switching is discussed in detail in the chapter entitled "Mechanics of a Task Switch" on page 157.

When an interrupt causes a task switch, the processor saves the entire processor context (i.e., its register set) in the interrupted task's TSS and then switches to the interrupt (or exception) handler task by loading the register set from the handler's TSS. The EFlags[NT] (Nested Task) bit is set to one. In performing the task switch, the processor also stores the 16-bit selector for the interrupted task's TSS in the Link entry in the handler's TSS. At the conclusion of handler execution, the last instruction in the handler task is an IRET. When the IRET is executed by the processor with EFlags[NT] set, the processor reloads the TR with the TSS selector (obtained from the handler's TSS Link field) for the task that was interrupted. This causes a task switch back to the interrupted task and the reloading of EFlags with its original value turns off the NT bit.

Figure 12-10: Task Gate Format

Task Gate Descriptor Format

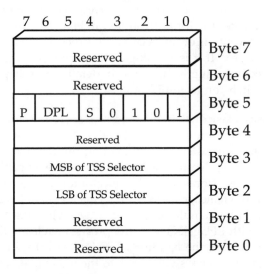

```
    7  6  5  4  3  2  1  0
   ┌──────────────────────────┐
   │        Reserved          │  Byte 7
   ├──────────────────────────┤
   │        Reserved          │  Byte 6
   ├──┬─────┬──┬──┬──┬──┬──┬──┤
   │P │ DPL │ S│ 0│ 1│ 0│ 1│  Byte 5
   ├──┴─────┴──┴──┴──┴──┴──┴──┤
   │        Reserved          │  Byte 4
   ├──────────────────────────┤
   │    MSB of TSS Selector   │  Byte 3
   ├──────────────────────────┤
   │    LSB of TSS Selector   │  Byte 2
   ├──────────────────────────┤
   │        Reserved          │  Byte 1
   ├──────────────────────────┤
   │        Reserved          │  Byte 0
   └──────────────────────────┘
```

P Bit	Segment Present bit.
DPL Field	Descriptor Privilege Level.
S Bit	System bit. When 0, indicates system segment. Must be 0 in a Task Gate descriptor.
Byte 5[3:0]	With S = 0, 0101b indicates Task Gate descriptor.
TSS Selector	Identifies the TSS descriptor that holds the base address, limit and attributes of the TSS for the task being switched to.

Note: A Task Gate descriptor may reside in the Global, Local or Interrupt Descriptor Tables.

Interrupt/Exception Handling in VM86 Mode

For a discussion of interrupt and exception handling when the processor is operating in virtual 8086 mode, refer to the chapter entitled "Virtual 8086 Mode" on page 265.

Exception Error Codes

The processor pushes a 32-bit error code (if the current code segment's default operand size is 16-bits, it's a 16-bit error code) onto the stack for certain types of software exception conditions. Table 12-7 on page 215 lists the exceptions that return error codes. The format of the error code is shown in Figure 12-11 on page 216. The error code indicates the following:

- Sets the EXT bit if an event external to the program caused the error. As an example, EXT = 1 if a hardware interrupt selected a task gate pointing to an invalid TSS selector in the IDT.
- Sets the IDT bit if the error is associated with an entry in the IDT. In this case, the Selector Index field indicates the IDT entry in question.
- A zero in the IDT bit indicates that the error is associated with an entry in the LDT or GDT. The state of the TI (Table Indicator) bit then indicates whether the entry in question resides in the GDT (TI = 0), or LDT (TI = 1). The Selector Index field indicates the table entry in question.

Table 12-7: Exceptions that Return Error Codes

Exception	Vector	Is Error Code Standard Format?
Double-fault	8	No. Always 00000000h.
Invalid TSS	10	Yes.
Segment not present	11	Yes.
Stack fault	12	Yes.
GP exception	13	Yes.
Page fault	14	Special format (see Figure 12-12 on page 216).
Alignment check	17	No. Always 00000000h.

Protected Mode Software Architecture

Table 12-7: Exceptions that Return Error Codes (Continued)

Exception	Vector	Is Error Code Standard Format?
Machine check	18	Processor model-dependent.

Figure 12-11: Error Code Format

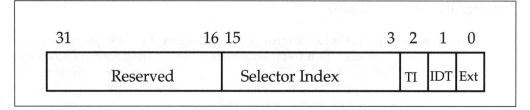

Figure 12-12: Page Fault Error Code Format

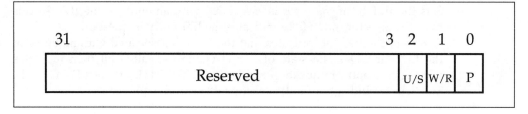

Resume Flag Prevents Multiple Debug Exceptions

When a debug instruction breakpoint exception occurs, the processors jumps to the debugger's exception handler. Because this exception is a fault, the CS:EIP return address value on the stack points to the instruction that caused the exception, rather than to the instruction that follows it. In the handler, the breakpoint is reported to the programmer. If the programmer chooses to resume the interrupted program and executes an IRET rather than an IRETD (interrupt return from debugger), execution of the interrupted program resumes at the same instruction and the same exception is generated again.

To prevent this, the exception handler should set the EFlags[RF] (resume flag) bit in the EFlags image on the stack. In addition, an IRETD rather than an IRET should be executed at the end of the exception handler. When the IRETD is executed, the processor loads the EFlags register from the stack, thus setting the

Chapter 12: Interrupt Sources and Handling

EFlags[RF] bit. Execution of IRETD with RF set causes the processor to resume execution of the interrupted program at the instruction that caused the exception, but not generate the instruction address breakpoint exception again.

Special Case—Interrupts Disabled While Updating SS:ESP

The Problem

Assume that the programmer executes the following code to switch to a different stack:

```
MOV  SS,AX          ;move new value into SS
MOV  ESP, StackTop ;move new top-of-stack offset into ESP
```

Now assume that the processor is interrupted after execution of the first move but before the second begins execution. When the processor pushes the CS, EIP and EFlags values onto the stack, it will be using the new stack segment descriptor to obtain the stack base address and the old ESP value—in other words, you've got a mess on your hands.

The Solution

To prevent this problem, x86 processors automatically inhibit recognition of interrupts and debug exceptions after either a move to SS or a pop to SS instruction until the instruction boundary following the next instruction is reached. If the LSS (load full pointer into SS) instruction is used (instead of two moves), this problem does not occur. The double-move method is often used, however.

13 Virtual Paging

The Previous Chapter

The previous chapter provided a detailed description of interrupt and exception handling in real and protected modes.

This Chapter

This chapter provides a detailed description of the processor's virtual paging mechanism. It discusses linear vs. physical addresses, the page directory, page directory entries, page tables, page table entries, page faults, the translation lookaside buffers, and Pentium paging extensions.

The Next Chapter

The next chapter describes how the x86 processor may be set up to operate as if segmentation does not exist. Memory appears to be a single linear array 4GB in size, rather than being subdivided into many segments of various sizes. Protection is implemented via the paging unit rather than using segmentation.

Pentium Pro Paging Extensions

For a detailed description of the paging enhancements implemented in the Pentium Pro processor, refer to the MindShare book entitled *Pentium Pro Processor System Architecture* (published by Addison-Wesley).

Problem—Loading Entire Task in Memory is Wasteful

Consider the following scenario:

1. A machine has 16MB of RAM memory.
2. The power-on self-test completes and the boot program reads (i.e., boots) the OS loader into memory.
3. The OS loader reads the entire OS into memory, consuming 6MB of memory. The OS is a multitasking OS, permitting the end user to start multiple programs. The OS rapidly timeslices between them, giving the appearance that all of the programs run simultaneously.
4. The user tells the OS to start a word processing program. In response, the

OS loads the entire program into memory, consuming 2.5MB of memory.

5. The user starts three more programs, each of which is loaded in its entirety into memory, consuming an additional 7MB of memory.

6. 15.5MB of memory is now in use and only .5MB remains free. The user attempts to start another program, causing the OS to respond that there is insufficient memory.

In this scenario, both the OS loader and the OS task manager manage the pool of free memory in a very inefficient fashion. The entire OS is loaded into memory even though large portions of the OS code may never be required during the current work session. Every time the user starts a program, the OS loads the entire program into memory. Once again, large portions of the application's code may never be required during the current work session. As an example, Word for Windows 6.0 implements hundreds of features, most of which are never called upon during a typical work session.

Solution—Load Part and Keep Remainder on Disk

Load on Demand

The OS loader should be designed to load only the portions of the OS:

- that are necessary to initiate applications programs
- that are used very frequently and must always reside in memory in order to yield good performance.

The remainder of the OS should be kept on disk until it is required.

Likewise, the OS applications program loader should be designed to load only enough of an applications program into memory to get it started. Additional portions of the applications program should only be read into memory upon demand.

Track Usage

After a portion of the OS or an application program has been loaded into memory, the OS should track how long it has been since the information was last used. If it hasn't been used for quite a while, the OS should eliminate it from memory. In the event that some of the information has been updated since it was read from disk, the OS should swap it back to disk before eliminating it from memory.

Capabilities Required

In order to implement the capabilities just discussed, the OS must have the following capabilities:

- Whenever an instruction (or the instruction prefetcher) initiates a memory code or data access, the processor must in some manner quickly **determine if** the target **information** is already **in memory (and, if so, where). If it isn't** in memory, the processor must be able to **quickly determine** the **mass storage address** of the required information so it can load it into memory to be accessed by the current program.
- The processor must have some way of **determining if** the block of **information has been accessed** since it was placed in memory, **and**, if so, **was it changed** (i.e., written to).
- Although not mentioned in the preceding discussion, it would also be nice if the processor could determine:
    - **if** the currently-executing program is permitted access to the information (i.e., it has **sufficient privilege**).
    - **if** the currently-executing program is **permitted to write** to the targeted area.

Problem—Running Two (or more) DOS Programs

Applications programs designed for the DOS environment are written using 8088 code and only access information in the first 1MB of memory space (i.e., from 00000000h through 000FFFFFh). Furthermore, each DOS application believes itself to be the only program executing and, as long as it doesn't mangle the OS (which also resides in the first 1MB area), it can access any location within the first 1MB of memory space.

If a multitasking OS were to load two or more DOS applications programs into the first 1MB of memory, the second one loaded would almost certainly overwrite a portion of the first one (thereby rendering it useless). Even if they occupied mutually-exclusive areas of the first 1MB (highly unlikely), each of the programs would feel free to build (i.e., write) data structures in the memory areas occupied by the other program(s).

In a word, anarchy!

Protected Mode Software Architecture

Solution—Redirect Memory Accesses to Separate Memory Areas

The OS can multitask multiple DOS applications by taking the following precautions:

- Load **each DOS** application **program in**to a **separate 1MB area** of memory.
- When a DOS program is executing, it only generates memory accesses within the first 1MB of memory. Since it actually resides in a different 1MB area other than the first MB, the processor must automatically **redirect** each of **its memory accesses to** the **1MB area** that **it really resides in**.

Global Solution—Map Linear Address to Disk Address or to Different Physical Memory Address

Both of the problems discussed earlier are solved by treating the memory address generated for each code or data access as a logical, or intermediate, address. The processor then **translates** (or redirects) the **address into** one of the following:

- a **physical disk address**. The OS programmer then reads the block of information from the specified disk device into an available block of RAM memory. The original memory access is then reattempted and the processor redirects the access to the block of memory that contains the information.
- a **physical memory address**. The processor substitutes the actual physical location of the information for the logical address submitted by the program.

In both cases, the program that initiated the memory read or write access is unaware of the fact that the memory address it generated has been redirected to somewhere else. All it knows is that it is permitted to access the desired item of information.

Paging Unit Is the Translator

The processor's paging unit makes both forms of address translation possible. It intercepts the logical memory address (referred to as the linear address by Intel) generated by the currently-executing program and converts it to a different memory address.

Linear Memory Space Divided into 1M 4KB Pages

In protected mode, the currently-executing program can generate memory accesses anywhere within the 4GB range from 00000000h through FFFFFFFFh. When the processor's paging unit is enabled, the memory address generated by the currently-executing program is called the linear address. From the paging unit's point-of-view, the 4GB linear space available to the currently-executing program is subdivided into 4KB (4096d locations) pages. When the page size is divided into the overall size of linear space, 4GB, there are 1M (2^{20}) linear pages. By definition, then, any memory access targets a location within one of these linear pages.

- The upper 20 bits of the linear address identify the linear page (1-of-1M).
- The lower 12 bits identify the exact target location (1-of-4096d) within the page.

Physical Memory Space Divided into 1M 4KB Pages

The processor's external address bus (on the 386, 486, and Pentium processors) consists of 32 address signal lines. This permits the processor to address any location in external memory from 00000000h through FFFFFFFFh, a 4GB range. This is referred to as physical memory space. As with linear memory space, the processor's paging unit views the 4GB physical memory space as consisting of 1M 4KB pages.

Mass Storage Space Divided into 4KB Pages

An OS that implements paging considers all of the information on mass storage devices as being divided into 4KB pages of information. As an example, a 1GB hard drive can be viewed as 256K pages of information.

Paging Unit Uses Directory to Remap Address

The upper 20 bits of the linear memory address identify the target linear page. Using the linear page address (1-of-1M pages), the paging unit must perform a lookup in a directory to determine the current location of the physical page (in physical memory or on a mass storage device). Since the linear page can be mapped to any of 1M physical memory pages, it would appear that the processor must maintain a directory with 1M entries. Each entry maps one linear page to its corresponding page in physical memory or to a page on a mass storage device. It should be fairly obvious that a table of this size cannot be kept in the processor itself. It is kept in memory.

Three Possible Page Lookup Methods

When a 32-bit linear memory address is submitted to the paging unit, the paging unit must somehow scan the directory in memory to determine where the page of information currently resides in physical memory or on a mass storage device. The sections that follow describe three possible methods that the processor's paging unit could perform the directory table scan.

First Method: Sequential Scan through Large Table

Using this method, the paging unit starts at the first directory entry and compares the target linear address to every entry looking for a match. If the last entry is reached without a match, the page isn't currently in memory. This method has the following characteristics:

- **each entry contains** a complete 20-bit linear page address and the corresponding 20-bit physical page address that it is mapped to. In addition, there would be a Page Present bit to indicate whether or not the page is currently in physical memory. In all, each entry is **41 bits** in length (5 bytes plus one bit of another byte).
- the entire table (containing 1M entries) is resident in memory all the time. The **table** alone **consumes approximately 5MB of memory** (just to keep track of the pages of information currently in memory).
- the amount of **time necessary** to determine that a page of information isn't currently in memory **would be colossal**.

Second Method: Index into Large Table

Use the 20-bit linear page address as a 20-bit table index to select a directory entry to compare against. Since only this specific linear page address would select this table entry, it wouldn't be necessary to store the 20-bit linear address in the entry. It's only necessary to store the physical page address it's mapped to, and to have a Page Present bit indicating whether the page currently resides in physical memory. This method has the following characteristics:

- As a positive, it's **fast**. The paging unit only has to read one entry to determine if the page is in physical memory and, if so, where.
- As another positive, **each** table **entry** only **contains 21 bits**: 20 to hold the physical page address and a Page Present bit.
- As a negative (and a large one), the **entire** 1M entry **table** has to be **memory resident** (consuming 1M x 21 bits/entry = approximately 3MB).

Third Method: Index into a Selected Small Table

The fast lookup provided by the previous method would be ideal if the table consumed considerably less memory. Consider a variation that has the following characteristics:

- From the perspective of the paging unit, a 32-bit linear address is viewed as illustrated in Figure 13-1 on page 226.
- The **4GB** of **linear** memory **space** is **divided into** 1M 4KB pages grouped into **1024d page groups** (see Figure 13-2 on page 227).
- **Each page group contains 1024d linear pages** (see Figure 13-3 on page 228).
- **Each page group has** its **own directory** consisting of 1024d entries. There can be 1024d page group directories.
- Each entry in a page group directory contains the location of the respective page (in physical memory or on disk) that the associated linear page is mapped to.
- **At a given moment** in time, only **some of the page group directories are resident in memory, while** the **remainder reside on disk.** The disk-resident page group directories are only loaded into memory on an as-needed basis.
- The paging unit's **master directory** in memory **identifies** the **page group directories currently in memory**, as well as those that are still on disk.
- **Each entry in the master directory contains** a **page group directory present bit** indicating whether the respective page group directory is present in physical memory **and**, if so, where (i.e., the **start physical memory address of the respective page group directory**).
- **Each entry in a page group directory contains** a **page present bit** indicating whether the respective page is present in physical memory **and**, if so, where (i.e., the **start physical memory address of the associated page**).

Whenever the currently-executing program must perform a memory access, the 32-bit linear address is submitted to the paging unit and the following actions are taken to remap the access to the correct physical memory page:

1. The **upper 10 bits** of the address **identifies the page group** and selects one of the 1024d master directory entries. In other words, they **select** the **page group directory** that keeps track of the physical location of each of the 1024d pages that comprise the target page group.
2. Assuming that the selected master directory entry's Present bit = 1, the selected page group directory is present in memory and its start physical address is obtained from the selected master directory entry.
3. The **middle 10 bits** of the address **identifies one of the 1024d pages within the selected page group**. It **selects the entry within the page group directory** that identifies the location of the respective 4KB page.
4. Assuming that page present = 1 in the selected page group directory entry, the target 4KB page is present in physical memory and the 20-bit start physical address of the page is obtained from the selected page group directory entry.
5. The paging unit forms the 32-bit physical memory address in the following manner:
   - The upper 20 bits (the 20-bit physical page address) is obtained from the selected entry in the selected page group directory.
   - The lower 12 bits of the linear address become the lower 12 bits of the physical memory address. This part of the linear address is never translated. It identifies the target location within the 4096d locations that comprise the 4KB page.

Figure 13-1: Paging Unit's View of 32-bit Linear Address

Figure 13-2: 4GB Linear Memory Space Divided into 1024d Page Groups

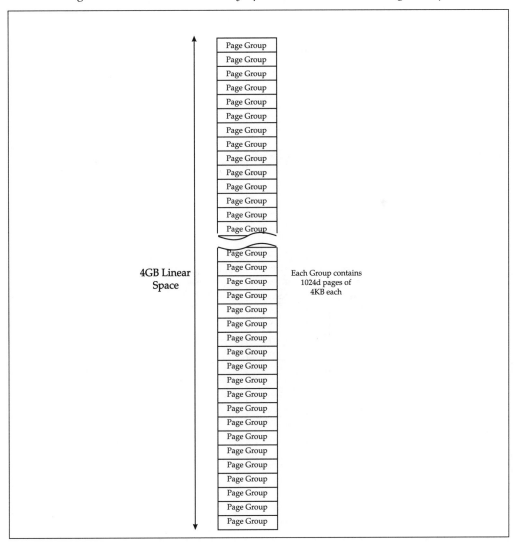

Figure 13-3: Each Page Group Consists of 1024d 4KB Pages

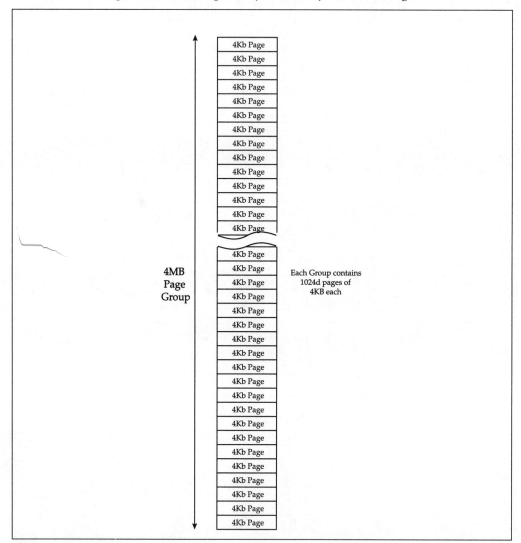

x86 Page Lookup Method

The method described in the previous section is the one implemented by post-286 processors. The pre-386 processors did not have paging capability. The sections that follow provide a detailed description of the x86 paging method.

Enabling Paging

The x86 processor's paging unit is only enabled by an OS that makes use of paging. Before enabling the paging unit, the OS programmer must create a **minimum of two tables** in memory:

- One is the **master directory, referred to as the page directory**. Each entry in the page directory points to a page group directory.
- The other is a **page group directory, referred to as a page table**. Each entry in a page table points to a physical page in memory.

Each page table can identify the physical location of up to 1024d linear pages, each containing 4KB of information (in other words, a total of 4MB of information).

After creating the tables in memory, the OS must store the physical base address of the master table, referred to as the page directory, in CR3. The upper 20 bits of the 32-bit physical base address are stored in CR3[31:11]. The lower 12 bits of the base address are assumed to be zero. The page directory must start on a 4KB address boundary. Figure 13-4 on page 229 illustrates the format of CR3.

The OS enables the paging function by setting CR0[PG] to one. Figure 13-5 on page 230 illustrates CR0. From that point forward, the paging unit intercepts all 32-bit linear memory addresses generated by the segment unit and performs its redirection function.

Figure 13-4: Control Register 3 (CR3)

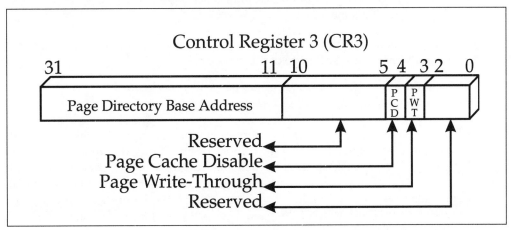

Protected Mode Software Architecture

Figure 13-5: Control Register 0 (CR0)

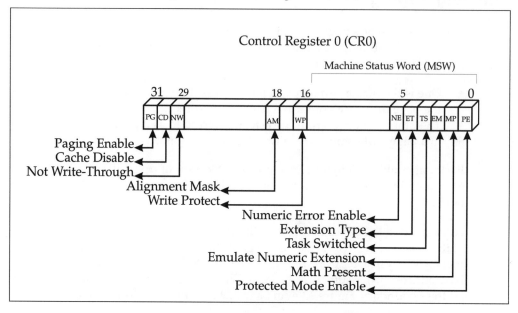

Page Directory and Page Tables

The paging unit's page directory contains 1024d 32-bit entries, each of which may contain the base address of a page table in memory. In addition, each entry contains a page table present bit that indicates if the respective page table is currently present in memory.

Each page table, in turn, contains 1024d 32-bit entries, each of which defines the physical location of a 4KB page of information:

- in physical memory (by specifying its base address), or
- its location on a mass storage device.

Each page table entry contains a page present bit to indicate whether the page of information is currently present in memory or not. If it is, the upper part of the entry contains the 20-bit, 4KB-aligned base address of the page in physical memory. If the page isn't present in memory, the upper part of the page table entry (bits [31:1]) can contain a mass storage address. Figure 13-6 on page 231 illustrates the relationship of the page directory, page tables and pages of information. CR3 identifies the base physical address of the Page Directory.

Figure 13-6: Page Directory, Page Tables and Pages

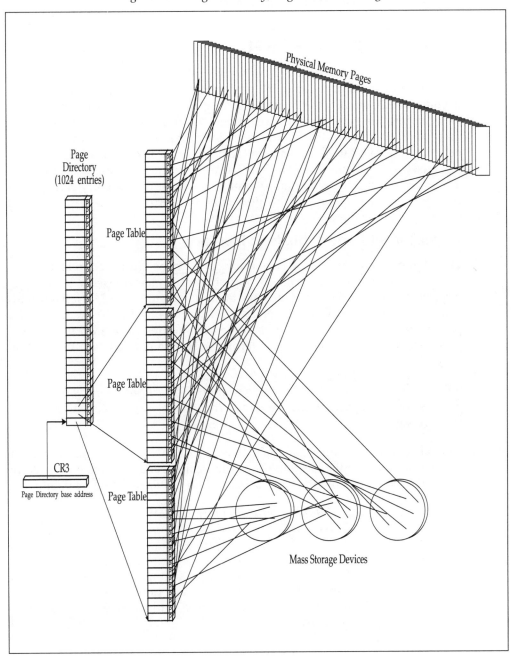

Protected Mode Software Architecture

Finding Location of Physical Page

Find the Page Table First

Refer to Figure 13-10 on page 237 during the following discussion. When the 32-bit linear address is supplied to the paging unit by the segment unit, the upper ten bits, [31:22], identify the target page group. The 10-bit group number is used to index into the page directory, selecting 1-of-1024d page group tables. Since each page directory entry is four bytes long, the paging unit multiplies the index by four to create the offset into the page directory. It then adds the resulting offset to the page directory base address (from CR3) to create the start address of the page directory entry in physical memory. The entry is read from memory and the page group table present bit (bit zero) is tested to determine if the target page group table is present in memory.

When Target Page Table Is in Memory

The paging unit interprets the page directory entry as illustrated in Figure 13-7 on page 235. Table 13-1 on page 232 describes each element of the page directory entry. $P = 1$ indicates that the page table is in memory, and $PS = 0$ indicates that the selected page directory entry contains the physical base address of a page table in bits [31:12] (rather than the base address of a 4MB page). 4MB pages are covered later in this chapter in the section entitled "4MB Pages" on page 257.

If $P = 0$, the page table is not present in memory. The actions taken by the paging unit are covered in the section entitled "When Target Page Table Isn't in Memory" on page 235.

Assuming that the proper page table has been located, the paging unit must access it to discover the location of the physical page. This topic is covered in the section entitled "Find the Page Using an Entry in Page Table" on page 238.

Table 13-1: Page Directory Entry Format

Field	Description
P bit	$P = 1$ if the **page table** is **present** in memory. If $P = 0$, the page table is on a mass storage device and bits [31:1] of the entry can be used by the OS to indicate the mass storage address.

Table 13-1: Page Directory Entry Format (Continued)

Field	Description
W bit	W = 1 if the page table is considered read/**writable**. When W = 0, the page table can be read (but cannot be written) by applications programs (executing at privilege level 3). The later versions of the 486 and all versions of the Pentium processor implement CR0[WP]. When CR0[WP] = 0, programs executing at the supervisor level (privilege levels, 0, 1, or 2) can both read and write all pages (regardless of the state of a page's W bit). When CR0[WP] = 1, pages with W = 0 can only be read by both applications and supervisor-level programs. Any attempt to write to a write-protected page when not permitted results in a GP exception.
U/S bit	U/S (**user/supervisor**) = 0 when access to the page table is restricted to programs executing at privilege levels 0, 1, or 2. When U/S = 1, the page table can be accessed by any program.
PWT bit	When **Page Write-Through (PWT) = 1**, the processor's (later versions of the 486 and all versions of the Pentium) internal and external cache controllers use a write-through policy when dealing with memory writes within the page table defined by this entry. This means that, on an internal cache hit, the new data is written into the internal cache and a memory write transaction is initiated to write the data to the external cache and system RAM memory. The processor's PWT output is asserted during the memory write bus cycle to instruct the external cache to write the data through to system RAM memory. When PWT = 0, a write-back policy is used to handle memory writes within the page of information defined by this entry. On an internal cache hit, the data is updated in the cache but isn't written to the external cache and system RAM memory. For a detailed discussion of write-back cache operation, refer to the MindShare books entitled *Pentium Processor System Architecture* and *ISA System Architecture*, both published by Addison-Wesley.

Table 13-1: Page Directory Entry Format (Continued)

Field	Description
PCD bit	When **Page Cache Disable (PCD)** = 1, the processor (later versions of the 486 and all versions of the Pentium) doesn't cache information from the page table pointed to by this entry. In addition, when the processor initiates a memory read or write transaction within this page table, it asserts its PCD output, instructing the external cache not to cache information from this address. PCD = 0 permits the processor to perform cache lookups, and, in the event of a cache miss, to cache the line from external memory. The processor's PCD output is deasserted during the cache line fill, giving the external cache permission to cache the line as well.
A bit	The processor automatically sets A (**accessed**) = 1 on any read or write access to the page table defined by this page directory entry. Once, set, the processor doesn't automatically clear this bit. This is the OS programmer's responsibility.
PS bit	PS (**page size**) = 0 indicates that the page directory entry points to a page table, while PS = 1 indicates that it points to a 4MB page. See the discussion of 4MB paging in the section entitled "4MB Pages" on page 257 for more information.
Avail	This 3-bit field is available to the OS for usage. It can be used to define additional, OS-specific page table attributes.
Page Table base address	The upper 20 bits of the selected page table's base physical memory address is stored in bits [31:12].

Figure 13-7: Page Directory Entry Format

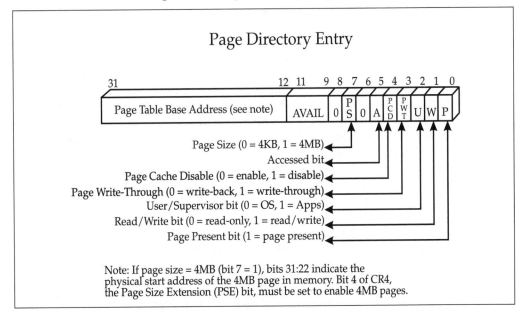

When Target Page Table Isn't in Memory

If P = 0 in the selected page directory entry, the target page table isn't currently in memory. This results in a page fault exception. The return address pushed onto the stack points to the instruction that submitted the 32-bit linear address to the paging unit. The processor latches the linear address into CR2, the Page Fault Address register (see Figure 13-8 on page 236), so that it may be examined by the OS's page fault exception handler. The following actions are taken:

1. The 32-bit linear address is stored in the Page Fault register, CR2 (see Figure 13-8 on page 236).
2. The processor generates a Page Fault exception and jumps through entry 14d (0Eh) in the IDT to the Page Fault exception handler routine.
3. The programmer reads the linear address that caused the Page Fault from CR2.
4. The upper 10 bits identifies the page table that needs to be read from disk to memory.
5. The OS may use the upper 10 bits (i.e., the page table ID) to index into the page directory and read the entry that caused the Page Fault. This entry could specify the mass storage address where the target page table resides (see Figure 13-9 on page 236).

6. A memory allocation call is made to the OS requesting the start address of an available 4KB block of physical memory.
7. A request is issued to the mass storage device driver to perform a 4KB read from the specified mass storage device into the memory buffer allocated for this purpose.
8. When the mass storage read has completed (signaled by a hardware interrupt) and the page table is resident in memory, the programmer inserts the page table base address into the page directory entry, the page table present bit is set to one, the writable bit is set to zero to protect the table from write attempts, the user/supervisor bit is set to zero to protect the table from accesses by applications programs, and the accessed bit is set to one to indicate that the table has been accessed.
9. The last instruction executed in the page fault handler is the IRET instruction. This causes the processor to pop the return address into CS:EIP from the stack and to resume execution at the same instruction that caused the page table fault.
10. The same 32-bit linear address is submitted to the paging unit for a lookup in the page directory. The same page directory entry is selected, but this time P = 1, indicating that the page table is in memory and its base address is contained in bits [31:12] of the page directory entry.

Now that the proper page table has been located in memory, the paging unit must access it to discover the location of the physical page. This topic is covered in the section entitled "Find the Page Using an Entry in Page Table" on page 238.

Figure 13-8: Page Fault Register (CR2)

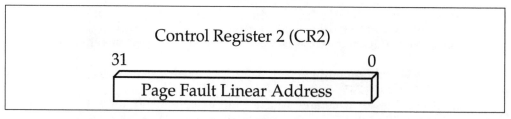

Figure 13-9: Page Directory (or Page Table) Entry when Page Table (or page) not Present in Memory

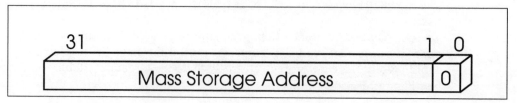

Figure 13-10: Page Table Lookup Mechanism

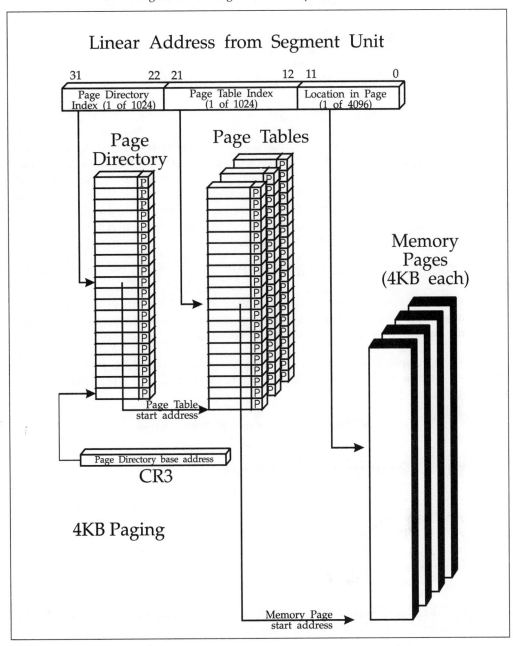

Find the Page Using an Entry in Page Table

Now that the correct page table has been located (see "Find the Page Table First" on page 232), the table must be accessed to obtain the location of the physical page in memory that the linear page is mapped to. The base address of the page table was obtained from the page directory entry (see Figure 13-7 on page 235). The middle 10 bits of the linear address identifies the page (1-of-1024d) within the page group and the corresponding entry in the page group's directory. The processor's paging unit indexes into the page table by multiplying the 10-bit page number by four (because there are four bytes per entry). The resulting offset is added to the table's base address to obtain the start physical memory address of the page table entry for the target page. Figure 13-11 on page 240 illustrates the page table entry associated with a page. The paging unit checks the P bit (page present) to determine if the physical page is currently in memory. The two sections that follow describe the actions taken when the page is in memory versus when it's not in memory.

When Target Page Is in Memory

When P = 1, the target physical page is in memory. It starts at the 4KB-aligned base address indicated in the entry's base address field. The paging unit creates the exact 32-bit address of the physical location in the page as follows:

- the upper 20 bits are obtained from the entry's base address field
- the lower 12 bits are supplied directly by the lower 12 bits of the 32-bit linear address

This 32-bit address is submitted to the processor's code or data cache for a lookup.

When Target Page Isn't in Memory

If P = 0 in the selected page table entry, the target page isn't currently in memory. This results in a page fault exception. The return address pushed onto the stack points to the instruction that submitted the 32-bit linear address to the paging unit. The processor latches the linear address into CR2, the Page Fault Address register (see Figure 13-8 on page 236), so that it may be examined by the OS's page fault exception handler. The following actions are taken:

1. The 32-bit linear address is stored in the Page Fault register, CR2 (see Figure 13-8 on page 236).
2. The processor generates a Page Fault exception and jumps through entry

14d (0Eh) in the IDT to the Page Fault exception handler routine.

3. The programmer reads the linear address that caused the Page Fault from CR2.

4. The upper 10 bits identifies the page group table and its respective entry in the page directory.

5. The programmer reads the indicated entry from the page directory and checks the P bit to determine if the page group table is in memory.

6. In this example the table is in memory (i.e., P = 1) and the programmer uses the middle 10-bit of the linear address in CR2 to select the entry in the selected page table.

7. The programmer reads the indicated entry from the selected page table and determines if the page is in memory (i.e., P = 1). In this case, P = 0, indicating that the page is not in memory.

8. Bits [31:1] of the entry in the selected page table could specify the mass storage address where the target page resides (see Figure 13-9 on page 236).

9. A memory allocation call is made to the OS requesting the start address of an available 4KB block of physical memory.

10. A request is issued to the mass storage device driver to perform a 4KB read from the specified mass storage device into the memory buffer allocated for this purpose.

11. When the mass storage read has completed (signaled by a hardware interrupt) and the page is resident in memory, the programmer inserts the page base address into the entry in the page table, the page present bit is set to one, and the accessed bit is set to one to indicate that the page has been accessed.

12. The last instruction executed in the page fault handler is the IRET instruction. This causes the processor to pop the return address into CS:EIP from the stack and to resume execution at the same instruction that cause the page fault.

13. The same 32-bit linear address is submitted to the paging unit for a lookup in the page directory. The same page directory entry and page table entry are selected, but this time P = 1 in both of them, indicating that the page is in memory and its base address is contained in bits [31:12] of the page table entry.

The page starts at the 4KB-aligned base address indicated in the entry's base address field. The paging unit creates the exact 32-bit address of the physical location in the page as follows:

- the upper 20 bits are obtained from the entry's base address field
- the lower 12 bits are supplied directly by the lower 12 bits of the 32-bit linear address

Protected Mode Software Architecture

This 32-bit address is submitted to the processor's code or data cache for a lookup.

Figure 13-11: Page Table Entry Format

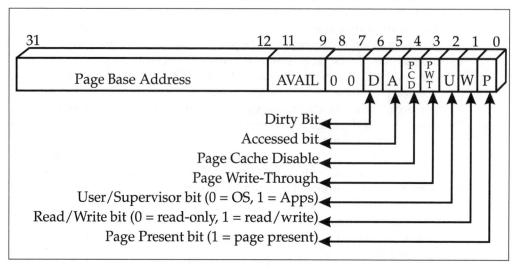

Checking Page Access Permission

There is no performance penalty incurred in order to perform the page privilege and access rights checks. The paging unit performs these checks in parallel with address translation. The two sections that follow describe the privilege level and access rights checks.

The Privilege Check

Segment Privilege Check Takes Precedence Over Page Check

The processor always evaluates segment-level protection before performing the page-level protection check. As an example, assume that a segment (code or data) has been defined as 64KB in length and starts on a page boundary (i.e., an address divisible by 4KB). Also assume that the DPL of the segment descriptor is set to three. This means that the segment may be accessed by a program with a CPL (current privilege level) of 0, 1, 2, or 3 (in other words it can be accessed by any program).

The segment encompasses 16 pages (16 * 4KB = 64KB). There is a separate page table entry for each page within the segment, each with a U/S bit (see Figure 13-11 on page 240) defining the privilege level necessary to access the page. In this example, some of the page table entries have U/S = 0, while other have U/S = 1. The CPL of the current program must have a privilege level of 0, 1, or 2 to access a supervisor page (U/S = 0), while any program can access a page with U/S = 1 (user access permitted).

When a code or data memory access is attempted, the processor first checks for sufficient privilege at the segment level before checking for sufficient privilege level to access the target page within the segment. If the currently-executing program doesn't have sufficient segment-level privilege, the page-level privilege check isn't performed and the access isn't permitted to proceed (i.e., it causes a GP exception). If, on the other hand, the segment privilege check passes, the page-level check is then performed. If it passes, the access is performed, otherwise it results in a page fault exception.

U/S Bit in Page Directory and Page Table Entries Checked

Both the page directory entry and the page table entry have a U/S bit. The page-level protection **check is performed based on the more restrictive of the two U/S bit settings**. The U/S bit in the page directory entry defines the privilege level necessary to access any page within the page group, while a page table entry's U/S bit setting defines the privilege level necessary to access any location within a specific page in a group. Table 13-2 on page 241 illustrates the affect of the four possible U/S bit combinations.

Table 13-2: Effect of U/S Bit Settings

Page Directory Entry U/S	Page Table Entry U/S	Page can be accessed by
0	0	Supervisor program.
0	1	Supervisor program.
1	0	Any program (supervisor or user).
1	1	Any program (supervisor or user).

Protected Mode Software Architecture

Accesses with Special Privilege

Regardless of the currently-executing program's CPL, the following accesses are have an implied privilege level of 0 (i.e., they have supervisor privilege):

* Accesses to segment descriptors in the GDT, LDT, IDT descriptor tables.
* Accesses to the privilege level 0, 1, or 2 stack caused by execution of a CALL instruction, or an interrupt or exception. This occurs when the called program or interrupt/exception handler resides within a code segment with a DPL of 0, 1, or 2.

The Read/Write Check

Whether a page is restricted to read accesses or permits both reads and writes is defined by the state of the W bit in both the page directory and page table entry, as well as by the state of CR0[WP] (note that this bit was reserved on the 386 and on early 486 processors; it was first introduced in the Pentium and then migrated to later versions of the 486). As with the U/S privilege check, the **read/write check is performed based on the more restrictive of the two W bit settings.** Even if a page is marked read-only, supervisor programs (i.e. privilege level 0, 1, or 2) have read/write access when CR0[WP] = 0. When CR0[WP] = 1, however, supervisor programs only have read access to a page marked read-only. An attempt to write to a page with read-only access results in a page fault exception.

Table 13-3: Effect of W and CR0[WP] Bit Settings

Page Directory Entry W Bit	Page Table Entry W Bit	CR0[WP]	Page accesses may be
0	0	0	Read-only by user programs. Read/write by supervisor programs.
0	1	0	Read-only by user programs. Read/write by supervisor programs.
1	0	0	Read-only by user programs. Read/write by supervisor programs.

Table 13-3: Effect of W and CR0[WP] Bit Settings (Continued)

Page Directory Entry W Bit	Page Table Entry W Bit	CR0[WP]	Page accesses may be
1	1	0	Read/write by all programs.
0	0	1	Read-only by all programs.
0	1	1	Read-only by all programs.
1	0	1	Read-only by all programs.
1	1	1	Read/write by all programs.

Page Faults

Page Fault Causes

Any one of the following events results in the generation of a page fault exception:

- Selected page directory entry's P bit = 0, indicating that the **page group's directory** is **not present** in memory.
- Selected page table entry's P bit = 0, indicating that the **target page** is **not present** in memory.
- Attempt to **write to** a **read-only page**.
- **Insufficient** page-level **privilege** to access the page table or the page.
- A **reserved bit set to one** in the page directory or page table entry.

If the page fault occurs due to page not present or page privilege access violation (privilege or write), the A and D bits are affected in the page directory entry, but not in the page table entry. The page table entry's A and D bits are only affected if the page access succeeds.

Second Page Fault while in Page Fault Handler

In the event that a second page fault occurs while handling a previous one, the processor automatically pushes the linear address (in CR2) that caused the first page fault onto the stack.

Protected Mode Software Architecture

Page Fault During Task Switch

During a task switch, the processor must access memory for the following reasons:

1. Read the GDT to obtain the TSS descriptor for the new task.
2. Read the values stored in the new task's TSS to check them for correctness.
3. Before switching to the new task, "snapshot" the processor register set in the current task's TSS.
4. Load the processor's register set with the values from the new task's TSS.
5. Resume execution using the new values.

A page fault may occur during any of these accesses. If a page fault occurs during number one or two, the exception occurs in the context of the old task. In other words, the old task's stack is used and the CS:EIP values pushed onto the stack point to the next instruction of the old task.

If the page fault occurs during number three or four, the exception occurs in the context of the new task. In other words, the new task's stack is used and the CS:EIP values pushed onto the stack point to the next instruction of the new task. If the OS permits page faults to occur during a task (i.e., the OS doesn't guarantee that the GDT and both the old and new TSSs are resident in memory), the page fault handler should be called through a task gate in the page fault's IDT entry.

Page Fault while Changing to Different Stack

The following instruction sequence is frequently used in pre-386 code to change to a new stack:

```
MOV   SS,AX          ;move stack segment pointer to SS
MOV   SP, StackTop   ;move top of stack offset to SP from memory
```

The second instruction fetches the top-of-stack value from memory and places into the SP register. There is no danger of a page fault when the second instruction is executed on a pre-386 processor because paging isn't implemented. However, a page fault could result when it is executed on a post-286 processor with paging enabled.

If a page fault were to occur at this point, the stack segment base address has been changed, but the stack pointer register still points to the top of the old stack. When the processor begins its automatic sequence to jump to the page fault exception handler, it pushes CS:EIP, and EFlags to the stack. If the page fault handler is at the same privilege level and in the same task, the register values are pushed into spurious memory locations. This can be prevented by using the LSS instruction instead of the two instruction sequence.

On the other hand, they are correctly pushed to a new stack (not the spurious one) if the page fault exception entry in the IDT contains a task gate, or if the exception handler is in the same task but at a higher privilege level.

Page Fault Error Code

In addition to latching the 32-bit linear address in CR2, a 32-bit error code is pushed onto the stack when a page fault exception occurs. Its format differs from that of error codes associated with other exceptions, however. The normal error code format is shown in Figure 12-11 on page 216, while that for a page fault is shown in Figure 13-12 on page 246. Table 13-4 on page 245 details the interpretation of the page fault error code that is pushed onto the stack.

- P = 0 when the fault occurs due to a page (or page table) not present
- P = 1 when the fault occurs due to a page protection violation.
- W/R = 0 when the access that caused the fault was a read.
- W/R = 1 when the access that caused the fault was a write.
- U/S = 0 when the program that causes the fault was executing at the supervisor privilege level (0, 1, or 2).
- U/S = 1 when the program that causes the fault was executing at the user privilege level (3).

Table 13-4: Page Fault Error Code Interpretation

P	W/R	U/S	Description
0	0	0	A program executing at supervisor privilege level (0, 1, or 2) attempted a read, resulting in a page table or page not present.
0	0	1	A program executing at user privilege level (3) attempted a read, resulting in a page table or page not present.
0	1	0	A program executing at supervisor privilege level (0, 1, or 2) attempted a write, resulting in a page table or page not present.

Table 13-4: Page Fault Error Code Interpretation (Continued)

P	W/R	U/S	Description
0	1	1	A program executing at user privilege level (3) attempted a write, resulting in a page table or page not present.
1	0	0	A program executing at supervisor privilege level (0, 1, or 2) attempted a read, resulting in a page protection violation.
1	0	1	A program executing at user privilege level (3) attempted a read, resulting in a page protection violation.
1	1	0	A program executing at supervisor privilege level (0, 1, or 2) attempted a write, resulting in a page protection violation.
1	1	1	A program executing at user privilege level (3) attempted a write, resulting in a page protection violation.

Figure 13-12: Page Fault Error Code Format

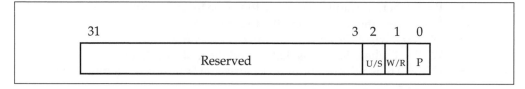

Usage of Dirty and Accessed Bits

A page of information in memory usually originates on mass storage and is copied into memory by the OS's page fault handler when the program requires access to one or more locations within the page. Whenever the processor accesses a page, it automatically sets the A (accessed) bit in the corresponding page table entry to one. On a write to any location within a page, the processor also automatically sets the D (dirty) bit. Once set, it's the programmer's responsibility to clear the bits (the processor will not clear them). A better name for the dirty bit would be the modified bit. When set, it indicates that the copy of the page in memory is no longer the same as the original page on mass storage. Of the two, the page in memory is fresh while the one on disk is stale. Note that the D bit is only implemented at the page-level (in the page table entry), not at the page table-level (in the page directory).

These bits can serve a number of purposes. Uses include:

- The OS can schedule a task to be executed on a **periodic** basis that **scans** the page table entries looking **for** any **pages that have been modified**. The page is copied to disk (to freshen the permanent copy) and the A and D bits are cleared by the programmer. This provides insurance that, in the event of a power failure, the information on disk has been updated to reflect all changes performed up until the most recent refresh.
- The OS can schedule a task to be executed on a **periodic** basis that **scans** the page tables (and the page directory) looking **for pages (or page tables) that have not been accessed in a while** (the algorithm implemented by the OS to "age" a page is OS-specific). These pages can then be eliminated from physical memory to increase the pool of free memory. The P bit is cleared to zero in the respective page table and page directory entries.
- **When** a **page fault occurs** because a page table or a page isn't in memory (P = 0), the page fault exception handler program must load the required page table or page into memory. In order to do this, the programmer must locate an unused 4KB page of physical memory to load the new page table or page into. If the free memory pool is running low, the OS programmer may have to **swap** a **page** currently in memory back **to disk to make room for** the **new page** table or page. The page directory and page tables can be scanned and the D and A bits checked to locate a page to swap out to disk. If the selected page is "clean," the programmer can clear its respective page table entry's P bit to mark it not present. The new page can then be loaded to that page in memory and its respective linear page's page table entry updated (P = 1 and the page's base address pointed to the physical page) to reflect the presence and location of the page.
- When the user indicates that the **system** is about to be **shutdown**, the OS scans the page tables and page directory and writes all modified pages to disk. Only when all modified pages have been written to disk would the user be given permission to power down the system.

Eliminating Page Location Lookup

Before the processor can access a memory location, the paging unit must perform two overhead memory reads to access the page directory and page table entries. This can have a severe effect on performance.

When a page is first accessed, the processor performs these two memory reads to obtain the page directory and page table entries. To eliminate the need to access this same page table entry for future accesses within the same page, x86 processors incorporate a relatively small, special-purpose cache that keep copies of the most-recently accessed page table entries. The size and organization of this cache can vary from processor to processor.

Protected Mode Software Architecture

386/486 TLB

The 386 and 486 processors each incorporate one cache, referred to as a translation lookaside buffer, or TLB. Figure 13-13 on page 249 illustrates the relationship of the TLB to the segment address generation logic, the paging unit, and the 486's internal cache (the 386 doesn't have an internal cache).

The 32-bit linear address created by the segment address generator is submitted to the paging unit for a lookup. The TLB is a very fast lookaside cache that sits off to the side and compares the upper 20 bits of the linear address (i.e., the target linear page number) to those stored in its entries. If there isn't a match, the paging unit (which is much slower than the TLB) is permitted to proceed with the two memory reads to obtain the page directory and page table entry. When the page table entry is obtained, two actions are taken:

1. The 32-bit physical memory address is created from the upper 20 bits of the physical page address (obtained from the page table entry) and the lower 12 bits of the linear address. The 32-bit physical memory address is submitted to the processor's cache for a lookup.
2. The paging unit makes an entry in the TLB consisting of approximately 45 bits (Intel doesn't define the content of a TLB entry, but it makes sense that it contain the elements listed below):
    *   A bit that indicates whether this TLB entry contains valid page mapping information.
    *   The upper 20 bits of the linear address. This is the linear page number.
    *   The upper 20 bits of the physical page address (i.e., the physical page number) that the linear page is mapped to.
    *   The PCD bit, indicating whether the page is defined as cacheable or not.
    *   The PWT bit, indicating whether the processor should use a write-through or a write-back policy in handling memory writes within the page.
    *   The U/S bit, defining the privilege level necessary to access the page.
    *   The W/R bit, defining the page as read-only or read/write.

Any subsequent accesses within the same linear page will result in a TLB hit. In the case of a TLB hit, the TLB inhibits the paging unit from generating the two memory reads. Instead, the TLB supplies the upper 20 bits of the physical page address, while the lower 12 bits are supplied directly by the lower 12 bits of the linear address. The 32-bit physical memory address thus created is submitted to the processor's internal cache for a lookup.

Figure 13-13: 486 TLB

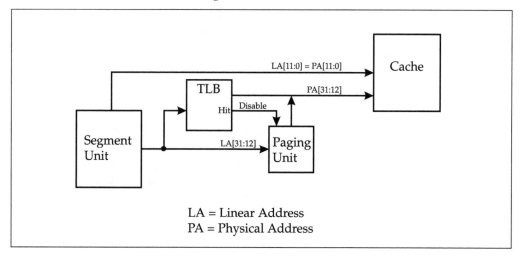

Pentium TLBs

The 386 and 486 processors used a single, unified TLB cache to store the physical start addresses and attributes of the most-recently accessed code and data pages. The Pentium processor implements separate code and data TLB caches. The discussion that follows assumes that the processor is a Pentium.

Memory accesses generated by the instruction prefetcher access code pages, while those generated by the integer and floating-point execution units access data pages. The actual code and data from the pages are cached in the processor's code and data caches, while the page table entries that define the start address and attributes of the most-recently accessed pages are cached in the data and code TLBs, respectively.

Figure 13-14 on page 252 illustrates the relationship of the Pentium's segment unit, paging unit, code TLB, code cache, data TLB and data cache. Code and data lookups are performed in the following manner.

Code Page Access

The segment address generator forms a 32-bit linear memory address for the instruction prefetcher by adding the contents of EIP to the code segment base address supplied by the selected code segment descriptor (in the GDT or LDT). The linear address is submitted to the paging unit and the code TLB simultaneously. Remember, however, that the TLB can be accessed much faster than the page directory and page table.

1. The upper 20 bits (the 10-bit page table and 10-bit page IDs) of the linear address is compared to a set of entries in the code TLB for a match.

2. Assuming that there is a miss on the code TLB, the paging unit performs a memory read to obtain the page directory entry and another to obtain the page table entry.

3. If either entry has P = 0, a Page Fault exception results and the page table or page must be obtained from disk.

4. Assuming neither memory access causes a Page Fault, the 32-bit physical addresses of the page directory entry and the page table entry are sequentially submitted to the data cache for a lookup (because page directory and page table entries are cached in the data cache as well as in the TLBs).

5. If both the page directory and page table entries are found in the data cache, the page start address and attributes are obtained very quickly. If either (or both) aren't found in the data cache, the processor must obtain the entry (or entries) from external memory. This causes a degradation in performance while the processor performs the bus transaction(s) necessary to obtain them.

6. Once it has the page table entry (and assuming P = 1), the paging unit obtains the 20-bit physical page address from the entry and forms the 32-bit physical memory address by appending the lower 12 bits of the linear address to the 20-bit physical page address. In addition, the code TLB makes a copy of the page table entry along with the upper 20-bits of the linear address (the page table/page IDs). The page attributes (e.g., U/S, W, etc.) are also stored in the TLB entry. Future accesses within the same code page will result in hits on the code TLB, obviating the need for the page directory and page table reads.

7. The processor submits the target physical memory address to the code cache for a lookup (if the page table entry's PCD bit = 0).

8. If the access results in a code cache hit, the requested code is immediately delivered to the instruction prefetcher to place in the prefetch queue.

9. If the access results in a code cache miss, the code cache issues a cache line fill request to the processor's bus interface unit.

10. The processor starts a memory read transaction with its CACHE# output asserted (indicating it wants to read a 32 byte cache line from memory), and sets its PCD output = 0 to indicate to the external cache (if present) that the address is cacheable.

11. The external cache or the main memory transfers the line of information back to the processor and the line is placed in the code cache and is also supplied to the instruction prefetcher for placement in the prefetch queue.

If the lookup in the code TLB had resulted in a hit, steps 2 through 6 are unnecessary. This can result in dramatic performance increases. At a given instant in time, the Pentium's code TLB can hold 32 page table entries, covering 128KB of memory space (32 pages of 4KB each). As long as the processor accesses only locations within these code pages, the paging unit doesn't need to perform the two reads usually necessary to obtain the page table entry. It only needs to perform the memory access to obtain the desired code from the page.

Data Page Access

Data page accesses utilize the data TLB and the data cache. The Pentium's data TLB can hold 64 page table entries, so it can keep track of the physical location of up to 256KB of data (64 pages of 4KB each).

Pentium TLB Structure

It was stated earlier that Figure 13-14 on page 252 is a simplified view of the relationship between the segment address generator, data TLB, data cache, code TLB, code cache and paging unit. The illustration has been kept simple in order to communicate the TLB lookup process clearly. In reality, the Pentium TLBs and associated logic consists of the following elements:

- A data TLB for 4KB pages. This is a 4-way, set-associative cache with 64 entries.
- A data TLB for 4MB pages. This is also a 4-way, set-associative cache and has eight entries.
- The Pentium processor's segment address generator can output a 32-bit linear address for both instruction pipelines (for a detailed description, refer to the MindShare book entitled *Pentium Processor System Architecture*, published by Addison-Wesley) simultaneously.
- The data TLB is dual-ported and can perform a lookup for linear addresses from both pipelines simultaneously.
- The code TLB is 4-way, set-associative and has 32 entries.
- The code TLB is single-ported because it only needs to perform lookups for addresses originated by the instruction prefetcher.
- The replacement algorithm used by the TLBs is pseudo least-recently-used (LRU) and is implemented with three bits. This is the same LRU algorithm used for line replacement by the 486 processor's internal code/data cache (for a detailed description, refer to the MindShare book entitled *80486 System Architecture*, published by Addison-Wesley).

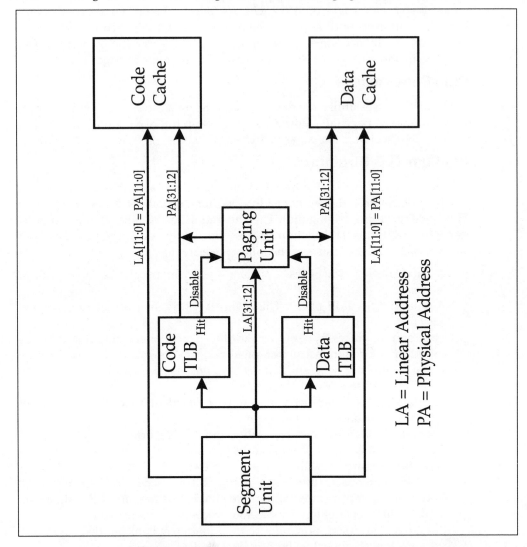

Figure 13-14: Pentium Segment Unit, TLBs, Paging Unit, and Caches

TLB Maintenance

Once a page table entry has been copied into the TLB, the paging unit no longer accesses the original entry in the page table in memory. Any access within a page with a cached TLB entry uses the mapping and protection information in the TLB rather than the entry in memory.

On the surface, it would seem that any change (i.e., memory write) that the OS programmer makes to a page table entry in memory can be detected by the TLB and that it can "snarf" a copy of the change to keep its TLB entry current. However, this is not the case. The TLB is not aware of writes performed to page table entries in the page tables in memory. Since this is the case, the OS programmer must take care to ensure that the TLBs always contain up-to-date page table entries. If this were not done, subsequent accesses within a page with a stale cached entry would use the old, stale mapping and protection information, rather than the fresh copy of the page table entry in memory. The sections that follow discuss the methods utilized by the OS programmer and the processor to ensure that the TLB doesn't use stale entries to perform address mapping and protection checks.

TLBs Cleared on Task Switch or Page Directory Change

CR3 contains the base physical address of the page directory in memory. Assume that the processor's TLBs have been caching page table entries from the page tables defined by the page directory currently pointed to be CR3. Placing a new value into CR3 identifies an entirely new set of page tables with different linear-to-physical address mapping and protection definition. By definition, this renders every page table entry currently residing in the TLBs stale. Any time a new value is loaded into CR3, the x86 processor therefore automatically clears all page table entries from the TLBs. A new value is loaded into CR3 under the following circumstances:

- **Task switch**. When a task switch occurs, the processor saves its current register set contents in the TSS of the old task and then loads its register set with the values from the new task's TSS. As a result, CR3 is loaded with a new page directory base address and all TLB entries are invalidated (eliminating all page table entries cached from the old set of page tables).
- **OS programmer loads a new value into CR3**. When a privilege level 0 program is executing, the programmer may choose to switch to a new set of mappings. This is accomplished by creating a new page directory and set of page tables and then loading CR3 with the base address of the new page directory. All TLB entries are invalidated (eliminating all page table entries cached from the old set of page tables).

Updating a Single Page Table Entry

The OS programmer may update individual page table entries using memory writes. Whenever the contents of a page table entry is altered, the programmer must explicitly instruct the TLBs to discard the affected page table entry from the TLBs. On the 486 and Pentium processors, this is accomplished by execution of the INVLPG (invalidate page) instruction. The 32-bit linear page address supplied as the instruction operand is used to perform the TLB lookup and invalidates a single page table entry.

The 386 does not implement the INVLPG instruction. When executing on a 386, the programmer must therefore load CR3 with a value when a page table entry has been changed. This causes the TLB to discard all TLB entries. From a performance standpoint, this is much less efficient than the 486 and Pentium's ability to delete a single page table entry from the TLB.

Note: The Pentium programmer's reference manual states that in most cases execution of the INVLPG instruction causes the code TLB to flush a single entry, but that, in some cases, it causes the entire code TLB to be flushed. The author has been unable to obtain an explanation of what these cases might be (and cannot think of what they might be).

Cache Issues

The OS programmer is responsible for setting up the page tables. In addition to the physical start address of the page in memory, each page table entry defines the 4KB page area as cacheable or non-cacheable. With respect to memory writes performed within the page, the respective page table entry instructs the processor's internal and external (if present) caches to utilize a write-through or a write-back policy in handling memory writes within the page.

The OS programmer must define the cacheability and write policy for three entities:

- the page directory
- each page table
- each page

The sections that follow describe the mechanisms that the programmer uses to define the cacheability and write policy for each of the three.

Page Directory Caching Policies

Some memory accesses target entries within the page directory. For each of these accesses, the processor must determine whether the contents of the location may be cached and, if the access is a write, whether to use a write-though or write-back policy with respect to the cache. The sections that follow describe how the OS programmer instructs the processor with respect to cacheability and write policy when performing accesses within the page directory.

Page Directory Cacheability

The processor must be instructed as to whether or not the locations within the page directory may be cached or not. This is accomplished with CR3[PCD] (see Figure 13-15 on page 257). CR3[PCD] = 0 permits the processor to cache entries from the page directory, while CR3[PCD] = 1 inhibits caching from the directory. The section that follows this one describes how the processor handles memory writes to the page directory when it is marked cacheable.

When the page directory is defined as cacheable (CR3[PCD] = 0), the processor performs data cache lookups for read and write accesses to the page directory. In the event of a cache miss on a read, the processor initiates a memory read transaction on its external bus and asserts its CACHE# output to request the entire 32-byte cache line that the page directory entry resides within. It also drives the state of CR3[PCD] and CR3[PWT] onto its PCD and PWT outputs to instruct an external cache (if present) regarding the cacheability of the page directory and its policy in handling a memory write (if this were a memory write). If external logic agrees that the addressed region of memory is cacheable, it asserts KEN# (cache enable) to the processor and transfers the line to the processor. The entire line is placed in the data cache and the requested page directory entry is supplied to the paging unit.

When the page directory is defined as non-cacheable (CR3[PCD] = 1), the processor bypasses the data cache for both read and write accesses within the page directory. On a read, it initiates the 4-byte (32-bit) memory read on the external bus, but does not assert its CACHE# output. This indicates to external logic that the processor does not want the entire cache line that contains the requested page directory entry. Rather, it only expects to read the requested 32-bit page directory entry. The processor also drives the state of CR3[PCD] onto its PCD output to inform the external cache (if present) that the access is not to be cached. When received from memory, the entry is routed directly to the paging unit (in other words, it is not placed in the data cache). On a write to a page directory entry, the processor does not perform a data cache lookup. Rather, it initiates a memory write transaction on its external bus (with its PCD output = 1) to update the page directory entry in memory.

Page Directory Write Policy

This section describes how the processor handles memory writes to page directory entries when the directory is marked cacheable (CR3[PCD] = 0). The manner in which the memory write is handled depends on the following factors:

- The state of CR3[PWT]. This is the page write-through bit.
- Whether the write results in a data cache hit or miss.

CR3[PWT] = 1 and Data Cache Hit. Since the write results in a hit on the data cache, the page directory entry is updated in the data cache. PWT = 1, indicating that the write data must also be written to external memory. The processor therefore initiates a memory write transaction to update the page directory entry in memory. The processor's PWT output is asserted, instructing the external cache (if present) to also write the data through to the directory in memory. If the write resulted in a hit on the external cache, its copy of the page directory entry is also updated. Using a **write-through policy** ensures that the page directory in memory is always kept up to date.

CR3[PWT] = 1 and Data Cache Miss. In the event of a data cache miss on a page directory write, the processor initiates a memory write transaction to update the page directory entry in memory. The processor's PWT output is asserted, instructing the external cache (if present) to also write the data through to the directory in memory. If the write resulted in a hit on the external cache, its copy of the page directory entry is also updated. Using a **write-through policy** ensures that the page directory in memory is always kept up to date.

CR3[PWT] = 0 and Data Cache Hit. Since the write results in a hit on the data cache, the page directory entry is updated in the data cache. PWT = 0, indicating that the write data doesn't necessarily have to be written to external memory (this is referred to as a **write-back policy**). There are three possible cases and the handling of the write is case-dependent:

- If the write **hits** on a data cache **line in** the **Shared** (i.e., S) **state**, this indicates that at least one other cache in the system has an identical copy of the line. The processor cannot just change its copy and not tell the other people that have copies. This would result in the other caches having stale copies and not knowing that they were wrong. The processor therefore initiates a memory write transaction to update the page directory entry in memory. The processor's PWT output is deasserted, instructing the external cache (if present) that it may also use a **write-back policy** in handling the write.
- If the write **hits** on a data cache **line in** the **Exclusive** (i.e., E) **state**, this indicates that no other cache in the system needs to be notified of the change. The processor's data cache is updated and the state of the cache line transitions from the E to the M (i.e., modified) state, indicating that it is no longer the same as the copy in external memory.
- If the write **hits** on a data cache **line in** the **Modified** (i.e., M) **state**, this indicates that no other cache in the system needs to be notified of the change. The processor's data cache is updated and the state of the cache line stays in the M state.

CR3[PWT] = 0 and Data Cache Miss. The processor has permission to use a write-back policy (PWT = 0) for writes to the page directory. A data cache miss results in the initiation of a memory write transaction to update the page directory entry in memory. The processor deasserts its PWT output, indicating to the external cache (if present) that it may (if capable; it may be strictly a write-through cache, however) use a **write-back policy** in handling the memory write.

Figure 13-15: CR3 Format

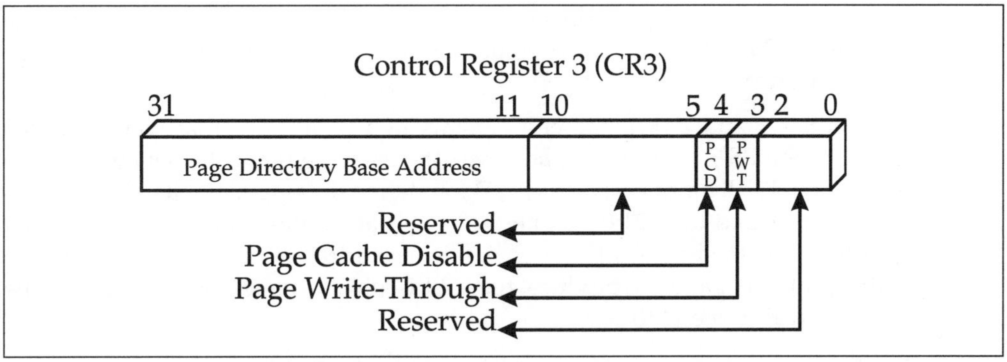

Page Table Caching Policies

Each page directory entry (with P = 1) points to a page table. The processor must be instructed regarding the cacheability of that page table and how to handle writes to entries within the page table. Like CR3, each page directory entry contains PWT and PCD bits that define the cacheability of the associated page table and how to handle memory writes to entries within the page table.

Page Caching Policies

Each page table entry (with P = 1) points to a page in memory. The processor must be instructed regarding the cacheability of that page and how to handle writes within the page. Like CR3 and each page directory entry, each page table entry contains PWT and PCD bits that define the cacheability of the associated page and how to handle memory writes to locations within the page.

4MB Pages

The paging unit implemented in the Pentium processor is a superset of the early 486's paging unit. Later versions of the 486 include the same paging-related enhancements as the Pentium processor. Intel has not publicly documented the changes, but information in publicly available documentation reveals enough to figure out most, if not all, of its new operational characteristics. The reader must note, however, that *this description is based on hopefully intelligent speculation on the author's part.*

To enable the paging extensions, the Page Size Extensions (PSE) bit in CR4 must be set to one. CR4 is illustrated in Figure 13-16 on page 258. When CR4[PSE] is set to one, the paging unit can map memory addresses to either 4KB or 4MB memory pages. When a linear address is presented to the paging unit for a lookup, the respective page directory entry is read and the state of bit seven, the Page Size (PS) bit, is checked. Figure 13-17 on page 259 illustrates the Page Directory entry.

When PS = 0 and P = 1, the entry points to a page table that identifies 4KB pages. When PS = 1 and P = 1, however, the entry defines a 4MB memory page (see Figure 13-18 on page 260). Bits [31:22] define the upper 10 bits of the page's base address and bits [21:0] define the page's attributes. The paging unit adds the offset specified in bits [21:0] of the linear address to the 4MB-aligned base address of the page to produce the 32-bit physical memory address to be accessed within the 4MB page.

As an example of its usage, a 4MB page would be handy for defining one contiguous, high-resolution display frame buffer in memory with one set of rules (i.e., read/writability, cacheability, write policy, necessary privilege level, etc.). Without the ability to define a 4MB page entry, the OS programmer would have to create and manage 256 page table entries, each with identical attributes, to define a 1MB video frame buffer with the same set of operational rules throughout. The same could be accomplished with a single 4MB page entry.

Figure 13-16: Control Register 4 (CR4)

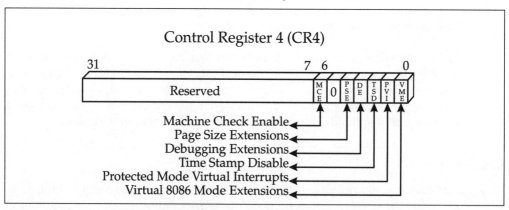

Figure 13-17: 4MB Page Directory Entry

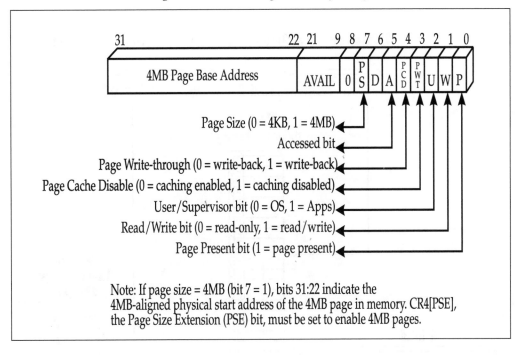

Note: If page size = 4MB (bit 7 = 1), bits 31:22 indicate the 4MB-aligned physical start address of the 4MB page in memory. CR4[PSE], the Page Size Extension (PSE) bit, must be set to enable 4MB pages.

Figure 13-18: 4MB Page

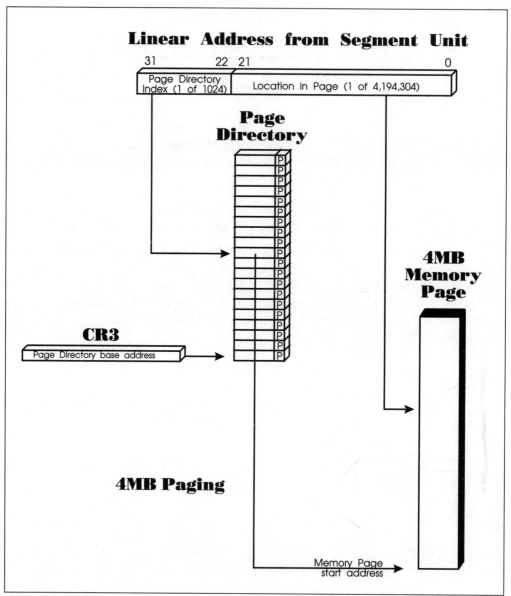

14 *The Flat Model*

The Previous Chapter

The previous chapter provided a detailed description of the processor's virtual paging mechanism. It discussed linear vs. physical addresses, the page directory, page directory entries, page tables, page table entries, page faults, the translation lookaside buffers, and Pentium paging extensions.

This Chapter

Many of today's OSs utilize the flat memory model. This chapter describes how the x86 processor may be set up to operate as if segmentation does not exist. Memory appears to be a single linear array 4GB in size, rather than being subdivided into many segments of various sizes. Protection is implemented via the paging unit rather than using segmentation.

The Next Chapter

The next chapter discusses virtual 8086, or VM86, mode. It describes:

- The problems typically experienced when running DOS programs in a multitasking environment.
- Creation of a VM86 task.
- Entering and leaving VM86 mode.
- The virtual machine monitor, or VMM.
- Memory address formation in VM86 mode.
- The use of paging to isolate DOS tasks from each other.
- Implementation of virtual video frame buffers.

Protected Mode Software Architecture

Segments Complicate Things

The use of segments complicates the programmer's life. The programmer should only have to think of what 32-bit memory location to access and not have to worry about what segment it's in.

Paging Can Do It All

If segmentation could be eliminated and paging substituted, the paging unit can provide complete protection, as well as demand mode paging. The paging unit provides the following checks on each memory access attempt:

- Privilege check using the page table entry's U/S bit.
- Read/write permission checking using the page table entry's R/W bit.

When a memory access is attempted, the paging unit deals with one of three cases:

1. The target **page** is currently **in memory** (P = 1 in the page table entry). Assuming that the currently-executing program has sufficient privilege to access the page and that it's not attempting to write to a read-only page, the access is permitted.
2. The target **page isn't in memory** (P = 0 in the page table entry). This results in a page fault exception. The page fault handler examines the 32-bit linear address and determines whether or not the target **page belongs to** the **currently-executing program**. If it does, the page is read into memory and the page table entry is updated with its location and P is set to one. The access that caused the fault is then restarted and completes successfully.
3. The target **page isn't in memory** (P = 0 in the page table entry). This results in a page fault exception. The page fault handler examines the 32-bit linear address and determines whether or not the target page belongs to the currently-executing program. If the **page doesn't belong to the program**, the OS alerts the end user that the program has a bug and shuts the offending program down.

Eliminating Segmentation

There is no way to disable the x86 processor's segmentation logic. However, if all segments are described (in the GDT) as starting at location 00000000h and are 4GB in length, segmentation is effectively eliminated.

The code segment is defined as a 32-bit code segment (D = 1), with a base address of 00000000h and a length of 4GB. Defining it as a 32-bit code segment has the following effects:

- All memory addresses generated by the EIP register are 32-bits wide, permitting access to any location in the 4GB code segment.
- All memory addresses generated by instructions for data accesses are 32-bits wide, permitting the program to access operands anywhere within the 4GB data segment.

Privilege Check

The code segment descriptor used by the OS would have its DPL set to 0, while the code segment descriptor used used by all applications programs would have its DPL set to 3. As described in the previous chapter, the CPL of the currently-executing program must first pass the segment descriptor's privilege check and then the page's privilege check.

Since an application program's code segment DPL is set to 3 (and the DPL becomes its CPL), it can successfully access any page with its U/S (user/supervisor) bit set to one, indicating user access permitted. However, if it attempts to access a page with U/S = 0, a GP exception results (because only programs with a privilege level of 0, 1, or 2 are permitted access to supervisor pages).

The code segment for the OS, however, has a DPL of 0 and the OS therefore executes at privilege level 0. It can access both user and supervisor pages.

Read/Write Check

Assuming that the currently-executing program has sufficient privilege to access a page, it is not permitted write access to a page if the page is write-protected. The OS, however, can write to a read-only page if CR0[WP] = 0, but incurs an exception if CR0[WP] = 1.

Each Task (including OS) Has Its Own TSS

When a task switch occurs, the processor automatically loads its segment registers with the values from the new task's TSS. The GDTR register is not loaded with a new value, however. This means that all tasks share the same GDT, but each can select a different set of segment descriptors within the GDT when it is started or resumed (via a task switch).

Protected Mode Software Architecture

Switch to Application Task

If the new task is an application program, the value loaded into the CS register from its TSS selects a code segment descriptor with a DPL of 3. This means the CPL of the task's entry program is 3.

A new value is also loaded into CR3, selecting the page directory used while the application task is executing. The task's page directory and its associated set of page tables describes the pages that the task is permitted to access and how it may access them (i.e., read/write or read-only). The task may be permitted to access up to 1M pages of information (4GB) some of which are contained in memory while others are on mass storage.

Switch to OS Task

If the new task is the OS, the value loaded into the CS register selects a code segment descriptor with a DPL of 0. This means the CPL of the task's entry program is 0. A new value is also loaded into CR3, selecting the page directory used while the OS task is executing. The task's page directory and its associated set of page tables describes the pages that the task is permitted to access and how it may access them (i.e., read/write or read-only; qualified by the state of CR0[WP]). The task may be permitted to access up to 1M pages of information (4GB) some of which are contained in memory while others are on mass storage.

15 *Virtual 8086 Mode*

The Previous Chapter

The previous chapter described how the x86 processor may be set up to operate as if segmentation does not exist. Memory appears to be a single linear array 4GB in size, rather than being subdivided into many segments of various sizes. Protection is implemented via the paging unit rather than using segmentation..

This Chapter

This chapter discusses virtual 8086, or VM86, mode. It describes:

- The problems typically experienced when running DOS programs in a multitasking environment.
- Creation of a VM86 task.
- Entering and leaving VM86 mode.
- The virtual machine monitor, or VMM.
- Memory address formation in VM86 mode.
- The use of paging to isolate DOS tasks from each other.
- Implementation of virtual video frame buffers.

The Next Chapter

The next chapter provides an overview of the floating-point unit.

A Special Note

The terms "DOS task" and "VM86 task" are used interchangeably in this chapter (because the vast majority of VM86 tasks are DOS tasks). It should not be construed, however, that only DOS tasks are candidates to be VM86 tasks. Any real mode task that must be executed by a multitasking OS should be set up as a VM86 task.

Protected Mode Software Architecture

DOS Application—Portrait of an Anarchist

The chapter entitled "Multitasking Problems" on page 17 discussed the many ways in which DOS programs are disruptive in a multitasking environment. They may attempt to access memory belonging to currently-suspended programs, communicate directly with IO ports, can call OS code (even routines they shouldn't be able to), disable interrupt recognition when they don't wish to be interrupted, and call BIOS routines to indirectly communicate with IO devices (thereby bypassing the OS). In addition, the task assumes that DOS is the OS it is interacting with when it may be a completely different OS. In this case, all OS calls initiated by the DOS task must be intercepted and passed to the host OS (or another program that substitutes for the DOS OS).

Solution—Set a Watchdog on the DOS Application

Intel's solution to this problem is to provide a hardware/software combination tasked with monitoring the behavior of an DOS program and intercepting all actions which may prove injurious to the overall multitasking environment. Intel implemented VM86 mode in the 386, 486 and Pentium processors for this purpose.

The OS creates a separate 32-bit TSS associated with each DOS task (it cannot be a 16-bit, 286-style TSS because the 286 TSS only has a 16-bit field for the Flag register image; it doesn't have a 32-bit EFlags register field containing the VM bit). When the OS creates the TSS for a DOS task, it sets the VM bit to one in the EFlags register image within the TSS. Whenever a task switch to a DOS task occurs, the processor copies the EFLags image from the task's TSS into the EFlags register, setting EFlags[VM] = 1. EFlags[VM] = 1 informs the processor that the current task is a DOS task and enables the processor's watchdog logic that monitors for anarchistic behavior. Note that "watchdog" is the author's term, not Intel's.

The VMM

When the processor hardware associated with VM86 mode detects that the currently-executing DOS task is attempting a potentially disruptive action, it suspends the VM86 task and jumps to the GP exception handler. As with any exception, before jumping to the exception handler, the processor first stores the current EFlags register contents on the stack. It then clears the EFlags[VM] bit, disabling VM86 mode. Upon entry to the GP exception handler, the programmer examines the VM bit in the EFlags image stored on the stack to determine if the exception was generated by a DOS task (i.e., EFlags[VM] = 1). If it was, the GP exception handler jumps to the watchdog program associated with that DOS task. If it wasn't, the body of the normal, protected mode GP exception handler is executed.

The watchdog program associated with a DOS task is referred to as the virtual machine monitor (VMM). The VMM's job is to determine the action attempted by the DOS task and to accomplish it in a manner that is not disruptive to the multitasking OS or the other suspended tasks.

Having emulated the potentially disruptive action in a benign fashion, the VMM program then resumes execution of the DOS task at the instruction after the one that caused the exception. In order to have full access to all of the processor's facilities to deal with problems, the VMM executes at privilege level 0.

When a GP exception occurs, the processor transfers control to the GP exception handler. The discussion in this chapter indicates that the GP exception handler code determines whether a VM86 task was executing when the exception occurred and that it jumps to the VMM program if this is the case. Please note that, rather than having the GP handler jump to the VMM program, the VMM program itself could serve as the GP exception handler.

Entering or Reentering VM86 Mode

Task Creation, Startup and Suspension

Create TSS

Before the multitasking OS initially starts a DOS task, it creates a 32-bit TSS for the task, setting the EFLags[VM] bit to one in the TSS's EFlags field. It also creates a TSS descriptor (in the GDT) that points to the task's TSS in memory.

Each Task Gets a Timeslice

A multitasking OS usually permits a task to execute for a predefined period of time, typically referred to as a timeslice. This is accomplished by triggering a hardware timer prior to starting (or resuming) the task. The task is then started and continues to execute until a hardware interrupt is generated by the timeslice timer (unless the task is interrupted prior to this for some other reason). This interrupt selects an IDT entry containing a task gate that points to the OS's task scheduler. The task that was executing is suspended and the new task (i.e., the OS task scheduler) is resumed.

Unlike many other processors (e.g., the PowerPC processor family), x86 processors do not incorporate a hardware "timeslice" timer to facilitate the timeslice approach to multitasking. Instead, the system designer must incorporate a hardware timer external to the processor. This timer is implemented as an IO device that can be programmed for the desired interval and enabled. The timer generates a maskable interrupt when it has expired.

Select DOS Task via Far Call or Far Jump

The task is started by executing a far jump or a far call that selects the TSS descriptor in the GDT. The offset portion of the target address is discarded.

When the processor determines that a TSS descriptor has been selected, it suspends the current task (in this case, the OS) by copying the majority of the processor's registers into the OS's TSS. It then switches to the new DOS task by loading the processor's register set from the DOS task's TSS. When the EFlags register is loaded from the TSS, EFlags[VM] is set to one, placing the processor into VM86 mode. In other words, the watchdog logic is activated just before the task starts (or resumes) execution.

Leaving VM86 Mode

The processor temporarily exits VM86 mode when an interrupt or exception occurs. The IDT entry selected by the interrupt or exception can contain one of the following descriptor types:

- **Task gate**. When the interrupt or exception selects an IDT entry that contains a task gate, a task switch occurs—the current task is suspended and another task is initiated.
- **Trap or an Interrupt gate**. A task switch does not occur when an entry containing a trap or an interrupt gate is selected. Rather, the processor executes the interrupt or exception handler pointed to by the selected IDT descriptor.

The sections that follow describe the two methods of leaving VM86 mode.

Task Switch Changes EFlags

While executing a DOS task in VM86 mode, a task switch results when an interrupt or exception selects an entry in the protected mode IDT that contains a task gate. A classic example would be the hardware interrupt generated by the timeslice timer. This interrupt typically selects an IDT entry that contains a task gate and a task switch occurs.

When the DOS task is suspended, the current contents of most of the processor's registers are saved in the DOS task's TSS. The copy of the EFlags register saved in the TSS has EFlags[VM] set to one. The processor's registers (including EFlags) are then loaded from the new task's TSS.

- If the new task is also a DOS task, the copy of EFlags read from the new task's TSS also has EFlags[VM] set to one and the processor reenters VM86 mode when the new task starts.
- If the new task is not a DOS task, the copy of EFlags read from the new task's TSS has a zero in EFlags[VM] and the processor exits VM86 mode when the new task starts.

Interrupt or Exception Clears EFlags[VM]

If an interrupt or exception occurs and selects an IDT entry containing an interrupt or trap gate, the current state of EFlags (including EFlags[VM]) is saved on the stack before the selected handler is executed. The processor then clears EFlags[VM] and VM86 mode is turned off for the duration of the handler's execution.

IRET Sets EFlags[VM]

At the end of the handler's execution, execution of the IRET instruction causes the EFlags register to be reloaded from the stack. Since the EFlags image on the stack has EFlags[VM] set to one, this automatically reenables the watchdog logic before execution of the interrupted DOS task is resumed.

Protected Mode Software Architecture

DOS Task's Memory Usage

1st MB Is DOS Memory

Each DOS task believes that it resides within and interacts with other programs residing within the first megabyte of memory space (the linear address range from 00000000h through 000FFFFFh).

Paging Provides Each DOS Task with Its Own Copy of 1st MB

If multiple DOS tasks are being run under a multitasking OS, each of them, when active, performs memory reads and writes within the first megabyte of linear memory space. The currently-executing DOS task can easily alter the contents of memory locations that are also being used by other DOS tasks that are currently suspended. This would obviously cause severe problems.

This problem can be avoided using the processor's virtual paging capability. When a task switch occurs to a DOS task, one of the registers loaded from the task's TSS is CR3. This register contains the base address of the page directory that maps linear memory addresses generated by the program to actual physical memory space. The OS sets up a separate page directory for each DOS task and initializes the CR3 image in each task's TSS with the start address of its respective page directory. The page directories for the DOS tasks are set up to direct memory accesses by each DOS task to a separate 1MB region of physical memory. In this manner, the currently-executing DOS task is prevented from corrupting data or code within another (currently-suspended) DOS task's megabyte of memory space. Whenever an DOS task generates a memory access within the first megabyte of linear memory space, the paging unit accesses the task's set of page tables and remaps the access to its own, dedicated megabyte of memory space.

Where VMM Resides

A DOS task is capable of performing memory accesses within the first MB of its linear memory address space. Some DOS tasks that were written to run on the post-8086 processors (i.e., 286 and later) can generate memory accesses within the linear memory address range from 0000000h through 0010FFEFh (for additional information, refer to "Dealing with Segment Wraparound" on page 271).

In order to ensure that the DOS task does not read or write the memory area occupied by the VMM, the VMM should be located above linear memory address 0010FFEFh.

Dealing with Segment Wraparound

8086 Processor

The 8088/8086 processors have 20 address lines. Memory addresses are formed by adding the programmer-specified offset to a segment start address. Consider the following code fragment:

```
MOV  AX, FFFF   ;set DS base address = FFFF0h
MOV  DS, AX     ;
MOV  AL, [0010h];read one byte into AL register
```

When the third instruction is executed, the processor extends the DS value by adding hex 0 on its lower end, yielding a data segment start address of FFFF0h. The offset 0010h is added to the base address, resulting in the 21-bit memory address 100000h. This is the first location of the second MB of memory space (i.e., the first location in extended memory). When the 8086/8088 processor outputs the address onto its 20-bit address bus to perform the memory read, the upper bit is stripped off. This results in a read from memory address 00000h, rather than 100000h. In other words, the processor wraps around to the bottom of the first MB of memory. With a segment base address of FFFF0h, any offset from 0010h through FFFFh causes a wraparound to locations near the bottom of memory.

Post-8086 Processors

Post-8086 processors have more than 20 address lines. When the same code fragment is executed, the processor can generate address 00100000h and access extended memory. If the offset specified by the programmer were FFFFh, the address generated would be 0010FFEFh.

Solutions

Some DOS programs depend on segment wraparound occurring while others deliberately use this method to access the extended memory directly above the first MB.

- **Wraparound Required by Task**. The currently-executing DOS task may require memory accesses to linear locations 00100000h through 0010FFEF to access the same physical memory locations as those that access linear addresses from 00000000h through 0000FFEFh. In this case, the task's page tables must be set up to map accesses within both ranges to the same area of physical memory.
- **Wraparound Not Required by Task**. The currently-executing DOS task may not want accesses to linear memory addresses 00100000h through 0010FFEFh to address the same memory as those to linear addresses 00000000h through 0000FFEFh. In this case, the task's page tables must be set up to map accesses within each range to different areas of physical memory.

Segment Register Interpretation in VM86 Mode

Whenever a new value is moved into a segment register and the processor is in protected mode (CR0[PE] = 1), the processor checks the state of EFlags[VM] to determine how to use the new value:

- When EFlags[VM] = 0, the processor is not in VM86 mode. It therefore treats the segment register value as a selector to select a descriptor from either the GDT or LDT. The selected descriptor defines the base address and size of the segment.
- When EFlags[VM] = 1, the processor is in VM86 mode. It therefore interprets the segment register value (plus a least-significant hex digit of 0h) as the segment's base address and the segment has an implicit length of 64KB.

Using Address Size Override Prefix

Although it is legal to use an address size override prefix to force an instruction to generate a 32-bit address, an exception results if the specified offset is greater than 64KB (i.e., > 0000FFFFh). A GP exception is generated if the processor is not addressing the stack, while a stack exception results if the processor is addressing the stack.

Privilege Level of VM86 Task

All VM86 tasks execute at privilege level three (in other words, they're under-privileged).

Restricting IO Accesses

The Problem

This section is a copy of the section entitled "IO Port Anarchy" on page 18 from the chapter entitled "Multitasking Problems". It is repeated here to eliminate the need to turn back to that section. It states the nature of the IO-related problem that must be dealt with in VM86 (and other) programs.

Assume that the currently executing task needs to initiate a disk access. To do this, it must program the disk controller's IO registers with the information defining the disk command type (e.g., disk read), the cylinder number, the head (or surface) number, the start sector number and the number of sectors to be transferred. This is accomplished by performing a series of OUT instructions that cause the processor to execute a series of IO write transactions to transfer the command and associated parameters to the disk controller. Now assume that the task has programmed some, but not all of, the disk controller's registers when the task's timeslice expires. The OS suspends the current task and starts or resumes another task.

The new task, having no knowledge of the suspended tasks, may decide that it also wants to issue a command to the disk controller. Assume that it does so and that the operation completes without error. Eventually, the OS suspends this task and reawakens the other task. This task doesn't even know that it was put to sleep and resumes execution at the point of suspension. In other words, it completes the series of IO writes to transfer the remainder of the request parameters to the disk controller. It has no idea that the initial parameters that it sent to the disk controller (before it was suspended) were overwritten by the other task while it was asleep. The end result will be that this task's disk operation will not occur correctly.

Generally speaking, the system's IO devices should be treated as a pool of shared resources to be managed by a central entity (the OS). Having one entity perform all communications with IO devices ensures that there will be no contention for IO devices between multiple tasks.

To accomplish this, the OS can not permit the tasks to talk directly to IO ports. In other words, any attempt to execute an IN or OUT instruction (or INS or OUTS) should cause the processor to trap (jump) to the OS. The OS then communicates with the IO device for the task.

The OS and/or processor could be configured to permit a task to access certain IO ports directly, but restrict access to other ports.

The sections that follow describe the methods used to monitor DOS task IO accesses in both IO and memory-mapped IO space.

IO-Mapped IO

IO Permission in Protected Mode

When the processor is in protected mode but is not in VM86 mode (i.e., EFlags[VM] = 0) and attempts to execute an IOPL-sensitive instruction (see page 142), the privilege check is performed in the following manner:

- If the CPL is numerically ≤ IOPL (i.e., program's privilege level is the same as or better than the IOPL), no exception is generated and the IO instruction is executed.
- If the CPL is numerically > IOPL (i.e., the program's privilege level is not as good as the IOPL) and the instruction is one of the IO instructions (IN, OUT, INS, or OUTS), the processor checks the current task's IO permission bit map (in its TSS) to determine if the current application is permitted to access the addressed IO port(s). If the bit map indicates that the task is permitted to access the indicated IO port(s), no exception is generated and the IO instruction is executed. Otherwise, a GP exception is generated.

The IO permission bit map is described in the section entitled "IO Permission Bit Map Offset Field" on page 144.

IO Permission in VM86 Mode

When the processor is in protected mode and VM86 mode (i.e., EFlags[VM] = 1) and attempts to execute an IO instruction (IN, INS, OUT, or OUTS), the privilege check is performed as follows.

- IOPL is not checked at all.
- The processor checks the current task's IO permission bit map to determine if the current application is permitted to access the addressed IO port(s). If

the bit map indicates that the task is permitted to access the indicated IO port(s), no exception is generated and the IO instruction is executed. Otherwise, a GP exception is generated.

The IO permission bit map is described in the section entitled "IO Permission Bit Map Offset Field" on page 144.

Memory-Mapped IO

The system may implement memory-mapped IO ports that are used to communicate with IO devices. Just as with IO-mapped IO ports, the OS should provide a mechanism that permits the current task to communicate directly with some memory-mapped IO ports while denying direct access to others. This can be implemented using the paging mechanism.

Segregate Ports into Two Groups of Memory Pages

The system designer can group the memory-mapped IO ports that tasks are permitted to access directly into one (or more) 4KB pages of physical memory space. Those memory-mapped IO ports that only the OS should be able to access should be grouped in one (or more) 4KB pages of linear memory space.

Set Up Task's Page Tables to Permit or Deny Access

In each task's page tables, memory-mapped IO accesses that are to be permitted should be mapped to the physical pages actually occupied by the memory-mapped IO ports. Conversely, map memory-mapped IO accesses that are to be denied to a pages that are marked not present (P = 0).

When the task attempts a memory access to a port that access is permitted to, the paging unit translates the linear memory address into the physical memory address of the port and performs the access.

When the task attempts a memory access to a restricted port, the paging unit selects a page table entry with P = 0 and a GP exception is generated. This invokes the task's VMM. The VMM can then examine the IO instruction attempted and the 32-bit linear address targeted and decide what to do (e.g., terminate the task, perform the access itself, etc.).

Handling Display Frame Buffer Updates

As discussed earlier, each DOS program "owns" a 1MB block of memory linear space that it thinks is the first megabyte of physical memory space. Many DOS programs update the display frame memory directly (rather than making a BIOS or DOS function call) by performing memory writes to the display frame buffer area (000A0000h through 000BFFFFh). The OS sets up the page tables for each VM86 task to direct all accesses within its linear address range 000A0000h through 000BFFFFh to a separate physical memory buffer (a "virtual" frame buffer) for each task.

Whenever a DOS task is resumed, the VMM can then copy the DOS program's "virtual" frame buffer into the physical frame buffer residing in physical memory in the range from 000A0000h - through - 000BFFFFh. At some point (due to timeslice exhaustion or some other interrupt), the OS suspends the VM86 task and transfers control to another task. If the next task is another VM86 task, the OS first copies the task's virtual frame buffer into the real frame buffer and then resumes the task. This ensures that the screen looks just as it did at the point when the task was suspended earlier.

IOPL-Sensitive Instructions

The Problem—Instructions with Side Effects

In addition to IO instructions, a DOS task may attempt to execute other instructions that may interfere with the multitasking OS or other tasks that are currently suspended, or that may attempt to call services provided by a nonresident OS (e.g., DOS) or the BIOS. These instructions are listed below:

- **CLI**. If the DOS task is permitted to execute the CLI instruction, the interrupt enable bit (EFlags[IF]) is turned off and the processor will not recognize subsequent external hardware interrupts received on its INTR input. Although the currently-executing DOS program may not care to be interrupted by IO devices at this point, an IO device that had been stimulated by another (currently-suspended) program at an earlier time may be signaling for service. The currently-executing program is completely unaware that this device was previously stimulated by another program and therefore thinks it can disable interrupt recognition without any ill consequences. This is obviously not the case in a multitasking OS.

- **STI**. If the DOS task is permitted to execute the STI instruction, the interrupt enable bit (EFlags[IF]) is turned on and the processor will recognize subsequent external hardware interrupts received on its INTR input. Although the currently-executing DOS program may not mind being interrupted by IO devices at this point, the OS (without the knowledge of the currently-executing program) may have disabled interrupt recognition for some reason. The currently-executing program is completely unaware of this and therefore thinks it can enable interrupt recognition without any ill consequences. This is obviously not the case in a multitasking OS.
- **PUSHF**. If the DOS task is permitted to execute the PUSHF instruction, the EFlags register is copied to the stack and the EFlag[VM] and EFlag[RF] bits are then cleared. This would disable VM86 mode, preventing the processor from continued monitoring of the VM86 task's behavior.
- **POPF**. When executed, the POPF instruction copies the EFlags image on the stack into the EFlags register. If the programmer had altered this image, a number of problems could result:
  - The VM bit could be cleared, disabling VM86 mode and preventing the processor from continued monitoring of the VM86 task's behavior.
  - The IF bit could be cleared and the processor would no longer recognize external hardware interrupts.
  - The IF bit could be set and the processor would recognize external hardware interrupts.
- **INT nn**. DOS programs call DOS or BIOS routines using the software interrupt instruction. Instead, the VMM should be invoked because DOS may not be present and/or because the DOS task cannot be permitted to ask BIOS routines to talk directly to IO ports.
- **IRET**. Like the POPF instruction, the IRET instruction copies the EFlags image on the stack into the EFlags register. If the programmer had altered this image, a number of problems could result:
  - The VM bit could be cleared, disabling VM86 mode and preventing the processor from continued monitoring of the VM86 task's behavior.
  - The IF bit could be cleared and the processor would no longer recognize external hardware interrupts.
  - The IF bit could be set and the processor would recognize external hardware interrupts.

The Solution—IOPL-Sensitive Instructions

For the reasons stated in the previous section, the x86 processor design provides a mechanism that automatically alerts the VMM if the DOS program attempts to execute one of these instructions when the EFlags[IOPL] field contains a value < 3. A GP exception results. In the GP exception handler, the programmer jumps to the VMM if the EFlags[VM] bit stored on the stack (when the exception occurred) = 1. The VMM then examines the instruction that caused the exception and substitutes an action (or series of actions) that accomplishes the same thing but in a manner that doesn't disturb the overall multitasking environment. For an example, refer to the section entitled "Attempted Execution of CLI Instruction" on page 292.

Interrupt/Exception Generation and Handling

Introduction

The topic of interrupts was covered in the chapter entitled "Interrupt Sources and Handling" on page 183. Basically, interrupts fall into two categories:

- Hardware-initiated interrupts.
- Software-initiated exceptions.

Software exceptions can be further divided into two categories:

- Software exceptions that result from an error while attempting to execute an instruction.
- Software exceptions that result from the execution of a software interrupt instruction (i.e., INT nn).

In all of these cases, the interrupt or exception type provides a one-byte index into the interrupt descriptor table (IDT), selecting an IDT entry (1-of-256d). The selected IDT entry contains the start address of the interrupt- or exception-specific handler routine that must be executed to handle the hardware or software condition.

Normally Only One IDT

Normally, there is only one IDT. When the processor is operating in real mode, the IDT starts at memory location 00000000h and contains 256, 4-byte entries. Each entry contains the physical memory start address of a handler.

When the processor is operating in protected mode, the IDT can start at any location in memory and contains up to 256, 8-byte entries. Each entry contains one of the following:

- An **interrupt gate descriptor**. Points to a protected mode handler. When an entry containing an interrupt gate descriptor is selected, the contents of EFlags is pushed onto the stack and the EFlags[IF] bit is then cleared, disabling hardware interrupt recognition while in the handler. Execution of the IRET at the end of the handler causes EFlags to be reloaded from the stack, automatically setting EFlags[IF], reenabling recognition of hardware interrupts.
- A **trap gate descriptor**. Points to a protected mode handler. When an entry containing a trap gate descriptor is selected, the contents of EFlags is pushed onto the stack, but, unlike the interrupt gate, the EFlags[IF] bit is not cleared, permitting hardware interrupt recognition while in the handler.
- A **task gate**. Points to the TSS for a separate task that acts as the handler for the condition that selected this IDT entry.

VM86 Mode—Tale of Two IDTs

A VM86 task is a real mode task that is executing under protected mode. The VM86 task has its own 1MB linear memory address space that it thinks is the first MB of memory consisting of locations 00000000h through 000FFFFFh. The **real mode IDT** exists within the task's 1MB linear space, residing in linear memory locations 00000000h through 000003FFh. Each of the 256, 4-byte entries points to a real mode interrupt or exception handler.

In addition to the real mode IDT, the OS's **protected mode IDT** is also in memory starting at the linear memory location contained in the IDTR register. The protected mode IDT contains up to 256, 8-byte entries.

Which IDT Is Used?

Although there are two IDTs when a VM86 task is executing, **interrupts or exceptions always select** an entry in the **protected mode IDT**, not the real mode IDT.

Processor Actions when Hardware Interrupt Occurs in VM86 Mode

If hardware interrupt recognition is enabled (EFlags[IF] = 1) and the processor's INTR input is asserted by the interrupt controller, the processor recognizes the hardware request upon completion of the currently-executing instruction. This discussion assumes that the system interrupt controller consists of either an 8259A programmable interrupt controller (PIC), or the Pentium's APIC is programmed for PIC-compatible mode.

Obtain Vector from Interrupt Controller

Two, back-to-back interrupt acknowledge transactions are generated. The first one tells the 8259A interrupt controller to prioritize the currently-pending interrupt requests from IO devices. The second one is a request to the interrupt controller for the interrupt vector number— an index into the interrupt descriptor table (IDT) in memory.

Use Vector to Select and Read Protected Mode IDT Entry

Using the vector to select a protected mode IDT entry, the processor reads the contents of the indicated IDT descriptor from memory. Assuming that the entry doesn't contain a task gate descriptor (which would result in a task switch), the processor checks the descriptor's DPL to see if it's set to three. If it isn't, the interrupt isn't permitted (a GP exception results).

The processor also checks to ensure that the handler's code segment has a privilege level of 0. This is accomplished by using the selector field of the trap gate or interrupt gate descriptor to obtain the code segment descriptor for the handler from the LDT or GDT. The handler's code segment DPL is then checked to ensure that the privilege level of the handler is zero. If it isn't or is defined as a conforming code segment, a GP exception is generated. In other words, it's a rule that all VM86 interrupt and exception handlers must have a privilege level of 0 (so that they have access to the full spectrum of processor resources to handle the event).

Switch to VM86 Task's Level 0 Stack

Refer to Figure 15-1 on page 281 during the following discussion. Before initiating execution of the handler pointed by the selected IDT descriptor, the processor automatically takes the following actions:

1. Temporarily saves the current SS:ESP values in an invisible processor register.
2. Reads the SS0:ESP0 fields from the VM86 task's TSS (see Figure 15-2 on page 282) and loads them into SS:ESP. SS:ESP then points to the top of the task's privilege level 0 stack.
3. Stores the current contents of ES, DS, FS, and GS on the privilege level 0 stack.

4. Stores the old SS:ESP values on the privilege level 0 stack.
5. Stores the current contents of EFlags on the privilege level 0 stack.
6. If the selected IDT entry contains an interrupt gate descriptor, the processor clears EFlags[IF] and EFlags[TF], disabling recognition of subsequent external hardware and single-step interrupts before entering the handler. The processor also clears EFlags[VM], permitting the handler to execute instructions that would cause an exception in VM86 mode.

   If the selected IDT entry contains a trap descriptor, the processor clears EFlags[TF], disabling single-step interrupts but permitting recognition of subsequent external hardware interrupts before entering the handler. The processor also clears EFlags[VM], permitting the handler to execute instructions that would cause an exception in VM86 mode.
7. Stores the current contents of CS:EIP on the privilege level 0 stack.
8. Clears ES, DS, FS, and DS registers to zero (refer to "Why Data Segment Registers Were Cleared" on page 286).

Figure 15-1: Privilege Level 0 Stack After VM86 Task Interrupted

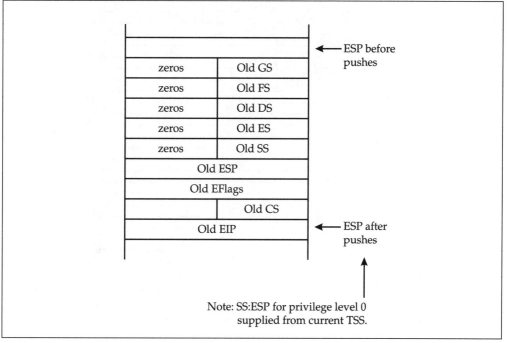

Protected Mode Software Architecture

Figure 15-2: 32-bit TSS Data Structure

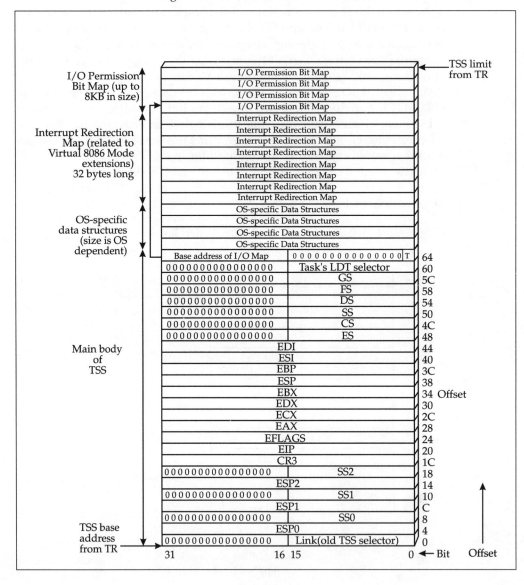

Chapter 15: Virtual 8086 Mode

Jump to Handler

The processor then loads the CS register with the segment selector field (Figure 15-3 on page 284 if it's an interrupt gate descriptor or Figure 15-4 on page 285 if it's a trap gate descriptor) from the selected entry in the IDT and loads EIP with the offset field from the IDT entry.

Using the table indicator and index fields in the CS register, the processor selects either the GDT or LDT and reads the code segment descriptor from the entry selected by the index in CS. This code segment descriptor supplies the base address of the code segment that contains the handler, while the offset field in the IDT entry supplies the offset of the handler's entry point within that code segment. The offset field is loaded into the EIP register.

The processor then resumes normal operation. In other words, it uses CS:EIP to fetch the next instruction—the first instruction of the handler.

If Handler Expects Values in Data Segment Registers

Remember that the processor automatically saved the values from the data segment registers on the privilege level 0 stack and then cleared them before entering the handler. If a particular handler expects values to be passed to it in the data segment registers, it must obtain the values from the privilege level 0 stack.

When Handler Must Know if Entered from VM86 Mode

When a handler must know whether or not it was entered from an interrupted VM86 task, it cannot test the state of EFlags[VM] to determine this (because EFlags[VM] was cleared by the processor before entering the handler). Rather, the programmer must test the state of the VM bit within the EFlags image that was pushed onto the privilege level 0 stack.

If Handler Must Return Values in Data Segment Registers

When the IRET instruction is executed at the end of the handler, the processor pops the original contents of the data segment registers (i.e., DS, ES, FS, and GS) back into those registers. Consequently, any handler that must return values in any of the data segment registers must store those values in the data segment register images stored on the privilege level 0 stack before executing the IRET.

Protected Mode Software Architecture

Figure 15-3: Interrupt Gate Descriptor Format

Interrupt Gate Descriptor

7 6 5 4 3 2 1 0	
4th byte of Offset	Byte 7
3rd byte of Offset	Byte 6
P	DPL	S	X	1	1	0	Byte 5
0 0 0	Reserved	Byte 4
MSB of Code Segment Selector	Byte 3
LSB of Code Segment Selector	Byte 2
2nd byte of Offset	Byte 1
LSB of Offset	Byte 0

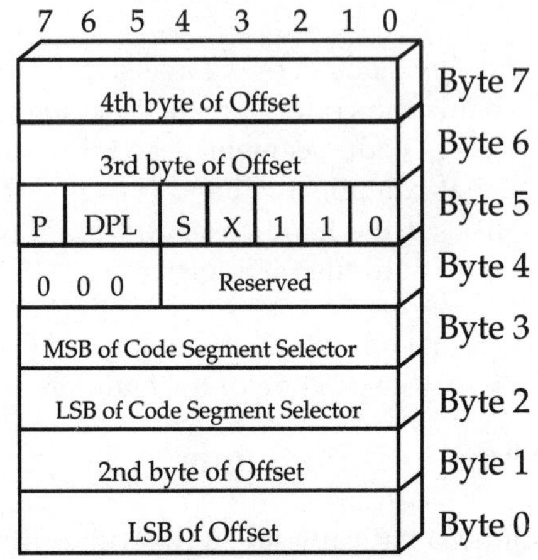

P Bit	Segment Present bit.
DPL Field	Descriptor Privilege Level.
S Bit	System bit. When 0, indicates system segment. Must be 0 in an Interrupt Gate descriptor.
X Bit	Identifies this as a 16 or 32-bit Interrupt Gate Descriptor. 0 = 16-bit. 1 = 32-bit.
Byte 5[2:0]	With S = 0, 110b indicates Interrupt Gate descriptor.
Offset	Offset of the interrupt service routine within the code segment referenced by this descriptor.
Code Segment Selector	Identifies the code segment descriptor in the LDT or GDT that contains the base address of the segment containing the interrupt service routine.
Note:	An Interrupt Gate descriptor resides in the Interrupt Descriptor Table, or IDT. The Code Segment descriptor it references may reside in the Global or Local Descriptor Tables.

Figure 15-4: Trap Gate Descriptor Format

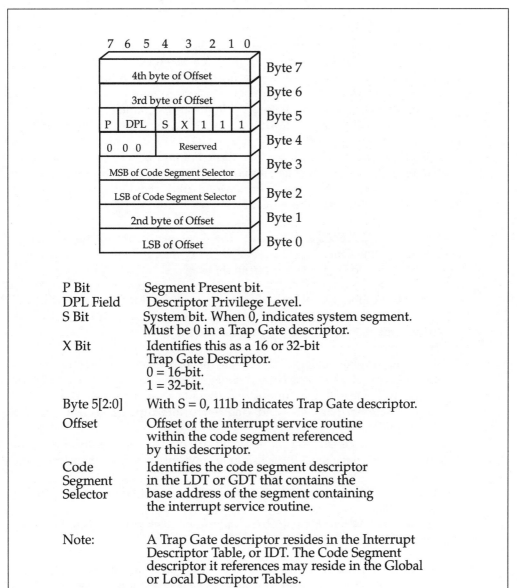

P Bit	Segment Present bit.
DPL Field	Descriptor Privilege Level.
S Bit	System bit. When 0, indicates system segment. Must be 0 in a Trap Gate descriptor.
X Bit	Identifies this as a 16 or 32-bit Trap Gate Descriptor. 0 = 16-bit. 1 = 32-bit.
Byte 5[2:0]	With S = 0, 111b indicates Trap Gate descriptor.
Offset	Offset of the interrupt service routine within the code segment referenced by this descriptor.
Code Segment Selector	Identifies the code segment descriptor in the LDT or GDT that contains the base address of the segment containing the interrupt service routine.
Note:	A Trap Gate descriptor resides in the Interrupt Descriptor Table, or IDT. The Code Segment descriptor it references may reside in the Global or Local Descriptor Tables.

Protected Mode Software Architecture

Exit Handler and Return to Interrupted VM86 Task

Why Data Segment Registers Were Cleared. Oftentimes, the code at beginning of a handler may save the contents of the data segment registers. The handler may not be specific to handling an interrupted VM86 task and it assumes that the data segment registers contain values that must be saved on entry and restored before exiting the handler. Since the interrupted task is a VM86 task, however, the data segment registers contain all zeros because the processor had cleared them. Before exiting, the programmer may attempt to restore the original values to the data segment registers. Since they are all zeros in this case, they all select entry 0 in the GDT. This is a null descriptor and selecting it will never result in an exception. If a non-zero selector were loaded back into a data segment register, it may select a segment descriptor that causes a protection exception. The processor cleared all of the data segment registers before entering the handler to prevent this possibility.

Execution of IRET Instruction. The final instruction in the handler is always an IRET instruction. When it is executed, the processor takes the following actions (refer to Figure 15-1 on page 281):

1. Pops the original CS:EIP values from the privilege level 0 stack into CS:EIP. The next instruction fetched (after the following steps have completed) will be the one that would have been executed if the VM86 task had not been interrupted.
2. Pops the original EFlags value from the privilege level 0 stack into the EFLags register. Since this copy of EFlags was made before the VM, TF and IF bits were cleared, the pop restores them to ones. This reenables recognition of external hardware and single-step interrupts, and also reenables VM86 mode.
3. Reads the VM86 task's stack base and top-of-stack pointer (SS:ESP) value from the privilege level 0 stack into an invisible processor register temporarily.
4. Reloads the data segment registers (DS, ES, FS, and GS) from the privilege level 0 stack.
5. Copies the VM86 task's stack base and top-of-stack pointer from the temporary holding register to SS:ESP.

The processor's register set has now been restored to its state at the point of interruption and the processor resumes normal operation. It uses CS:EIP to fetch the instruction that would have been executed next if the VM86 task had not been interrupted.

Processor Actions when `INT` `nn` Executed in VM86 Mode

When the `INT` `nn` instruction is executed, the processor determines if the EFlags[IOPL] field is set to a privilege level numerically < 3 (the CPL of the VM86 task) and generates a GP exception if it is (because the `INT` `nn` instruction is an IOPL-sensitive instruction). Assuming that it's not, the `INT` `nn` is executed. The nn value supplies the vector used to select an IDT table entry. The processor does not generate interrupt acknowledge transactions on its external bus to obtain the vector.

This discussion assumes that the selected IDT entry does not contain a task gate descriptor. Aside from the vector source, in all other respects the actions taken by the processor when executing an `INT` `nn` instruction are identical to those that it takes in response to a hardware interrupt (see"Processor Actions when Hardware Interrupt Occurs in VM86 Mode" on page 279).

Processor Actions when Exception Occurs in VM86 Mode

Exceptions occur for a variety of software-related problems that may be encountered while attempting to decode or execute an instruction. The various causes are discussed in the section entitled "Software-Generated Exceptions" on page 190.

The type of exception dictates the vector used to select an IDT entry. This discussion assumes that the selected IDT entry does not contain a task gate descriptor. Although the source of the vector differs, the actions taken by the processor in response to a software exception are the same as those taken in response to the execution of an `INT` `nn` instruction (see the previous section). It should be noted that, unlike hardware interrupts or `INT` `nn` instructions, some exceptions push an error code onto the stack (see Figure 15-5 on page 288).

Figure 15-5: Privilege Level 0 Stack after Exception with Error Code

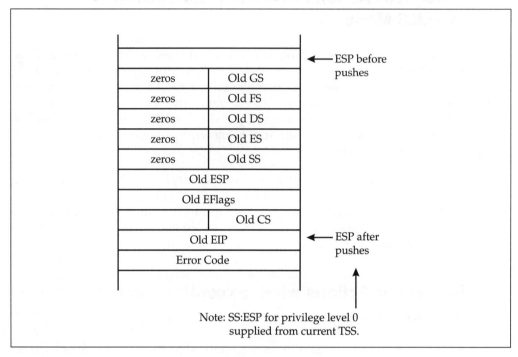

Execute Protected Mode Handler or Pass Control to VMM

As previously discussed, when an interrupt or exception occurs while a VM86 task is executing, the processor vectors to the appropriate protected mode handler and starts executing it. In the protected mode handler's entry code, the programmer must determine whether to service the interrupt or exception or to pass control to the VMM.

Upon entry to a specific protected mode handler, the **designer of a specific protected mode handler has two options**:

1. **Handle all events of this type with the protected mode handler.** In this case, the programmer doesn't care whether the event occurred during a VM86 task or a regular, protected mode task. The body of the protected mode handler is executed.

2. **Handle events** of this type that occur **during** execution of regular, **protected mode tasks by executing** the body of the **protected mode handler. If** the **interrupted task is a VM86 task**, however, **pass control to** the **VMM**.

When option 2 is used, the programmer examines the EFlags[VM] bit pushed onto the privilege level 0 stack by the processor to determine whether or not to pass control to the VMM.

*   If **VM = 0**, the **interrupted task is not** a **VM86 task**, so the body of the **protected mode handler is executed**.
*   If **VM = 1**, the **interrupted task is** a **VM86 task**. At this point, the protected mode handler may **jump to the VMM** and let it decide how to handle the event. In this case, it provides the VMM with its vector number.

The next section discusses possible actions taken by the VMM when a protected mode handler passes control to it.

VMM Chooses Response Based on Vector

When a protected mode handler passes control to the VMM, it supplies it with its corresponding IDT vector. This tells the VMM what type of interrupt or exception occurred. The action taken by the VMM is defined by the event type, as well as the OS implementation.

Based on the vector supplied to it by the protected mode handler, the VMM has two basic options:

1. Handle the event within the VMM.
2. Pass control to the real mode handler that corresponds to the vector number received from the protected mode handler.

The sections that follow describe both options.

VMM Passes the Ball to a Real Mode Handler

Pass Control to Real Mode Handler. The programmer must take the following actions to pass control to the corresponding real mode handler:

1. Multiply the vector of the protected mode handler being executed by four (because the real mode IDT consists of four bytes per entry) to obtain the offset into the real mode IDT.

Protected Mode Software Architecture

2. Since the real mode IDT starts at linear memory address 00000000h, the offset obtained in the previous step is the start linear address of the corresponding real mode IDT entry (you could add a base address of 00000000h to it, but what's the point?).

3. Read the new CS:EIP value from the real mode IDT entry. This is the entry point of the corresponding real mode handler.

4. Obtain the interrupted VM86 task's EFlags, CS:EIP values from the privilege level 0 stack and store them on the VM86 task's privilege level 3 stack (level 3 stack's base and top-of-stack values are obtained from the SS:ESP values that were pushed onto the privilege level 0 stack). These return values will be used when the IRET instruction is executed at the end of the real mode handler (see step 9).

5. Read the CS:EIP return address previously saved on the privilege level 0 stack by the processor. This address points to the VM86 task instruction that would have been executed next if the task had not been interrupted. Save this return address to be used later (see step 3 in "Real Mode Handler Executes" on page 290).

6. Store the real mode handler entry point address into the privilege level 0 stack in place of the address just read and saved.

7. Execute an IRET instruction. This pops the start address of the real mode handler into the CS:EIP registers. In addition:
   - the EFlags image from the privilege level 0 stack is popped into the EFlags register. Since the VM bit = 1 in this image, VM86 mode is reenabled.
   - the VM86 task's stack base and top-of-stack are popped into SS:ESP.
   - the data segment (DS, ES, FS and GS) register values are popped into their respective data segment registers.

8. The processor begins execution of the real mode handler. Execution of the real mode handler services the interrupt or exception.

Real Mode Handler Executes. The real mode handler executes, servicing the event that caused the interrupt or exception.

Exit Real Mode Handler Back to VMM. At the conclusion of the handler's execution, the following actions are taken:

1. The IRET instruction at the end of the real mode handler is executed. Since IRET is an IOPL-sensitive instruction (and assuming that the IOPL < 3) and the handler is executing with EFlags[VM] = 1, the attempt to execute it causes a GP exception.

2. The processor saves CS:EIP, SS:ESP, EFlags, DS, ES, FS, and GS on the privilege level 0 stack. It then clears EFlags[VM], [IF] and [TF] and jumps to the protected mode GP exception handler. The VM bit on the privilege level 0

stack is examined and, because VM = 1, the GP exception handler jumps to the VMM.

3. The VMM replaces the previously-saved (see step 5 in "Pass Control to Real Mode Handler" on page 289) pointer to the interrupted VM86 task into the privilege level 0 stack.

VMM Resumes Interrupted VM86 Task. Once the real mode handler has passed control back to the VMM and the VMM has cleaned up the stack, it returns to the interrupted VM86 task:

1. The VMM executes an IRET instruction (the IRET executes successfully because the processor is no longer in VM86 mode), causing the processor to pop the previously saved values (CS:EIP, SS:ESP, EFlags, DS, ES, FS, and GS) from the privilege level 0 stack.
2. The processor resumes execution of the VM86 task.

VMM Handles Event

Rather than passing control to a real mode handler, the VMM may choose to handle the event itself. This would certainly be the case if the VM86 task had attempted one of the following:

- Direct access to an IO port and the corresponding bit in the TSS's IO permission bit map is set. In other words, the VM86 task attempted to access an IO port that only the multitasking OS is permitted to access, resulting in a GP exception. The protected mode GP handler passed control to the VMM because the interrupted task is a VM86 task.
- Attempted execution of an IOPL-sensitive instruction when EFlags[IOPL] = 3. In other words, the VM86 task does not have sufficient privilege to execute the instruction, resulting in a GP exception. The protected mode GP handler passed control to the VMM because the interrupted task is a VM86 task.

Each of these cases results in a GP exception, interrupting the VM86 task. Since the GP exception is a fault, the return address that is pushed onto the privilege level 0 stack points to the instruction that caused the exception. The processor jumps to the protected mode GP handler. The GP handler checks the state of VM bit in the EFlags image on the privilege level 0 stack to determine if the interrupted task is a VM86 task. In these cases, VM = 1 indicating a VM86 task was interrupted. The GP handler therefore jumps to the VMM and passes its vector number, 13d.

Protected Mode Software Architecture

Using the return address that was pushed onto the privilege level 0 stack, the VMM examines the VM86 task's instruction that caused the exception. The following sections describe the typical actions taken by the VMM for these cases.

Attempt to Access Forbidden IO Port. The VM86 task attempted to access an IO port that it is not permitted to access directly (because the OS and other tasks would not be aware of the change in the IO device's state caused by the IO access). The action taken by the VMM is implementation-specific. Some typical actions might be:

- The VMM is part of the OS and acts as the central point for communication with all shared IO devices. The VMM may perform the IO access and keep track of the IO device's current state. It is the author's opinion that this would be the most commonly-used method.
- The VMM may decide to terminate the VM86 task.
- The VMM may ignore the IO access attempt. In other words, it may choose to resume execution of the interrupted VM86 task at the instruction after the IO instruction that caused the exception.
- If the instruction is an IO write (OUT or OUTS), the VMM may simply update a copy of the IO port's contents that is maintained in memory (in other words, a virtual copy of the IO port). If the instruction is an IO read (IN or INS), the VMM may return the contents of a virtual copy of the IO port that is maintained in memory.

Attempted Execution of CLI Instruction. The VM86 task has attempted to disable recognition of external hardware interrupts (because it doesn't want to be bothered by interrupts during execution of a critical piece of code). The processor did not successfully execute the instruction, so interrupt recognition is still enabled. There are three possible cases:

- the VMM checks the state of the IF bit in the EFlags image on the privilege level 0 stack and determines that **interrupt recognition had already been disabled (by the VMM or OS) at some earlier point in time**. In this case, the VMM adjusts the return pointer on the privilege level 0 stack to point to the instruction following the CLI that caused the exception, and then executes an IRET to **resume execution** of the interrupted VM86 task **at the instruction that follows the CLI**.
- the VMM may know that this is a **safe time to disable interrupt recognition** (because there are no high-priority interrupts expected). In this case, the **VMM** could choose to **execute** a **CLI** instruction, adjust the return pointer on the privilege level 0 stack to point to the instruction following the CLI that caused the exception, **and** then execute an IRET to **resume execution** of the interrupted VM86 task **at the instruction that follows the CLI**.

- the VMM may know that this **not a safe time to disable recognition** of hardware interrupts. The text that follows provides a detailed description of this case.

The multitasking OS cannot permit the VM86 task (which doesn't know of the existence of the multitasking OS or other, currently-suspended tasks) to summarily disable interrupt recognition. At an earlier point in time, another task may have stimulated an IO device (e.g., a disk interface) to perform an operation and generate an interrupt when it has been completed. The device may complete the requested operation and generate the interrupt while the VM86 task is executing. Furthermore, the device may be quite sensitive to being serviced on a timely basis. The VM86 task is unaware of any of this.

Based on the attempted execution of the CLI instruction, the VMM will note (in a memory location somewhere) that the currently-executing task prefers not to be interrupted. In other words, the **VMM maintains a virtual copy of EFlags[IF] bit in software**. It alters the return address on the privilege level 0 stack to point to the instruction that follows the CLI and then executes the IRET to resume execution of the interrupted VM86 task at the instruction that follows the CLI.

If a hardware interrupt should subsequently occur, the VM86 task is interrupted and the hardware interrupt's protected mode handler then passes control to the VMM. If the VMM knows that the interrupting device requires fast servicing, it immediately executes either the protected mode or real mode handler to service the device. In other words, it ignores the preference of the VM86 program that it not be interrupted. In this case, the VM86 task was interrupted even though it preferred not to be. The VMM designer should make every attempt to accomplish the check just described as expeditiously as possible and return control to the interrupted task. Otherwise, the interrupted VM86 task may not function correctly (because of the lengthy delay imposed by the VMM's software overhead necessary to determine whether to service the hardware interrupt right away or to defer servicing it until the task's timeslice has expired).

On the other hand, the VMM may determine that the interrupting device can stand some delay in being serviced and that the virtual copy of the EFlags[IF] bit indicates that the VM86 task prefers not to be interrupted. In this case, the VMM would set a bit in a VMM-specific data structure (let's call it the **deferred interrupt data structure**) indicating that the specified interrupt handler should be executed when the VM86 task completes its timeslice. It then executes the IRET instruction to resume execution of the interrupted VM86 task. Later, when the VM86 task's timeslice has expired and a task switch occurs back to the OS, the OS checks the deferred interrupt data structure (mentioned earlier) to determine if the servicing of any hardware interrupt(s) was deferred. If it was, the OS calls the respective interrupt handler(s) to service the hardware device(s).

Attempted Execution of STI Instruction.
If the VM86 task attempts to reenable interrupt recognition, one of three cases is true:

- the VMM checks the state of the IF bit in the EFlags image on the privilege level 0 stack and determines that interrupt recognition is already enabled. In this case, the VMM adjusts the return pointer on the privilege level 0 stack to point to the instruction following the STI that caused the exception, and then executes an IRET to resume execution of the interrupted VM86 task at the instruction that follows the STI.
- the VMM may know that this is a **safe time to enable interrupt recognition**. In this case, the **VMM** could choose to **execute a STI** instruction, adjust the return pointer on the privilege level 0 stack to point to the instruction following the STI that caused the exception, **and** then execute an IRET to **resume execution** of the interrupted VM86 task **at the instruction that follows the STI**.
- the VMM knows that this is not a safe time to reenable recognition of hardware interrupts. In this case, the VMM adjusts the return pointer on the privilege level 0 stack to point to the instruction following the STI that caused the exception, and then executes an IRET to **resume execution** of the interrupted VM86 task **at the instruction that follows the STI**.

Attempted Execution of PUSHF Instruction.
If the DOS task is permitted to execute the PUSHF instruction, the EFlags register is copied to the stack and the EFlag[VM] and EFlag[RF] bits are cleared. This would disable VM86 mode, preventing the processor from continued monitoring of the VM86 task's behavior. The VMM could emulate this in a benign fashion, copying the EFlag contents to the VM86 task's stack (SP:ESP are on privilege level 0 stack) without clearing EFlag[VM]. The VMM adjusts the return pointer on the privilege level 0 stack to point to the instruction following the PUSHF that caused the exception, and then executes an IRET to **resume execution** of the interrupted VM86 task **at the instruction that follows the PUSHF**.

Attempted Execution of POPF Instruction.
When executed, the POPF instruction copies the EFlags image on the stack into the EFlags register. If the programmer had altered this image, a number of problems could result:

- The VM bit could be cleared, disabling VM86 mode and preventing the processor from continued monitoring of the VM86 task's behavior. The VMM must copy the data from the VM86 task's stack into the EFlags register, ensuring that the VM bit remains set to one.

- The IF bit could be cleared, disabling the processor so it would no longer recognize external hardware interrupts. The VMM could treat this attempt to disable interrupt recognition in the same manner as an attempt to execute a CLI instruction (see "Attempted Execution of CLI Instruction" on page 292).
- The IF bit could be set, reenabling the processor to recognize external hardware interrupts. The VMM could treat this attempt to enable interrupt recognition in the same manner as an attempt to execute a STI instruction (see "Attempted Execution of STI Instruction" on page 294).

Attempted Execution of INT nn Instruction. Many VM86 tasks utilize the INT nn instruction to call the real mode OS or BIOS services. An attempt to execute an INT nn instruction when the EFlags[IOPL] field < 3 results in a GP exception. The processor executes the protected mode GP exception handler. The handler checks the VM bit in the EFlags image on the privilege level 0 stack to determine if the interrupted task is a VM86 task. If it is (VM = 1), the GP handler passes control to the VMM. The VMM must then determine what to do in response. There are two basic cases:

1. The VMM determines that it is not legal for the VM86 task to call the target vector. In this case, the VMM would be forced to terminate the VM86 task.
2. The VMM determines that the VM86 task is attempting to call a DOS or BIOS service.

In the second case, the VMM must choose one of the following options:

1. Pass the call to a real mode handler. This is accomplished in the manner already described in "VMM Passes the Ball to a Real Mode Handler" on page 289.
2. Pass the call to the protected mode OS to handle. When the OS has completed the request, the VMM then returns control to the interrupted VM86 task at the instruction immediately following the INT nn instruction.

Attempted Execution of IRET Instruction. As discussed earlier, in some cases the VMM may pass control to a real mode handler to service an interrupt or exception. VM86 mode is reenabled when control is passed to the real mode handler. At the conclusion of the real mode handler, attempted execution of the IRET instruction results in a GP exception. The protected mode GP handler passes control back to the VMM, which in turn passes control back to the interrupted VM86 task. This was described in detail in "VMM Passes the Ball to a Real Mode Handler" on page 289.

Protected Mode Software Architecture

Using Separate Task as Handler in VM86 Mode

If an interrupt or exception occurs while a VM86 task is executing and the vector selects a protected mode IDT entry that contains a task gate, a task switch occurs. The processor suspends the VM86 task and starts up the task that is being used to handle the interrupt or exception. Upon entry to the new task, EFlags[NT] (nested task; see Figure 15-6 on page 296) is set. The TSS selector (see Figure 15-2 on page 282) for the VM86 task is stored in the Link field of the new task's TSS.

When the IRET is executed at the end of the task, the set NT bit forces the processor to perform a task switch back to the interrupted task. The processor uses the GDT selector stored in the TSS Link field to locate the VM86 task's TSS. The processor's register set is reloaded from the VM86 task's TSS and execution resumes at the next instruction.

Figure 15-6: EFlags Register

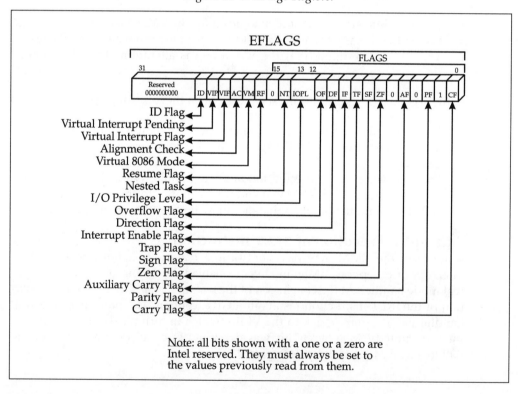

VM86 Mode Extensions

By now, it should be somewhat apparent that there is a lot of software overhead involved when the processor must intercept potentially disruptive actions initiated by a VM86 task. When one of these attempts is detected, the processor executes the protected mode GP handler which in turn transfers control to the VMM. The VMM must then determine the proper action to take.

- The VMM must decide whether the real or protected mode handler should handle an interrupt or exception event.
- The processor prevents the VM86 task from altering the state of the interrupt enable bit in the EFlags register.

The Pentium processor and later versions of the 486 processor implement the CR4 register (see Figure 15-7 on page 299). Setting CR4[VME] to one enables extended capabilities that permit faster handling of these disruptive actions.

The description of these extended capabilities was under non-disclosure until the Pentium Pro processor was introduced. At that time, Intel included a description in the processor data books. The sections that follow provide a brief introduction to these topics. A detailed description of these capabilities can be found in MindShare's *Pentium Pro Processor System Architecture* book (published by Addison-Wesley).

Virtual Interrupt Enable Bit

When the processor's VM86 mode extensions are enabled (CR4[VME] = 1), a new EFlags bit, EFlags[VIF], becomes available (see Figure 15-6 on page 296).

When operating in VM86 mode with the extensions enabled, the processor operates differently when an attempt is made to execute an instruction (CLI or STI) that would alter the state of the processor's IF flag bit. The discussion that follows assumes that CR4[VME] = 1.

As stated earlier, the multitasking OS must be in sole control of the interrupt enable bit. When an attempt by a VM86 task to execute the CLI instruction is detected with an IOPL < 3, the processor doesn't generate a GP exception. The CLI clears the virtual IF bit (EFlags[VIF]), rather than the actual EFlags[IF] bit. Detection of an attempt to execute the STI instruction causes EFlags[VIF] to be set to one (rather than the EFlags[IF] bit). The VIF bit takes the place of the virtual copy of the IF bit software had to maintain (see "Attempted Execution of CLI Instruction" on page 292).

Software Interrupt Redirection

When the processor is operating in VM86 mode and the VM86 extensions are enabled (CR4[VME] = 1), the processor uses the software interrupt vector (a number between 0 and 255d) to index into the interrupt redirection bit map in the VM86 task's TSS. This is a 32-byte bit map (pictured in Figure 15-8 on page 300) that defines the action to be taken for each of the 256 interrupt vectors (32 bytes x 8 bits/byte = a 256 bit map). The base address of the IO permission bit map field in the TSS identifies the start address of the IO permission bit map and the end address (plus one) of the interrupt redirection bit map. When the OS initially sets up the TSS for a VM86 task, it selects the states of the up to 256 bits in the redirection bit map to indicate which software interrupt types are to use the real mode handlers and which use the protected mode handlers.

Hardware Interrupt Redirection

Hardware interrupts are never redirected. They are always vectored through the protected mode interrupt table.

Figure 15-7: CR4 Register

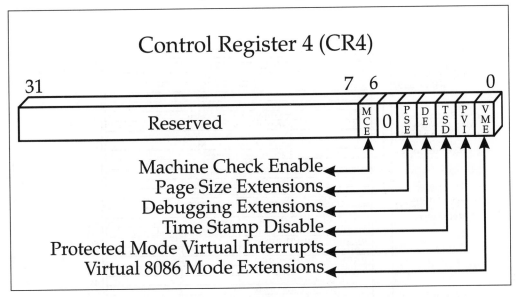

Figure 15-8: 32-bit TSS Format

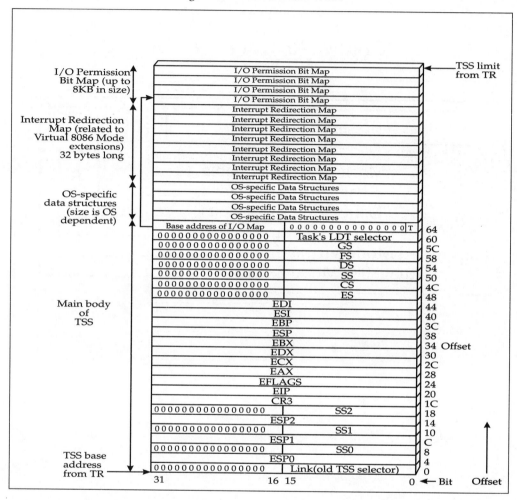

Figure 15-9: EFlags Register

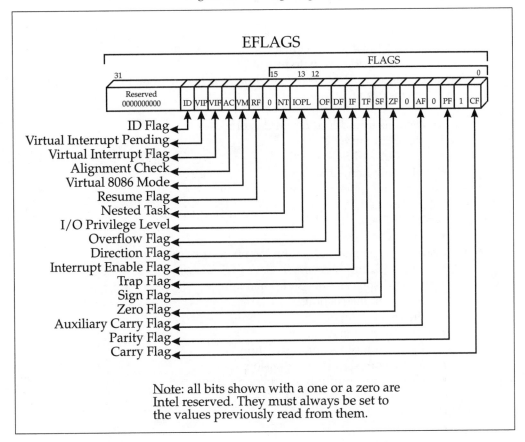

Note: all bits shown with a one or a zero are
Intel reserved. They must always be set to
the values previously read from them.

Registers Accessible in VM86 Mode

A program operating in VM86 mode has access to all of the 8086 registers, as
well as the two additional data segment registers—FS and GS. The FS and GS
segment override prefixes may be used. As an example:

```
MOV AH, FS:[0100] ;read byte from location 0100h in FS
                  ;data segment into AH register
```

Protected Mode Software Architecture

Instructions Usable in VM 86 Mode

In addition to the 8086 instruction set, a VM86 task may utilize instructions that access the FS and GS data segment registers. Instructions may make use of the operand size override prefix to utilize 32-bit (rather than 8- or 16-bit) operands. The following is a list of post-8086 processor instructions that may be utilized by a VM86 task:

- Instructions introduced on the 286 processor
  - PUSH immediate data
  - PUSHA and POPA
  - Multiply immediate data
  - Shift and rotate by immediate count
  - INS and OUTS
  - ENTER and LEAVE
  - BOUND
- Instructions introduced on the 386 processor
  - LSS, LFS, and LGS
  - Long-displacement conditional jumps
  - Single-bit instructions
  - Bit scan instructions
  - Double-shift instructions
  - Byte set on condition instruction
  - Move with sign/zero extension
  - Generalized multiply instruction
- Instructions introduced on the 486 processor
  - BSWAP
  - XADD
  - CMPXCHG
- Instructions introduced on the Pentium processor
  - CMPXCHG8B
  - CPUID

Index

Index

Index

Index

Index

Index

Index

Technical Seminars

PCI System Architecture
PCI Software Environment
PCMCIA System Architecture
486 System Architecture
EISA System Architecture
CardBus System Architecture
Pentium System Architecture
Plug and Play System Architecture
ISA System Architecture
PowerPC Hardware Architecture
PowerPC Software Architecture

MindShare courses are presented at your site and are tailored to suit the needs of the audience.

To Contact MindShare

Email: mindshar@interserv.com
Web Site: www.mindshare.com
Compuserve: 72507,1054
Phone: (214) 231-2216
Fax: (214) 783-4715

MindShare, Inc.
2202 Buttercup Drive
Richardson, TX 75082

Note: New courses are constantly under development. Please contact MindShare for the latest course offerings.